Don Quixote in the Archives

Edinburgh Critical Studies in Renaissance Culture

Series Editor: Lorna Hutson

Titles available in the series:

Open Subjects: English Renaissance Republicans, Modern Selfhoods and the Virtue of Vulnerability
James Kuzner
978 0 7486 4253 3 Hbk

The Phantom of Chance: From Fortune to Randomness in Seventeenth-Century French Literature
John D. Lyons
978 0 7486 4515 2 Hbk

Don Quixote in the Archives: Madness and Literature in Early Modern Spain
Dale Shuger
978 0 7486 4463 6 Hbk

The Girlhood of Shakespeare's Sisters: Gender, Transgression, Adolescence
Jennifer Higginbotham
978 0 7486 5590 8 Hbk

Friendship's Shadows: Women's Friendship and the Politics of Betrayal in England, 1640–1705
Penelope Anderson
978 0 7486 5582 3 Hbk

Untutored Lines: The Making of the English Epyllion
William P. Weaver
978 0 7486 4465 0 Hbk

Visit the Edinburgh Critical Studies in Renaissance Culture website at www.euppublishing.com/series/ecsrc

Don Quixote in the Archives

Madness and Literature in Early
Modern Spain

Dale Shuger

EDINBURGH
University Press

© Dale Shuger, 2012

Edinburgh University Press Ltd
22 George Square, Edinburgh

www.euppublishing.com

Typeset in 10.5/13 Adobe Sabon
by Servis Filmsetting Ltd, Stockport, Cheshire, and
printed and bound in Great Britain by
CPI Group (UK) Ltd, Croydon, CR0 4YY

A CIP record for this book is available from the British Library

ISBN 978 0 7486 4463 6 (hardback)
ISBN 978 0 7486 4464 3 (webready PDF)
ISBN 978 0 7486 4916 7 (epub)
ISBN 978 0 7486 4915 0 (Amazon epub)

The right of Dale Shuger
to be identified as author of this work
has been asserted in accordance with
the Copyright, Designs and Patents Act 1988.

Contents

Acknowledgements

It is a commonplace among Cervantine critics for the author, of course only following the example set out in *Don Quixote* itself, to identify with his or her subject of critical analysis. If, in writing a book about insanity, I have managed to escape a total identification with my subject, it is thanks to the guidance, support and assistance of many friends, colleagues and institutions. I would like to thank the New York University Department of Spanish and Portuguese and the Columbia University Latin American and Iberian Cultures Department, and the archivists and librarians at the Archivo Histórico and Biblioteca Nacional in Madrid and the Archivo Diocesano in Cuenca, and the editors at Polifemo Press for permission to reprint material from Chapter 2 which first appeared in *USA Cervantes* (Madrid: Polifemo, 2009). Carlos Alonso, Gian Maria Annovi, Patricia Grieve, Kenneth Krabbenhoft, Jacques Lezra, Graciela Montaldo, Jesús Rodríguez Velasco, Kathleen Ross and Jane Tylus all provided me with valuable suggestions and criticism. I thank Eunha Choi, Alexandra Falek and Ysette Guevara for their moral and academic support. This project would never have been possible without the intellectual generosity of two people who, without ever having met me, provided me with bibliographic and archival materials that represented years of their own work. Many of the cases of madness I was able to track down came from Jean Pierre Dedieu's database for the Toledo tribunal, and his felicitous decision to add an 'L' for *locura* in the entries of his database. Sara Nalle's book *Mad for God* was an inspiration, and I am eternally grateful for her willingness to share with me her entire transcription of the Bartolomé Sánchez case.

I may be the mother of my work, but this book also has a fairy godmother, a grandmother and a daughter (of sorts). Without Georgina Dopico Black, I never would have discovered that the Baroque was even more fun than the Neobaroque. She was my advisor, friend and reader through the earliest years of this project. I have the rare fortune of having a mother who is also an early modernist, and without her advice, support, editorial eye and genes, I literally and figuratively would not be here. Finally, there is my dog, Sancha Panza, who in the toughest of times, reminded me to eat, sleep and keep my wits about me.

Note concerning the Translation

All translations from unpublished archival sources are my own, unless otherwise noted. I have sought to provide the most direct and literal translations possible, but because it is difficult to capture the vocabulary and rhythms of these depositions and judicial proceedings in English, I have included the original in the main text. I have modernised spelling and punctuation, and used italics when the handwriting or the condition of the file made it difficult to decipher.

I have used Edith Grossman's translation of *Don Quixote*; as per custom, each quote is identified by the Part (I or II) and chapter. (*Don Quixote*, a new translation by Edith Grossman. Introduction by Harold Bloom. Translation copyright © 2003 by Edith Grossman; introduction copyright © 2003 by Harold Bloom Reprinted by permission of HaperCollins Publishers.) Translations of all secondary sources are my own, unless otherwise noted.

Series Editor's Preface

Edinburgh Critical Studies in Renaissance Culture may, as a series title, provoke some surprise. On the one hand, the choice of the word 'culture' (rather than, say, 'literature') suggests that writers in this series subscribe to the now widespread assumption that the 'literary' is not isolable, as a mode of signifying, from other signifying practices that make up what we call 'culture'. On the other hand, most of the critical work in English literary studies of the period 1500–1700 which endorses this idea has rejected the older identification of the period as 'the Renaissance', with its implicit homage to the myth of essential and universal Man coming to stand (in all his sovereign individuality) at the centre of a new world picture. In other words, the term 'culture' in the place of 'literature' leads us to expect the words 'early modern' in the place of 'Renaissance'. Why, then, 'Edinburgh Critical Studies in *Renaissance Culture*'?

The answer to that question lies at the heart of what distinguishes this critical series and defines its parameters. As Terence Cave has argued, the term 'early modern', though admirably egalitarian in conception, has had the unfortunate effect of essentialising the modern, that is, of positing 'the advent of a once-and-for-all modernity' which is the deictic 'here and now' from which we look back.[1] The phrase 'early modern', that is to say, forecloses the possibility of other modernities, other futures that might have arisen, narrowing the scope of what we may learn from the past by construing it as a narrative leading inevitably to Western modernity, to 'us'. Edinburgh Critical Studies in Renaissance Culture aims rather to shift the emphasis from a story of progress – early modern to modern – to series of critical encounters and conversations with the past, which may reveal to us some surprising alternatives buried within texts familiarly construed as episodes on the way to certain identifying features of our endlessly fascinating modernity. In keeping with one aspect of the etymology of 'Renaissance' or 'Rinascimento' as 'rebirth', moreover, this series features books that explore and interpret anew elements of the critical encounter between writers of the period 1500–1700 and texts of Greco-Roman literature, rhetoric, politics, law, oeconomics, *eros* and friendship.

The term 'culture', then, indicates a licence to study and scrutinise objects other than literary ones, and to be more inclusive about both the forms and the material and political stakes of making meaning both in the past and in the present. 'Culture' permits a realisation of the benefits to be reaped after two decades of interdisciplinary enrichment in the arts. No longer are historians naïve about textual criticism, about rhetoric, literary theory or about readerships; likewise, literary critics trained in close reading now also turn easily to court archives, to legal texts and to the historians' debates about the languages of political and religious thought. Social historians look at printed pamphlets with an eye for narrative structure; literary critics look at court records with awareness of the problems of authority, mediation and institutional procedure. Within these developments, modes of research that became unfashionable and discredited in the 1980s – for example, studies in classical or vernacular 'source texts', or studies of literary 'influence' across linguistic, confessional and geographical boundaries – have acquired a new critical edge and relevance as the convergence of the disciplines enables the unfolding of new cultural histories (that is to say, what was once studied merely as 'literary influence' may now be studied as a fraught cultural encounter). The term 'Renaissance' thus retains the relevance of the idea of consciousness and critique within these textual engagements of past and present, and, while it foregrounds the Western European experience, is intended to provoke comparativist study of wider global perspectives rather than to promote the 'universality' of a local, if far-reaching, historical phenomenon. Finally, as traditional pedagogic boundaries between 'Medieval' and 'Renaissance' are being called into question by cross-disciplinary work emphasising the 'reformation' of social and cultural forms, so this series, while foregrounding the encounter with the classical past, is self-conscious about the ways in which that past is assimilated to the projects of Reformation and Counter-Reformation, spiritual, political and domestic, that finally transformed Christendom into Europe.

Individual books in this series vary in methodology and approach, sometimes blending the sensitivity of close literary analysis with incisive, informed and urgent theoretical argument, at other times offering critiques of grand narratives of the period by their work in manuscript transmission, or in the archives of legal, social and architectural history, or by social histories of gender and childhood. What all these books have in common, however, is the capacity to offer compelling, well-documented and lucidly written critical accounts of how writers and thinkers in the period 1500–1700 reshaped, transformed and critiqued the texts and practices of their world, prompting new perspectives on what we think we have learned from them.

Lorna Hutson

Note

1. Terence Cave, 'Locating the Early Modern', *Paragraph* 29.1 (2006), pp. 12–26 (14).

Introduction

Had Miguel de Cervantes, while doing research for his book, been able to google the word 'madness', he would in all likelihood have crashed his server. Early modern Spain saw an increased preoccupation with madness in almost every sector of society; for different reasons and in different ways, jurists, theologians, artists, advisors and the royal court all found themselves debating, exploring or dealing with madness and madmen. Yet the madnesses spoken of in elite literature, festivals, legal codes and medical manuals were not always the same, just as the madness spoken of in sixteenth-century Spain does not necessarily refer to the same actions or have the same significance as madness in four-teenth-century Germany or twenty-first-century America. We know that Cervantes chose to call the protagonist of his masterpiece a 'madman', but which 'madness' did he mean?

A few of the many discourses of madness swirling around in early modern Spain have, in subsequent centuries, been privileged as critical frameworks from which to read the madness of Cervantes's most famous protagonist. Not surprisingly, given *Don Quixote's* privileged status in the literary canon, the most common reading has emphasised a literary genealogy. The critic who wishes to trace a constellation of literary madness has any number of star charts to choose from; early modern European literature features furious lovers (the epic lovers who Don Quixote explicitly imitates), melancholy lovers (in countless *come-dias* and romances, including many of the characters in the intercalated stories of *Don Quixote*), buffoons or fools (the *graciosos* of the *comedia* and the court), objects of satire (the patients in Garzoni's or Beys's madhouses), and the satirical voices themselves (Erasmus's Dame Folly, Cervantes's own 'licenciado Vidriera'). Madness's frequent association with inversion makes it all the more difficult to pin down: by definition, it can mean one thing and its opposite (hence the endless paradoxes of the mad-sane, or 'madness of Christ'). 'Madness' in these works can be ludic or tragic, real or feigned, pathetic or terrifying, a locus of non-sense or a locus of truth. Perhaps the *only* thing we could say that all of these meanings of madness have in common is that none of these works emphasises the hallmarks of contemporary madness: subjective (psychological) crisis; social and institutional crisis; an experience whose cure, cause, meaning, definition and demarcation cannot, by and large, be stated with certainty. Madness in early modern visual arts and literature, in contrast, is all about certainty: characters are mad or they are not; they go mad for a reason (love, sin, sorcery); and, as widely diverse as the symbolic possibilities are, their madness symbolises something (even if that something is nothing more than the principle of inversion itself).

It may be precisely because of its allegorical stability (there may be several allegorical readings, but, for any specific text or image, the reader/viewer can easily distinguish which symbolic madness is present and thus draw the correct symbolic conclusions) that madness is so common a theme in satire, sermon, allegory and didactic literature. These are literary forms whose primary purpose is *docere*. A defining characteristic of the novel, in contrast to the satire or the allegory, is the shift toward a verisimilar, rather than a symbolic, treatment of characters and plot. (This is not to say that many novels do not contain symbols, but in general symbolic readings are supplements to equally plausible verisimilar readings. Moby Dick may be Nature or God, but he is also a whale). So while at first glance it might seem intuitive to place Don Quixote's madness into a literary genealogy, we should return to ask whether the novel's formal, generic innovations would not suggest a shift in its central theme as well. If Don Quixote's madness is a stepchild of Dame Folly and Orlando, then who might be his real parents?

This work will argue that a study of archival materials – principally over one hundred insanity defences pleaded before the Spanish Inquisition – reveals that there was an experience and a discourse of madness in early modern Spain that is not the one we find in the literary canon, and then that Don Quixote's madness differs from that of his fellow literary *furiosi* precisely because it engages this 'other' madness. It is sometimes assumed that the historicist reading necessarily *reduces* a text it to its most basic mimetic or polemic function. However, this assumes a false dichotomy between 'art' (outside of time) and 'history' (outside of art). *All* texts are produced in a time and place and that time and place is defined as much by literary ideas as by kings, wars and laws. To argue that a work of art engages a social discourse of its day is not to *reduce* it to political propaganda or to claim that the author is merely imitating life it is simply to shift the network of engagement from one type of discourse (philosophy, poetry etc.) to another (economics, law, politics). Nor are these literary and extra-literary networks mutually exclusive: a work as complex as *Don Quixote* engages all sorts of material, reflecting, refracting and refashioning each, and, importantly, stitching networks together in new ways – parodying a social discourse by placing it in a certain type of literary language, or laying bare the implicit assumptions of a literary convention by transposing its setting to a specific historical moment. It would seem obvious to recognise this in a work whose very premise depends on the uncomfortable relation between Dulcinea and Toboso, Don Quixote and la Mancha. In this study I will argue that, in fact, the historicist reading is intimately related to literary characterisation, because what we find in historical and archival documents shows that Cervantes's frame of reference was the popular madness of his own society, that Don Quixote's madness is, like *Don Quixote*, novelistic. Indeed, Walter Reed has argued that the defining characteristic of the novel is its 'confrontation' with 'those human fictions . . . which lie beyond the boundaries of the prevailing literary canon.'[1] Because *Don Quixote* is a novel, we *must* read it in its 'confrontation' with extra-literary discourse. And, I will argue, it is because of its 'confrontation' with extra-literary *madness* that *Don Quixote* becomes a novel.

Critical Tendencies

The critical literature on madness in *Don Quixote* is sufficient to fill an ageing nobleman's library, but we can group critical tendencies into three main categories. The first and largest group of scholars do not see madness as fundamental to the work, or at least it is not the focus of their inquiry. This group includes readers of the so-called 'hard' school, who see *Don Quixote* as primarily comic and therefore argue it is anachronistic to speak of psychologies or philosophical questions, or social actualities. For these readers, *Don Quixote* is not really about a mad man, nor really about 'men' at all: 'madness' is a starting point that permits parody, play or pratfalls.[2] Other readers in this category, while not so openly rejecting a 'realist' reading of madness, consider Don Quixote's madness principally as inviting an experiment or investigation of philosophical and aesthetic questions, and thus also subordinate elements of psychology to questions of art and form.[3]

At the other end of the spectrum is a second, smaller group of critics who have focused almost exclusively on Don Quixote's psychology, either drawing on sixteenth-century or modern medical theories. Critics of this first sort have focused on the parallels between Don Quixote's character and the humoral types described in Juan Huarte de San Juan's *Examen de ingenios para las ciencias* (1575), and more broadly on the idea of the melancholic in Renaissance literature.[4] It is inarguable that Cervantes draws on the medical theories of his day in his initial characterisation of Quixote. However, the polemic as to whether Quixote was actually choleric or melancholic[5] or the rigorous consideration of exactly which of the faculties of Quixote's brain is damaged[6] may give insight into Don Quixote as a character, but it has nothing to say about *Don Quixote* as novel. Critics who seek to apply theories from schools of modern psychology either end up anachronistically projecting motivations and meanings that the text simply cannot support or inserting *Don Quixote* into a teleological narrative which reciprocally affirms the validity of Freud's (Jung's, Lacan's etc.) theories and then validates Cervantes for anticipating/intuiting them.[7] The theory, be it humoral or Oedipal, obscures the novel – the creation of a world with language and the details of that language and that world.

The third group of critics do read madness as central to the novel. The most traditional of these readings focuses on the intertextuality between Erasmus's *The Praise of Folly* and *Don Quixote*.[8] According to this reading, *Don Quixote*'s madness – or rather the fact that Don Quixote is considered mad – reveals a world upside down, where vice is rewarded as virtue, and true virtue is labelled as madness. For Erasmus, the idea of a virtuous folly (or a virtue deemed foolish) comes directly from Paul's exhortation to his fellow disciples to be 'fools for Christ'.[9] Later schools of criticism have continued this reading, although no longer relying on or tracing it to a direct Erasmian influence. The Romantics secularise the Erasmian critique; for them, the main dynamic of the novel is society's repression of and violence towards, not now the true Christian, but the true hero, the true genius. While the Romantic reading is socio-historically rooted in the sense that it sees Cervantes using madness principally to reveal and criticise social dynamics, it considers these dynamics to be universal and timeless; there is no attempt to tie Cervantes's critique or Don Quixote's madness to specific sixteenth-century practices or institutions.

Two authors from the mid-twentieth century have been influential in turning critics toward what initially seems a socio-historically specific reading of madness in the *Quixote*. Mikhail Bakhtin's reading of *Gargantua y Pantagruel* led critics to consider the subversive potential of carnival in Renaissance literature.[10] Agustin Redondo, James Iffland and others have traced the genealogy of the festival in early modern Spain and seen the motifs and the logic of carnival in *Don Quixote*.[11] Where the Romantics saw the hero as being marginalised by his designation of madness, Bakhtinians see the inversions in the margins as liberating, subversive acts against the centre. After the publication of Michel Foucault's *Folie et déraison: Histoire de la folie à l âge classique*,[12] critics turned back to the Romantics' focus on dominant institutions, seeking to ground the universalist notions of the Romantics in a particular time and place. Despite their differences, however, Erasmians, Romantics, Bakhtinians and Foucauldians all share a reading of madness in *Don Quixote* as a symbolic state which reveals the hypocrisies and tensions of society. Madness is the general state of a society turned upside down; it is not a psychological condition experienced and defined by subjects in a society that may be upside down, but is the only one they know.

The Bakhtinian and Foucauldian readings are historicist, in the sense that Bakhtin and Foucault make claims about literary texts based on claims about the Baroque historical period. However, both Bakhtinians and Foucauldians draw on a limited range of materials to make claims about the understanding of madness in society as a whole: Foucault assumes that literary and artistic representations correspond to popular narratives, while Bakhtin and his followers assume that representations during Carnival can be generalised to the rest of the year.[13] Were we to find evidence of non-literary or non-Carnival narratives of madness in early modern Spain that challenged the existing readings, these would necessarily require us to rethink Foucauldian and Bakhtinian readings of *Don Quixote* – not the archival turn itself, but the archives they turn to, and hence the conclusions they make about Renaissance and Baroque society.[14] In this work I will argue that the archives of the Spanish Inquisition provide evidence of other narratives. I am not arguing that Don Quixote's madness is taken from any real-life case or that Cervantes had access to Inquisition archives, but rather that the depositions and interrogations before the Inquisition reveal dynamics present in the society at large.

Because my argument does not claim that Cervantes knew or was writing about any specific case, I have used archival accounts from approximately a one-hundred-year period, from 1540 to 1650, and across Spain. While Spain's material situation certainly changed over this period, there is no reason to think that the general experience and representation of madness changed significantly during this time. Some of the cases are so Quixotic that one is tempted to suspect that life is imitating art; however, the continuity of the cases over a period stretching back to the mid-sixteenth century makes this unlikely. These later *locos* did not 'find themselves' in *Don Quixote* and, despite what the author of the prologue claims, neither Don Quixote nor *Don Quixote* can be found 'buried in the archives of La Mancha' (I,5). What lie in the archives are hints of an experience and discourse of madness which Cervantes is clearly drawing on – not mimicking, but modifying, parodying, critiquing, expanding – in the creation of a character and a novel.

In order to argue that this 'other' madness is Cervantes's principal referent in *Don Quixote*, it will be necessary to examine the multiple discourses of madness circulating in Cervantine Spain. In Chapter 1, I provide a survey of these discourses, in order to see where they coincide with and where they differ from Cervantes's treatment of the theme. I will focus on 'madnesses' less familiar to Cervantine criticism, although many of the socio-historical discourses I discuss will look familiar to readers of Erasmus and Ariosto. The juxtaposition of these narratives makes it apparent that Baroque Spain recognised no single, stable allegorical meaning of madness, and offered no clear way of separating out 'madness' from other forms of marginal or unreasonable behaviour. Whereas literature and moral tracts tend to present madness as already-made-legible, archival documents, particularly Inquisition records, attest to an unprecedentedly visible yet illegible spectacle of unreason. Inquisition documents are hardly unbiased historical sources, and in Chapter 1 I will consider the effects of the Inquisition on ideas and representations of reason, as well as the material and theoretical complexities of using Inquisition materials.

The fact that madness in Cervantes's day was a pervasive social problem does not in itself prove that Cervantes was writing about that madness in *Don Quixote*. The fact that early modern madmen shared certain symptoms with Don Quixote is not proof that Cervantes was interested in the social, emotional and philosophical questions that these symptoms raised in society.[15] Yet in order to argue that Cervantes is building upon the dynamics of madness he might have seen in his own society, it is necessary to show that the manifestations of this madness do bear *some* resemblance to Don Quixote's symptoms. To this end, it is important to get an idea of the beliefs and behaviours that made a sixteenth-century Spaniard 'mad' in the eyes of friends, neighbours and authority figures, and this is the question I turn to in Chapter 2. Based on an analysis of archival accounts, I will argue that, while early modern Spaniards were hardly consistent in their interpretations of various types of unreason, the narratives of those deemed mad do share certain underlying dynamics: delusions of grandeur, inability to adjust action to context, a combination of loss of physical and verbal control, and an obsession or confusion about writing and representation.

This symptomatic overlap is necessary to sustain the idea that Cervantes is addressing a verisimilar concept of madness, but the exploration of symptomatic parallels in this chapter is equally important in developing an understanding of how Cervantes modifies those symptoms: how he modifies 'the real' and when he departs from verisimilitude altogether. These are the questions I ask in the remainder of the work, focusing in each chapter on a different aspect of the madman's lived and represented experience. In Chapters 3 and 4, I focus on the madman's social world: his interactions with his family, friends, neighbours and authorities. Inquisition documents give us new insight into the social experience of madness in early modern Spain because the tribunal's strategy for confirming an insanity defence involved questioning a wide range of social actors about their opinions and reactions to unreasonable behaviour, including many members of society whose voices would never otherwise pass into written discourse. In *Don Quixote* and in the archival accounts, commoners, law officials, clergymen and doctors struggled to determine if a person acting strangely was criminal, drunk, possessed or confused; whether this was a permanent or temporary condition; what its causes and cure might be; and their own responsibilities in interacting with that individual. The social dynamics that emerge in the testimonies have striking parallels with those we find in many of the scenes of *Don Quixote*. The similarities do more than simply prove that Cervantes's scenes on the road and in the inns of La Mancha are, in some aspects, realistic: they direct our attention to complexities and questions that are lost in many critical readings (Menippean, Romantic, Foucauldian, Bakhtinian) that depend on broad generalisations about all interactions between people and institutions, the sane and the mad.

The archives reveal that individuals' interactions with the mad changed according to their familiarity with the madman and their own authority or institutional affiliation, but this does not mean that authority figures uniformly sought to silence or punish the madman, or that his fellows encouraged him in the name of carnivalesque disorder. The archives allow us to understand early modern ethical ideas about laughter, punishment, censorship, mercy, love and respect that differ from our own. Understanding the ethical *map* of sixteenth-century Spain helps us understand the specific *route* that Cervantes charts for his protagonist. This can have profound implications for the reader, since the presumption by both 'hard' and 'soft' readers of *Don Quixote* of a stable and largely static relationship between Don Quixote and his fellow travellers is directly related to the stable and static relation that each school of criticism proposes between reader and text. The 'hard' school sees harmless laughter in the fictional world and argues that the reader should laugh; the 'soft' school sees abuse in the text and argues that the reader should condemn the abusers and identify with the abused. Thus the recognition of the complexity of the ethical acts within the text may require us to rethink and complicate our own reaction *to* the text.

John Jay Allen argues that our reactions towards Don Quixote shift from laughter to identification as the work progresses, as we get to 'know' the protagonist.[16] The archives, too, identify familiarity as the key factor determining ethical relationships with the mad. I divide Chapters 3 and 4 according to the type of relationships examined: in the former, I focus on Don Quixote's interactions with strangers and acquaintances, and, in the latter, on the interactions between Don Quixote and those who know him well, particularly Sancho. I show how Cervantes consistently develops Sancho's character and his relationship with Don Quixote through changes in the squire's understanding of his master's madness, and through an exploration of the ethical decisions such an understanding compels him to make. Cervantes uses the fundamental ambiguity and insecurity which, the archives tell us, was at the heart of mad-sane relationships to create both a rounded complex character and a dynamic human relationship, leaving the realm of archetypal stock figures in his literary wake.

The remaining chapters of the book turn away from the social world and towards the representation of the individual (recognising, of course, that neither of these can exist independent of the other), to make the argument that the defining elements of the novel can be seen to emerge from the crisis of self supposed by madness. It is not my intention to propose a fixed definition of the novel, nor to declare that *Don Quixote* is the first; the category of the novel is permeable and, as Diana de Armas Wilson notes, it has 'risen' many times in different socio-historical contexts.[17] Still, we can identify certain general elements that tend to define the novel against other genres, without supposing that these elements constitute a checklist of 'novel-ty': attention to the real and everyday, the development of verisimilar human relationships, a turn towards psychological introspection, and a resistance to totalising interpretations. In Chapters 5 and 6, respectively, I focus on these latter two categories. In Chapter 5, I argue that it is precisely the questions that a non-allegorical madness elicited in Baroque Spain that spurred artists and non-artists alike to think in new ways about interiority: the relations between perception, thought, will and self. In order to understand others behaving irrationally, individuals had to ask new questions about the invisible processes behind their actions; in order to understand themselves, those who suspected their own reason had to ask new questions about what their experiences meant. In *Don Quixote*, we can trace the turn toward psychological introspection to the authorial choice of a mad protagonist.[18] The archives give accounts of jurists and theologians eliciting self-narratives in order to make them intelligible and to assimilate them to existent narratives of unreason; Cervantes, not bound by an institutional imperative, can explore in further depth and with ambiguity and irony how psychic processes construct or deconstruct a stable sense of self. I argue that, far from presenting two fixed worldviews (realist and idealist) or even exploring the intersection and destabilisation of either as a philosophical exercise, Cervantes is interested in how an individual character explains his world to others and explains the world to himself, and how madness interrupts these processes. The madman's struggle to reconcile self and world does, in novel and archive, sometimes produce humorous paradoxes which might, in another context, be simple or satirical jokes (many critics read some of Quixote's rationalisations of unreason as precisely that). However, Cervantes is not using his character principally as a vehicle for humour: he is exploring how the sense-making process constitutes the character and, at the same time, how the reader gets a sense of an individual who exists – who has feelings, morals, a place in the world – beyond his madness.

In Chapter 6, I turn to the implications this struggle to make the self legible has for language and literary form. The effects of madness on language and its role in a certain sort of experimental, Modernist literature – Conrad, Artaud, Woolf, Faulkner –has been amply studied. I argue that many of the formal experiments in *Don Quixote* – the shifts in narrative perspective, destabilisations of omniscience and questioning of stable systems of meaning – can also be seen as artistic strategies to convey the tension between coherence and incoherence, meaning and nonsense, that is at the heart of the early modern subjective experience of madness.[19] *Don Quixote* is not *As I Lay Dying* because madness is not yet principally understood as a space of 'absolute transgression'[20] that exists at or beyond the limit of culture and society. Early modern madness is still very much an experience that society, culture and language struggle to incorporate. What Foucault and his followers see in terms of 'absolutes' – madness as 'absolute transgression' or literature as 'the sole channel by which madness has been able . . . to speak its own name'[21] – is, in early modern Spain, a space of negotiation and tension. Literature does not yet see its goal as breaking with society, and society has not yet fully 'broken' with the madman. A work about early modern madness will be a work of partial transgressions, a freeing of language, an experimentation with form that does not yet presuppose a rupture. It is precisely because society is still implicated in the experience of the madman (and vice versa) that it is useful, and essential, to read *Don Quixote* in the context of socio-historical accounts of madness.

This book is a study of one work and one historical moment, but it suggests new ways of thinking about the relationship between madness and novels, literature and history. In my final pages, I attempt to open a dialogue with specialists in other periods and national traditions. Indeed, it is with an aim toward dialogue and discussion that I set out to write this book. The world of Cervantine criticism is densely populated, and this work, like any other, marks out its territory at times by opposition and at times by exclusion of other critical approaches. I do not, however, propose to offer the only or the correct reading of Don Quixote's madness, and much less of *Don Quixote*. If we value Cervantes above and beyond most of his contemporaries, it is because his works are so infinitely complex, because they offer themselves to a multitude of readings which can contradict each other without necessarily being incompatible. I take as my own the stance articulated by Mercedes Alcalá Galán: 'It is a matter of opening debate, promoting thought and reflection, and establishing a dialogue with the texts.'[22] It is my hope to introduce a dialogue with very different texts (archival, novelistic), but also to show that these very different types of texts are in dialogue with each other.

Notes

1. Reed: 5.
2. See Russell and Close, *Romantic Approach to Don Quixote*, for the most strictly 'hard school' reading. Van Doren, Serrano Plaja, Torrente Ballester and Gorfkle emphasise the ludic or theatrical elements of Quixote's madness.
3. For example, Spitzer, Casalduero, *Sentido y forma del Quijote*, Avalle-Arce.
4. Huarte de San Juan. The connection between Huarte de San Juan and Cervantes was first studied by Rafael Salillas. See also Iriarte. For readings on melancholy in Renaissance literature, see Klibansky, Soufas, García Gilbert, Bartra.
5. Positions taken, respectively, by Green and Soufas.
6. Avalle-Arce: 99–143.
7. For Freudian and Lacanian readings of the work, see Johnson, *Madness and Lust*, El Saffar and Wilson, Sullivan, Garcés. For a psychiatric perspective, see Castilla del Pino, Bailón Blancas, *Cervantes y la psiquiatría* and *Historia clínica del caballero Don Quijote*.
8. Erasmus, *Praise of Folly*.
9. 1 Cor. 4.10.
10. Bakhtin, *Rabelais and His World*.
11. See: Molho; Márquez Villanueva, 'Planteamiento de la literatura del "loco" en España'; Redondo; Iffland.
12. Foucault, *Madness and Civilization*. This is a translation of Foucault's own

abridgement. In 2006, the complete work was finally published as *History of Madness*. All translations in this study come from the earlier work, but I have consulted the complete volume.

13. The qualitative difference between the type of archival material Foucault cites in support of his claims about the early modern period (paintings, plays) and the Enlightenment (hospital and judicial records) is striking.

14. By non-literary I simply refer to documents whose primary intent was not circulation and consumption as literature. Bureaucratic documents certainly do contain literary elements and, conversely, primarily literary texts had functions beyond giving aesthetic pleasure.

15. Indeed, I will argue in Chapter 5 that the symptomatic overlap between Tomás Rodaja, the protagonist of Cervantes's short story 'El licenciado Vidriera' and documented cases of glass delusions does not indicate an engagement on the part of Cervantes with madness as a lived experience. Cervantes Saavedra, *La española inglesa*.

16. Allen.

17. Wilson.

18. *Don Quixote* contains episodes (particularly the intercalated stories) which do not foreground psychological introspection, or any of the other novelistic features I discuss in these last chapters. This work will focus on the central, novelistic narrative, but we can both respect the heterogeneity and specificity of the non-novelistic moments and still note that the absence in these episodes of the sort of madness that we find in the archives and in the main plotline supports the main point: the intimate connection between a new form of madness and a new form of literature.

19. For studies of narrative structure and formal experimentation that do not consider the role of madness, see: Mancing; López Navia; Martín Morán; Parr, *Anatomy of Subversive Discourse* and *Touchstone for Literary Criticism*.

20. Foucault, *Madness and Civilization*: 287.

21. Felman: 15.

22. Alcalá Galán: 21. Of course I do not mean to suggest that she is the first or the only author to adopt this critical position.

Chapter 1

Many Madnesses

What did madness mean – what did it mean to be mad – in early modern Spain? Individual works of literature, or particular institutional discourses, often have clear answers to that question. However, institutional discourses and works of literature coexist in a broader social setting, and in the social setting of Baroque Spain there were many confusing and conflicting 'meanings' – including a reluctance or inability to find any clear meaning at all – of madness. In order to understand what madness 'means' in *Don Quixote*, it is important to present a picture of madness in Baroque Spain.[1] Rather than assume that *Don Quixote*, as a literary text, will be principally in dialogue with other literary texts, or that *Don Quixote*, as a novel, will be principally in dialogue with a socio-historical reality – and indeed, rather than assuming any fixed relation between literature and society – we may postpone these questions and begin by looking at *all* of these realities, literary, socio-historical and others, and then judge which seem to offer the most productive dialogue with *Don Quixote*.

Secularised Madness

Much of the modern imaginary of madness comes from ancient texts: Freud and Oedipus, Nietzsche and Dionysus, Sybil[2] and the Sybils. The three cases represent three variations on divine madness: Oedipus is punished by the gods; Dionysus is a god; Sybil is possessed by the gods. The Greeks also conceived of a physiological madness; Hippocrates' theories of the humours were the prevailing medical theory for melancholy and mania into the Renaissance.[3] Yet, since we have no first-person accounts of ancient experiences with madness, our ideas are shaped by philosophy and literature; in the former, unreason is disorder and a failing,[4] for the latter, madness is almost always associated with the gods. During the medieval period, the connection between madness and the gods persisted, but now rationally inexplicable events and experiences were explained through a Christian narrative of sin, redemption and grace. In her survey of medieval interpretations of madness, Corinne Saunders shows that there was a diversity of representations and interpretations – madness could be understood as demonic possession, physical illness, passionate excess – but each of these was ultimately tied back to 'God's providential patterning of the universe'.[5] God worked in various ways, but the loss of reason ultimately reflected back to 'the Passional disorder of the Fall, and thus . . . a state of sin.'[6] Madness was a divine punishment or test, and could only be met with repentance and piety. Its symptoms may have varied but its meaning was clear, and it fitted into a narrative whose roles and end were already written.

The Renaissance brought a general secularisation in European culture. Men did not necessarily become less faithful, but increasingly human affairs were considered the realm of human reason. The narrative of divine and demonic madness did not disappear, but it became one of many possible interpretations, and 'master allegories' are all or nothing. The sixteenth century affords a plethora of interpretations, from the humoral to the supernatural, of madness. Indeed, the obsession with discernment of spirits, and between true essences and false appearances in general, is one of the defining characteristics of the Spanish Baroque. Furthermore, madness was only one possible explanation for unreason: the seemingly furious or delusional figure might also be drunk, a fraud or a heretic. The 'man on the street' confronted by a man raving about Moors and morals had to choose not just between madman or sane, not just between visionary and demoniac, but between all of these (and feigned visionary/demoniac to boot). It becomes impossible to speak of one meaning, or one societal response to madness.

Rethinking Foucault: Madness in Spain

For Michel Foucault, whose *Madness and Civilization* is regarded by literary critics as the most important work on madness, in the Renaissance madness was always understood as evil, and the response was always punishment;[7] a century later madness meant scandal and the response was confinement and 'organized exhibition'.[8] The influence of Foucault's *Madness and Civilization* in Cervantine scholarship is somewhat inexplicable for, after a brief initial chapter which cites no archival material,[9] Foucault speaks neither of Spain nor of anything prior to the 1656 founding of l'Hôpital Général in Paris. In recent decades, a number of books have shown conclusively that many of the basic premises of *Madness and Civilization* do not apply to Spain. Studies of asylum archives in Valencia (by Hélène Tropé)[10] and Seville (by Carmen López Alonso)[11] show that there was no mass confinement of the mad, and yet most Cervantine critics suppose that the social dynamics which gained their institutional visibility in 1656 Paris were already underway in 1600 Spain (or they ignore the time-and-space gap entirely).[12] Foucault charts a social movement: from mass exclusion to symbolic omnipresence to mass confinement. What the Spanish archival scholarship reveals, by contrast, is a period in which mad*men* (and not just texts and images) were pervasive in public life, and they did not unequivocally represent evil. Spanish historical documents point to a 'great coexistence' rather than a 'great confinement'.

There were fewer institutions for the mad (or in which the mad would have been lumped together with the sick or the poor) in Spain than in France or England,[13] and the character of these institutions was markedly different from their French or English counterparts. In Spain, patients had more interaction with the public, and had a decent chance to return as full-time members to that public. The relative lack of semijudicial structures of social control has two main causes, one economical, the other theological. Even in the years of relative prosperity, Felipe II's external focus did not leave much time or money for internal investments. Spain's foreign engagements and internal economic woes (bankruptcy was declared in 1575, 1597 and 1607) made the sort of commitment and continuity required for long-term social planning impossible. The State was incapable of funding centralised institutions; instead, as Enrique González Duro writes, individual private charitable groups founded 'in an anarchic manner, a diverse and dispersed institutional system'.[14] Initial efforts under Felipe II to stem the inefficiency inherent in a system made up of small private charities were abandoned, and by the 1590s the situation had reverted to, and even surpassed, the previous disorder.[15]

The decline of the Spanish economy in the late sixteenth century is not, however, enough to explain the relative absence of Foucauldian hospitals. In fact, Foucault argues that the purpose of the hospitals was to address an economic crisis – the formation of an urban underclass of beggars, invalids, criminals and, mixed in with this 'undifferentiated mass', the mad – by removing them all from public space and finding some way to make them productive.[16] The same crisis of poverty and homelessness which Foucault charts in France and England occurred, if anything, earlier and on a larger scale in Spain, as evidenced by the proliferation in the early 1500s of pronouncements and plans to control or combat it.[17] Unlike in Protestant Europe, however, reform projects met with strong resistance from conservative sectors of the Church, who believed that any state intervention in the exercise of charity deprived the Christian of his ability to complete his sacramental obligations. While the debate had many voices and went on for decades, the main issues can be seen in the polemic between Juan Luis Vives and Domingo de Soto. It is worth looking in some detail at this debate, as it reveals much about the nature of sixteenth-century public poverty and the position of the mentally ill within the larger 'great unwashed'.

In 1526 Luis Vives published his recommendations to address the poverty crisis, thus becoming 'the first Catholic thinker to question the very heart of the medieval concept of charity, posing the problem of the poor in socio-economic terms and proposing laic, state-based solutions'.[18] He challenged the traditional Catholic sacramental practice of charity, maintaining that its at-all-costs preservation was actually pernicious to the spiritual health of the Church and its members, as it fomented a situation which encouraged public blasphemers, and 'one had to see their rabid quarrels, curses, libels, blows, murders, and all for money'.[19] The problem was not just the desperate need of so many but the violence and blasphemy which these needy displayed in public: that telling 'one had to see'. This certainly supports Foucault's ideas about the true motives behind public health and state charity movements, but it also confirms the visible and public nature of deviant behaviour in the 1500s. The failure of Vives's (and later Giginta's and Pérez de Herrera's) proposals in Spain would suggest that such public aberrance continued through Cervantes's lifetime.

In addition to highlighting the visibility of unreason, Vives's writings raise another issue which has important resonances with *Don Quixote*: feigned versus true madness. Vives was not insensitive to the plight of those truly unable to work, but he suspected that the majority of the public problems were caused by those who faked incapacity and thus took advantage and perverted Catholic charity. In other words, he suspected that the majority of the mendicants were of the picaresque and not the apostolic variety. The need for a Catholic reform that would preserve the virtue of charity made it necessary as never before to distinguish between the truly ill and the fakers. Vives wrote that 'it would be necessary to rely on the opinion of physicians, and those who deceived or faked any illness would be severely punished'.[20] The social reform called for a new precision, or at least certainty, of scientific diagnosis. Vives expected that this scientific knowledge could certify both physical and mental illnesses, and he recognised the validity of both as legitimate 'excuses' for mendicancy. The attention he paid to the mad suggests that insanity was frequently evoked as a defence for public violence and blasphemy, it being easier to fake a mental illness than a physical one. But just as it is easier to fake madness than plague, it is harder to discern the fakers. Furthermore, more was at stake in the diagnosis of the mentally ill than the physically infirm, since mental illness specifically attacked that which is divine in man. As the Spanish playwright and satirist Alonso Jerónimo Salas de Barbadillo put it, the insane were deprived of 'the most noble action that a rational creature can perform, which is, to think well . . . [madness] takes from his soul its most valued possession'.[21] Christians were asked to provide charity for men and women with suffering bodies, but they had no greater obligation than to aid suffering souls.

The divergence of outcomes for 'true' and 'feigned' madmen placed unprecedented weight on the precision of diagnosis. In Vives's programme, further precision was required after this initial distinction, as different types of madness would require different societal responses. Once in the hospital, it would have to be determined 'whether the madness is natural or stems from a particular occurrence, if there are hopes of health or if it is a hopeless case'. Among the mad, Vives wrote:

> some require comforts and nourishment; others a gentle and kindly treatment so they are tamed bit by bit like wild animals; others teaching; and there will be others who require punishment, but let it be used in such a way that it not cause them to become even more furious; first and foremost, insomuch as is possible, we must procure to introduce in their spirits that calm under which sanity and health easily return to the understanding.[22]

Vives had clearly defined the different treatments that correspond to 'some' and 'others' but he had not provided the diagnostic criteria to make these divisions. Priests, barbers, innkeepers and university students had to form their own criteria and ideas about the treatment each diagnosis might demand.

In his *Deliberación de la causa de los pobres*, Domingo de Soto voiced the Church's objections to Vives's proposal: principally, that it displaced charity from the street to the hospital, and from the everyday Christian to the medical professional. The power of conservative sectors of the Church in Spain meant that Vives's ideas, which guided reforms in England and Bruges, met insuperable resistance in Spain. In the following decades, the separation of alms and state was debated among the Catholic community, while in the meantime the *Cortes* continued to pass *cédulas* (royal decrees) which they then failed to enforce.[23] The Council of Trent signalled the end for the voices of institutional reform, as the Counter Reformation generally favoured an entrenchment of the Catholic orthodoxy, for whom 'any Vives-inspired proposal was branded as pestilential, pernicious, and injurious for the Church'.[24] The sheer dimensions of the crisis led to some movement in reform projects in the later decades of the sixteenth century, and, in the years in which Cervantes was writing the *Quixote*, the whole Vives/Robles-Soto debate was re-enacted. In 1598, Cristóbal Pérez de Herrera published his *Discursos del amparo de los legítimos pobres y reducción de fingidos*, in which he estimated the population of 'feigned beggars' in Spain at over 150,000. He expounded on the dangers of such a huge and visible population of fakers: they not only threatened Catholic morality but also national security, as many beggars were Moorish and Turkish spies. The stakes for discerning fakers were thus stepped up one notch further and the task of discernment again passed to science. Pérez de Herrera, himself a doctor, called for 'an examination of the poor in the presence of a physician or surgeon'.[25] Those who were confirmed to be 'legitimately poor' due to mental or physical illness would be interned in shelters but given licences to beg for alms during the day. Thus even if perfect diagnosis were possible and Pérez de Herrera's reforms had been fully carried out – neither of which happened – the truly mad would still have been a visible public presence. In reality, a few shelters did begin to operate, but the project was sharply curtailed after Felipe II's death. According to the editor of *Amparo de pobres*, Michel Cavillac, the mendicant population of Spain reached 500,000 by 1608 and a million by 1617.[26]

Wholly Foolish and Holy Fools

The ordinary Spaniard confronted with irrational behaviour had more than two diagnostic options. The behaviour of madmen might not only resemble that of the malingerer but it also could resemble the behaviour of a divinely inspired mystic, a demonically possessed sinner, or a faker of either of these. The Church's ambiguous attitude towards street prophets and visionaries promoted the free reign of a certain type of public spectacle and disorder, and thus made these decisions very common ones. The tradition of religious and secular street prophets warning of impending apocalyptic doom dated back to the Middle Ages, and these figures tended to proliferate in times of political and economic crisis. During the late medieval period, several of these charismatic prophets garnered huge followings and created mass havoc.[27] However, time and distance from the most destructive prophet-led disasters made intense repression seem unnecessary by sixteenth-century Spain. Richard

Kagan paints a picture of the ambiguous state of the street prophet in Cervantes's time:

> In theory the Spanish church, following the general tenets of the Counter-Reformation, took a dim view of any lay person who claimed to have the 'prophetic gift'. Yet in practice most seers were either tolerated or ignored, so long as they did not openly espouse heretical concepts or ideas. The Spanish crown also tolerated the vitriol of self-proclaimed street prophets . . . as long as the prophet had only a scattered following.[28]

The Church assumed that, through less drastic mechanisms of popular inculcation and correction, it could instil a disregard for strange and heretical ideas that would make spectacular and costly repression unnecessary. In theory, the public, well-educated as to the ephemeral and delusory causes of dreams and visions, would simply discount the street prophet as *loco* and thus his words and thoughts would have no influence. (Women were considered more susceptible to mystic experience – divine and, more typically, demonic – and the same behaviours which might, in a man, be written off as inconsequential results of a natural disturbance were interrogated and interpreted supernaturally or criminally when they came from a woman).[29] This was not merely a policy of convenience devised to minimise cost and effort; the State's profession of indifference was a positive assertion that these seers were not 'valid' enough individuals to merit official attention. Mounting an extensive official repression might have the reverse effect of mobilising the visionary's support, converting his/her cause into a larger popular struggle. During the medieval period, when it was generally believed that the madman possessed 'a magical aura and a heuristic surplus value', and that he was 'the representative of a counter-reality who somehow had important things to say',[30] such a strategy would have been impossible. However, the early modern Church depended on – and relentlessly promulgated – the idea that what might seem to be supernatural or preternatural was in fact a meaningless humoral disturbance, if not deliberate fraud. The distinction between these two categories, however, led to the same sort of diagnostic problems that social reformers faced in separating the disabled from the indolent. Andrew Keitt describes the 'flood of theological treatises, confessors' manuals, and handbooks on the discernment of false raptures and revelations' which appeared at the end of the sixteenth century, all meant to 'clarify the causal categories' to which these phenomena belonged.[31] Church officials condemned 'an epidemic of self-proclaimed prophets and miracle-working visionaries' in these years, yet there was hardly consensus on the matter. Keitt calls the period 'a "Hundred Years' War"' between competing models of conceptual legitimacy ... Doctors provided medical diagnoses, demonologists held forth on the scope of demonic agency, and inquisitors probed the workings of God's providential order'.[32] In the give and take between these competing approaches, official representatives were often compelled to enter 'irrational' debates, to accept and implicitly give credence to illogical premises in order to show that their extensions were false (conversing with 'demons' in order to prove the fraudulence of a supposed possession, for example). The reader should recognise a pattern Cervantes exploits and parodies in many of Don Quixote's dialogues.

The a priori discounting of the prophet was an ideal way to avoid the risks of official recognition – even for the purposes of refutation – of professed visionaries. There were two problems with this strategy, however. First of all, there is the essentially visionary nature of Christian history; the Church of Revelation, St Francis and Santa Teresa could not very well discount *all* visions. This had been a preoccupation since the beginning of the Church, but the sixteenth century was a time of heightened scholarly speculation on the ways of interpreting visions, and it was also a time of heightened preoccupation about the possibility of 'truly' supernatural dreams that were demonic, rather than divine, in origin.[33] Added to the divisions and ambiguity among the elites was the perseverance among the Spanish *pueblo* of a fascination with omens, prophecies and dreams. The popular *relaciones de sucesos* show that every sort of royal event or natural anomaly was subjected to prophetic interpretation, while mystic predictions of the future were eagerly awaited every New Year. Kagan writes that:

> the 1580s constituted another moment in Spanish history when street prophets suddenly proliferated ... oneiromancy [was] a regular feature of daily life ... Priests necessarily served as dream interpreters for their parishioners. Confessors, however, faced competition from free-market dream analysts, village wizards, and 'wise women'.

The Church condemned these, but to little effect. Kagan cites an estimate of over 10,000 'such individuals' in Spain.[34] Insofar as these visionaries advised a few illiterate neighbours whether to marry Anselmo or Lotario, the Church let them be. Only when their prophecies directly threatened the State did authorities step in.

The Church found itself then in a contradictory position. They expected people to discount religious or political prophesiers as *locos* but tacitly accepted (by failing to prosecute or publicly debunk) the free reign of prophesy in other areas. Of course society and visions do not break down so neatly into safe and dangerous content. The case of

Lucrecia de León shows the confused and inconsistent responses that institutions and people had when dreams (or in other cases, visions) crossed these lines.[35] The records of Lucrecia's trial reveal that everywhere – from Felipe II's court to the home of a *doncella recogida* to the street, not to mention in the Inquisition tribunal itself – people were speaking and acting in ways that motivated their peers and the authorities to ask questions about their mental state, and that the answers differed widely.[36]

Hallucinators, or those who faked hallucinations/visions, formed part of the much larger spectrum of public unreason. Let us step back a moment and imagine a Castile with 300,000 men, women and children in the streets, the plazas, the highways. Every description of this atmosphere – from picaresque to policy – as well as basic common sense suggests that the combination of idleness and desperation would lead to a fair amount of public violence and blasphemy. The free flow of wine would have added to the 'unreasonable' aspects of this violence (the Inquisition trial of Adán Carballo offers the revealing tidbit that 'se acostumbra por via de limosna a dar de beber a los pobres mendigantes que llegan a pedir' ['it was customary to give something to drink {i.e. wine} as alms to the poor beggars who come to ask for charity']).[37] The 'privileged' place of the mentally ill in Catholic theological teachings on charity, as well as the special status which the 'truly' ill held in reform programmes such as Pérez de Herrera's – insomuch as these ever got off the ground – gave added incentive for those who were most rational (in the sense of knowing what was in their best interest and acting to achieve it) to appear insane. We can imagine a scenario of interaction and incitement between and among the irrational (whether mentally ill or drunk) and their imitators, along with a constant interrogation of both groups by doctors, clerics, alms-givers and each other in an effort to distinguish one group from the other. We can imagine what such a cycle of unreason, and reason probing unreason, might look like to a hypothetical chronicler, but we should keep in mind that no one had the luxury of being a hypothetical observer. Every politician, cleric and man-on-the-street was compelled to interact with and judge this spectacle, and part of this decision depended on a mechanism to distinguish between the criminal and the *loco*. Not everyone came to the table with the same criteria or tools for this diagnosis; the individual's knowledge (of science, of theology), his range of social influences and interactions (what sermons he had heard, what folk traditions he shared), and his economic or social stake in the determination, all came to bear in the ways he made this decision and how this decision affected his course of action.

Before looking at the resonances of these multiple judgements and interactions with *Don Quixote*, we should fill in other aspects of sixteenth-century Spain which led to a nearly constant interaction with possible insanity. Thus far we have been discussing how the Catholic Church's power in Spain led to an increased presence of 'irrationals' (those so defined by their neighbours) who had not been processed by any institution. However, early modern Spain was hardly an institutional vacuum; the huge bureaucracies of Church and State did not affect popular life in the same way that Foucault describes in France and England, but they were certainly a powerful presence.

Rethinking Foucault: Madhouses in Early Modern Spain

While, as we have seen, the majority of mad-sane interactions occurred without any institutional mediation, there were a number of institutions in early modern Spain dedicated specifically to the care of the mentally ill. As opposed to the warehouses of undifferentiated misery Foucault describes, the constitutions of these hospitals clearly differentiated the mentally ill both from the physically infirm and from the able-bodied poor. I use the word 'care' here intentionally, because, at least in theory, these institutions were charitable and saw themselves as principally medical (within the limits of sixteenth-century medicine). The founding charter of the Hospital of Córdoba, for instance, specified that the asylum was for 'the suffering and the ill' and *not* beggars 'of the sort who wander from door to door'.[38] Spain, in fact, could boast the first such institution in all of Europe. Fray Gilaberto Jofré, as legend has it, was moved by the scene of a mentally ill man being harassed by street urchins to wonder why Spain should show such charity to the physically sick and yet allow the mentally ill to go unprotected.[39] Thus the very motivation for this first asylum, which officially opened its doors in 1419, was a recognition of the difference and special needs of the mentally ill. It is worth noting here the dynamic out of which the Valencia hospital emerged; this combination of compassion and cruelty is one we see again and again in the documents of the period and explored in the *Quixote*.

Within the next fifty years, a spate of similar institutions were founded across Spain: in Toledo, in Barcelona, in Córdoba, in Zaragoza, in Seville. Unfortunately, they seem to have been particularly flammable; almost all of these burned down once or various times in their history, taking their early modern archives with them. Still, from the documentation that has survived, it seems clear that there were notable differences between the Spanish hospitals and the institutions Foucault describes.[40] Not only did they have far fewer inmates and keep them for shorter times but also the residents who were interned there were hardly sealed off from the society at large. The public entered and the residents went out from the asylums under a variety of auspices. A mention of a few of the patient-public interactions should give an idea of the variety of contexts in which patients and public interacted, as well as the plurality of interpretations that governed these interactions.

Even during the course of one week, the mad could run a symbolic gamut. Hélène Tropé studies the range of roles played by the Valencia asylum patients during Holy Week, beginning with the Holy Thursday ceremonies at the hospital. On that day, the *locos* were reminders of Christ's teachings about the relative merits of wealth and meekness, and a selected twelve of them essentially became the Twelve Apostles. The constitution of the hospital specified that, on Holy Thursday, the entire population of the asylum be treated to a sumptuous dinner, to be served and enjoyed before the Administrators began their own. Then followed a ceremony in which the Administrators re-enacted Jesus' washing of the Apostles' feet before the Last Supper, with the selected twelve *locos* as the Apostles.[41] The constitution also specified that the Administrators' wives repeat the ceremony with the female inmates.

In treating the madmen as the Apostles, the townsmen were following Saint Paul's instructions to be 'fools for Christ' as well as tapping into more ancient associations of madness with holiness or divinity. At the same time, in humbling themselves to serve a feast to and wash the feet of these most miserable of subjects, they were following Christ's injunctions to care for the poor and innocent. Since the mad were often seen as symbols of abjection and innocence, stricken in that faculty which God reserved for man alone, pious men (or those seeking to project a pious image) could no more efficiently exercise their obligation to charity than through the support of an asylum. There seems to have been an element of nationalist and local pride in the zeal with which towns favoured their asylums even as other medical and social institutions fell into decline. Carlos V granted the hospital in Zaragoza 'extraordinary . . . favours and privileges'[42] and Felipe II gave the administrators of the hospital in Barcelona (El Hospital de la Santa Creu) exclusive rights to all box-office receipts for *comedia* performances in that city.[43] Even when Spain's economy was in a shambles, citizens continued to fund the asylums. After the original hospital in Valencia was destroyed by fire in 1610, there was a city-wide campaign to rebuild, and all the most important city figures and institutions, secular and ecclesiastic, donated. Tropé concludes:

The enthusiasm with which all – the great and the humble – responded to the call of the collectors for funds for the reconstruction is a testament to the extent to which, in the civic mentality, the Casa de los Locos was considered something important and necessary. These donations reveal the general consensus with regard to the community's assistance of the *locos* and their integration into that same community.[44]

Nor did the citizens' interaction with the *locos* end with an annual donation. A select group of *locos* accompanied the hospital administrators throughout the city on a daily basis asking for contributions, and these *colectas* garnered significant sums.[45] Their success again presents to the modern mind confusing questions of laughter and charity. On the one hand, the *locos* were dressed in bright and extravagant colours and at least until the 1560s travelled on mules (while the official charity collectors rode horses), 'provoking laughter as much through the extravagance of their outfits as through the association of the *locos* with the mules'.[46] On the other, Tropé theorises that the ostentatious marking of the *locos* 'in reality, constituted the privileged occasion for new relationships between the *locos* and the citizens, and an intent on the part of the administrators of the Hospital to re-integrate the *locos* of their institution into the urban sphere'.[47] In order to 'overcome the ancient negative vision of madmen – bothersome and discordant individuals *par excellence*' – it was necessary to clearly identify the subjects as *locos* and to physically associate them with the institution which had brought about their transformation.[48] On festive holidays, the hospital played up the burlesque element of the money-gathering ritual. At Easter and Christmas 'the *locos* asked for alms under the guidance of a burlesque character, called the "little bishop [*bisbet*]"', but during Holy Week the *colecta* took on very solemn overtones: after the Last Supper ritual, the *locos* went through the streets, plazas and churches of the city (surely packed for Holy Week services) begging for alms. The whole city could thus 'demonstrate to the humble figure of the poor *loco* evidence of its affectionate compassion'.[49]

Tropé's research not only reveals the great variation in the symbolic meaning of madness and the range of emotions it inspired but also confirms the visibility of *locos* in Spanish society, even of the minority 'locked up' in an institution. She observes a marked increase in the number of *colectas* circulating just after the 1597 bankruptcy – exactly the period when Cervantes would have been writing the *Quixote*. Tropé also notes that some of the *locos* worked in the adjacent medical hospital (el Hospital General), as watchmen, cooks and servers,[50] another opportunity for interaction with the rest of society in situations without prescribed narratives.

Carmen López Alonso's research in the Seville asylum archives shows similar interactions (and Cervantes lived in Seville during at least some of the period he wrote *Don Quixote*). The Seville staff also sent *locos*, along with hospital staff, into the streets to take collections. As López Alonso says, 'part of the mad had direct contact with the people . . . and the daily life of the city'. They too were accompanied by Brothers in special habits, designed to 'incite the compassion of the public'.[51] The story of the Seville hospital's most successful fundraiser, one Don Amaro, emphasises the ambiguous relations of compassion and humiliation with which early modern Spaniards reacted to madmen. Amaro was a once-prominent lawyer in the city who had gone mad and entered the asylum. After an initial period of fury and dementia, he became manageable enough to go out with the fundraisers. On the collection rounds, he would stop and deliver tirades, which were transcribed and collected.[52] The published sermons – having passed through chains of interpretation and editing that are impossible to reconstruct – bear many of the hallmarks of carnivalesque satire (inversion of hierarchies, libellous sexual imprecations against authorities), but, precisely because Amaro and his public did not meet each other during the carnival calendar or in a festival context, it is impossible to write off the moments of antagonism and the threats of violence that are written into the sermons (within irreverent but coherent commentary, sudden interjections of 'arrear, cornudos, a otra parte' ['Get moving, cuckolds!'] or 'Si me bajo de aquí, perro judío, cornudo . . . contigo hablo . . . si me bajo de aquí, Dios dijo lo que será' ['if I get down from here, Jew dog, cuckold . . . I'm talking to you . . . if I get down from here, God knows what will happen']) as harmless, carnival violence. The response of the public does not fit into any single 'reading' of madness; he evoked laughter, scorn, donations and the patronage of the city's archbishop. Were the people he antagonised or who mocked him the same people who gave him alms? Were they, in a sense, paying for their entertainment? Or did others fill his cup out of pity for the ridicule he received from the mockers? How did the *hermanos* who always accompanied him understand and see their obligations to Christian charity, the hospital's budget and public order? Did Don Amaro see himself as the crusading voice of truth, as a *bufón*, or was he unaware of the way his public and patrons saw him? We cannot know, but it seems certain that the *hermanos*, the hospital administrators, the public spectators, the archbishop and Amaro himself had different understandings of what Don Amaro's madness *meant*.

The admission records of the hospital confirm the multiple motivations behind internment and challenge a Foucauldian notion of the insane hospital as a dumping ground for those who threatened the social

status quo. The majority of patients were brought to the hospital by concerned citizens who saw them wandering in the streets. In some cases,
López notes, it seemed to be a case of locals 'protecting the madman
who "wandered through the streets being mistreated"' while in others
'we can also discover the opposite situation, the madman who is sent to
the Hospital to protect those who he, in a furious state, was injuring'.[53]
They were, however, not merely trying to render invisible disturbing
elements of society. All of the hospital charters specified charitable
treatment with the goal of a cure. From Córdoba: the mad should be
attended 'according to their illness, administering them food, drink, and
necessary medicines, and they should remain in the Hospital until they
are cured and convalesce and then are sent off with the grace of God'.[54]
And while physical restraints were used when absolutely necessary to
control violence, all evidence – the accounts of witnesses, the records
of staff and patient activities, and the inventories of the space and
equipment in the asylums – indicates that the cages and chains which
Foucault describes were only methods of last resort in the Spanish institutions of Cervantes's time. In general, treatment consisted of medical
care and, wherever possible, a reintegration into productive society.[55]
The language of the charters and the scant documents available from
admissions and discharges (many of the patients *were* released, at least
ostensibly 'cured') are strikingly lacking in charged rhetoric or symbolic
narratives. While madmen might represent an Apostle one day a year
or the folly of *Don Carnal* on another, they could also, on other days,
represent nothing more than sick people who needed physical care, for
their own sake and that of others.

Revisiting Bakhtin: Madness and *Fiesta*

Where Foucault focused on the institutions created to control and
limit the threatening potential of madness, Bakhtin emphasised the
extra-institutional power of unreason to subvert institutions and con-
trols. Correspondingly, literary critics of the *Quixote* who rely on a
Foucauldian theoretical framework are likely to see Quixote's madness
– or, rather, society's need to brand him as mad – as tragic, while the
Bakhtinian reader will focus on the liberating force of the text's inversion of mad and sane. While Bakhtin, like Foucault, wrote about a time
and place other than Cervantine Spain, the Bakhtinian lens would initially seem the more promising one, as seventeenth-century Spain was
indeed a period marked by festival and theatrical representations, and
madness or folly was a common theme. However, it is important to look

more closely at these festive representations of madness before we judge that Cervantes's madness is indeed carnivalesque.

Bakhtin saw popular festivals as an 'authentic' popular expression, apart from and subversive of dominant traditions: festivals in sixteenth- and seventeenth-century Spain were, however, shaped and organised by the Church and government (national or local), with ties to popular tradition *and* dominant institutions.[56] Indeed, the increased prominence of *fiestas de locos* (and *fiestas* in general) in the decade prior to the publication of the first part of the *Quixote* was largely promoted by the most dominant figure of all: the king. After an agonising illness, Felipe II died and was succeeded by his young son Felipe III, more *bon vivant* than *buen gobernador*. The change of power, according to Agustín Redondo, 'provoked a complete change in atmosphere. There was a true release. The liberating power of laughter, of carnivalesque madness, was rediscovered.'[57] The Crown sponsored elaborate pageants which featured 'an inversion of hierarchies and the rules imposed by dominant groups, a return to innocence, the release which comes with the temporary suspension of the norms of daily life'.[58] While the word *madness* was applied to this inversion of hierarchies, there is a difference between such a general atmosphere and the specific representation of *locos*. There were *locos* in the traditional carnival pageant, but as Redondo points out, 'the carnival "*loco*" does not suffer from mental illness . . . even when the costume is the same. The carnival *loco* gives the qualifier of "mad" or "simple" . . . to himself, he, unlike the demented person, knows what his "madness," his "simplicity" consists of'.[59] That these roles were usually played by actors, within a theatrical context and narrative which performers and spectators alike recognised, should make us pause before assuming that such representations were characteristic of the interactions with the (possibly) mad in that 'daily life' that carnival inverted.

The participants in the State-sponsored pageants often belonged to the Court's stable of 'madmen, dwarves, and men of pleasure'.[60] The royal entertainment corps consisted principally of three types: those with some physical irregularity or deformity, the jesters or *truhanes* who feigned madness or simplicity, and the truly mad or simple. The third group was by far the smallest. José Moreno Villa notes that sometimes the entry of a new *loco* in the palace was marked with the note 'from Zaragoza' because of the madhouse there from which the royal family recruited *locos*.[61] The king's 'talent scouts' would consult with the hospital administrators to choose the 'right' type of *loco*, although sometimes, Moreno Villa notes, the same registers record a prompt return to the hospital, 'returned, doubtless, for not providing diversion for the Court or perhaps because the individual's pathological state exceeded the desired limits.'[62] We get a good idea of the actual mental state of most of the Court performers from the letters of one *truhán*, Alonso Enrique de Guzmán. Defending his choice of profession, he wrote that 'I have always been . . . short on wealth but never on wits. I suffered from too much of the latter rather than a lack of the former.'[63] The 'madness' in the palace pageants was a scripted or ritualised satire, rather than a complex of physical and verbal loss of control.

In general, the atmosphere of festive buffoonery of the Court and the madness in *Don Quixote* have been overemphasised, and the difference between 'true' madmen and their imitators overlooked.[64] The majority of the court jesters were very deliberately playing a role. The court occasionally put on public plays for carnival or other festivals in which these actors played the parts of carnival monarchs.[65] Still, as Fernando Bouza Álvarez affirms, in general 'assuming the role of the nobility or even royalty, seems to have been a court game more than anything else'.[66] The public knew that when the royal *locos* went home they were no longer queens and counts, and that when carnival was over the *rey de gallos* (or the *obispillo*, or the *rey de fadas*, or any number of variants of parodic representations of royalty) returned to his ordinary status.

Most carnival celebrations were not directly staged by the court but were part of centuries-old local traditions. The performers here were the townspeople themselves. Still, by Cervantes's time, it was difficult to speak of a 'popular' festival tradition which had not been embedded in a narrative of Catholic order and piety. And most importantly, despite their apparent disorder, carnival festivities were marked off – in time, in morality – from the rest of daily life. The carnival is a framed event, and the participants recognise and accept this (when they cease to do so, as Umberto Eco points out, carnivals become revolutions).[67] We need not take a firm stance as to whether carnival ultimately destabilises power or neutralises destabilising energies in order to appreciate that the same events and terms experienced within the carnival space would be interpreted very differently in the world beyond the frame. With respect to madness then, we should be wary of assuming that the comic, satiric, carnival interpretation of madness operated outside a few authorised spaces. It would be a mistake to argue that such public representations of madness had no effect on non-carnival interactions, but there were many other competing understandings which affected day-to-day relationships with the unreasonable.

The Inquisition as Source

The *fiesta de locos* and the washing of the Valencia patients' feet on Holy Thursday, while differing in tone and in the relation established between 'sane' and 'mad', share an allegorical narrative that depends on an inversion of worldly values. These disparate rituals both have a prescribed tone and interpretation. It would seem that madness in early modern Spain, while perhaps not tied to *one* allegorical narrative, was still fundamentally seen in symbolic terms. However, we are perhaps limited by our sources: sermons, satires, *comedias* and romances sought primarily to instruct (*delectare* and *movere* were always subordinate to *docere*), to use symbols to convey messages. Symbolic clarity may simply come with the medium. The reader has no reason at this point to suppose that *Don Quixote* is not also using madness in this way and for these ends, except perhaps for a sense that *Don Quixote*, distancing itself from romance and satire in many other ways, might logically be expected to present its central trope in a new way. But let us suspend this question for a moment, and ask whether there *is* another madness, one that occurred largely among the illiterate (or if literate, disinclined to write) and, secondly, if this other madness might have other symbolic meanings, teach other lessons, or perhaps refuse to teach or symbolise something else at all. This might seem the literary equivalent to the Zen question of trees falling in the forest. We would love to discover the secret video recorder left in the woods, or the invisible, omniscient and entirely reliable *historiador* who followed around the objects of our scholarly interest, but we also know, from *Don Quixote* as from Kurosawa, that no historian and no historical source is a transparent window to the truth. Unless we despair of knowing anything about the past then, we must think through the sources available, consider what the biases and lacunae of each text might be, and how those judgements shape our interpretation of what the texts say.

The flourishing critical field of 'law and literature' studies provides us with examples of methodological strategies and possibilities for reading legal records as a historical source without losing sight of the context in which they are produced and/or their subjective, narrative quality.[68] The bulk of these works emphasize the shared humanist culture of 'men of letters', and thus focus on canon or civil law. The Inquisition would seem to represent the opposite of this tradition, both because of its anti-humanist ideology and because its procedures would seem to preclude the inclusion of voices other than the Inquisitors' own. It is, thus, not surprising that few early modern Spanish literary scholars have drawn on its archives. Yet the Inquisition files do not consist solely of terrible edicts or torture-induced confessions: the Tribunal's judicial procedures produced texts at every step of an investigation and, as a result, the files incorporate and mediate different voices (the Inquisitors, writing individually and in the name of the institution they represented; defendants; witnesses; learned consultants; Inquisition personnel, etc.).[69] Many of the documents were not for public consumption; these are the raw materials that the Church would later process and adjust for propagandistic goals, but in themselves they include everything from openly heretical statements to critiques of Inquisition practice to seemingly irrelevant digressions. Within the archives are over one hundred trial transcripts or other documents regarding trials in which a defendant either pled insanity or for whom insanity was alleged.[70] If we truly wish to understand madness in early modern Spain, how can we not at least look at these accounts and think about their possible reliability as historical sources?

What, then, are the possible symptoms and risks of the *mal d'archive*[71] when it comes to accounts of madness? The Inquisition texts could be unreliable on two levels: at the level of the individual accounts embedded as testimonies and depositions (i.e., the witnesses and accused are lying) and at the institutional level (i.e., the scribe was not recording what really happened). Let me begin with the former. The Inquisitors acknowledged that the insane person was incapable of will, and therefore of heresy; thus, insanity, if proven to the Inquisitors' satisfaction, meant absolution or suspension of the case. It is only logical then, that many suspects before the Inquisition claimed or performed insanity in order to escape prosecution. However, for the purposes of the current study, it scarcely matters whether any individual was lying when he claimed he had been mad: the way in which an early modern Spaniard feigned madness, the ways that authorities attempted to counter such imposture, and the interpersonal and linguistic structures that this challenge produced are what interests us, not any precise count of madmen in early modern Spain.[72] Furthermore, the repetition of certain words, symptoms and dynamics from case to case and tribunal to tribunal show that, regardless of whether individual witnesses were telling the truth about *their* mental state, this was the way mental illness was thought of during the period. It should be noted that most of my accounts come not from the accused themselves but from secondary witnesses to the events leading to an arrest, or friends and family who were called as 'character witnesses' to fill out a picture of the defendant's mental state. These witnesses were not on trial and outside the prosecution of rings of Judaizers and *moros* (and none of the madmen I cite were arrested as Judaizers or Muslims) – witnesses were not tricked into self-incrimination. The best evidence that outside witnesses did not feel pressured by the Inquisition to give any particular narrative is the frequency with which witnesses in the same case disagreed in their accounts of events and their interpretations of the accused's mental states. Finally, no witnesses were tortured, and in only one of the cases I cite was the accused tortured. Because the Inquisitors considered torture to be a completely legitimate procedure, they did not hesitate to write down when it was employed. The scrupulous detail about the torture used in many other *procesos* allows us to accept at face value the absence of torture in those cases where it is not mentioned.

What, then, about the idea that the *procesos* themselves are not an accurate representation of what went on in the proceedings? As Sara Nalle writes in the introduction to *Mad for God,* her groundbreaking study of one early modern madman, the court record 'is not the equivalent of a tape recording . . . the spoken language underwent some conventional modifications. Irrelevant responses were dropped, and all speech that was preserved was converted into the third person, past tense.'[73] I will return in my final chapter to the difficulties presented by this subjective determination of what was 'irrelevant' and other occasional intrusions by the scribes, but in general we can assume that the written account was a faithful transcription, as the entire testimony was read back to the defendant at the end of each *audiencia* and he was asked to ratify it. Such a ratification was obviously made in a context of pressure and vastly unequal authority, but in several *procesos* I consulted the defendant registered objections and these were also recorded and changes were made. Unless we are to make the Borgesian assertion that the whole process of ratification, including the refusal to do so, was a creation of the Inquisition, we can generally accept that the written transcript 'does represent what was said for the record'.[74] The scribes were taking notes because the hierarchical, bureaucratic structure of the Inquisition required that precise records of each case pass from the local tribunals to the *Suprema* and vice versa. In order for the *Suprema* to maintain centralised control over its vast network, it had to know exactly what was happening in each and every case. Since an insanity defence generally posed problems for the Inquisitors, letters between *Suprema* and tribunal usually went back and forth several times during these *procesos*. The *Suprema* kept close tabs on its tribunals, calling officials to Madrid or rotating them to other posts. It would have been difficult to carry out any sort of fraud for very long.

Madness and the Inquisition

I hope to have addressed the principal qualms which have led to the omission of Inquisition sources in previous studies of *Don Quixote* and to have suggested some of the possibilities the archives may hold. It should be noted that I am in no way asserting that Miguel de Cervantes ever came before the Inquisition or saw an Inquisition document (there is no evidence that he did). The archival material contains accounts of patterns of social interaction and processes of judgement that occurred every day on Manchegan roads: *these* are what any early modern Spaniard could have and must have seen. The Inquisition not only produced records of early modern madness, however, but also affected the nature of that madness. It is not a coincidence that so many defendants pleaded insanity before the Inquisition, while in secular courts it seems to have been relatively rare, although the insanity defence was equally valid in both.[75] This can be explained by the Inquisition's particular status as a tribunal of faith. While secular courts also consider will and intention, their emphasis is on proving and punishing acts. There are no secular crimes which exist *solely* in the realm of thought. In contrast, the Inquisition's end goal was a purification of belief and thought. It is true that a heresy declared in the public square received a harsher punishment than one offered in one's home, but this was because the public heresy had a greater chance of propagating itself, weakening the faiths of others.[76] In a secular trial, intentions and beliefs are generally irrelevant; at the most, they may mitigate the punishment, but they rarely determine guilt and innocence. In contrast, *every* case before the Inquisition involved an interrogation of nuances of thought. Even in the prosecutions of the least thought-based crimes under the Inquisition's jurisdiction (violence to a *familiar*, falsification of genealogy), the sincerity and extent of repentance carried a weight unknown to secular proceedings. As María Sacristán writes: 'for the Holy Office, it was very important to know the mental state of those denounced, since what the Tribunal punished was not the sinful act in itself, but rather the intention which induced a Christian to commit it'.[77] Anything that impeded the accused's capacity for reason or mitigated his/her intentions – not just madness but drunkenness, overwhelming emotion, ignorance, youth – justified a lesser punishment, or entitled him to go free. The Inquisitors were constantly forced to make judgements about mental states, and in their search to do so they called upon 'professionals' – priests, physicians, surgeons – but they also asked witnesses of the deviant behaviour – often peasants, women, fellow prisoners and other figures whose opinions rarely filter into the written record – to speculate about the internal state of persons they had observed.

Furthermore, the Inquisition's presence – even in its absence, thanks to the network of 'embedded' *familiares* – meant that the interrogation of thought that marks the *procesos* became a constant feature of public life. When the Inquisitor made his visit, he emphasised to the community that it was their duty as Christians not only to be vigilant about their own faith but also to protect their friends and neighbours from error and sin. The faithful Catholic understood it as his duty to monitor the orthodoxy of speech all around him, and then make judgements as to the thought behind it. If the words were proffered without will because the speaker was crazy, no sin had been committed. (Every document and testimony I read confirms that this was a shared belief at all levels of society. Debates swirled around the methods and proof of this internal state, but there was no debate – in the Church, the law, or the *pueblo* – about the essential innocence of the truly insane.) The citizen thus had no motive to denounce the mad blasphemer. The soul of the speaker was not in danger as he was not capable of sin, nor was the soul of the listener in danger of complicity in allowing a sin to go unpunished. The listener's responsibility as a Christian was to humanely remove the speaker from any context in which he might affect others, and then make sure that any other witnesses shared his opinion of the speaker's capacity and, consequently, his dismissal of the proffered blasphemy. Coming to such a consensus and advising others necessarily led to further discussions about the speaker's mental state and the exchange of personal criteria for making a diagnosis, exactly the sort of interchange which dominates discussions along Cervantes's trails and inns.

The constant interrogation of neighbours' interiority inevitably led to a climate of self-interrogation. The records show a surprising number of self-denunciations and spontaneous confessions resulting from an internalised self-Inquisition.[78] If we accept as a basic component of many forms of insanity a temporary loss of self-control, we can see how this tendency toward self-judgement would be heightened among such a population. The epileptics, the manics, the delusionals would face, in their moments of clarity, the terrifying task of reconstructing and accounting for their speech and actions, the disjunction between what they perceived and what those they trusted reported to them. The resulting confusion created a general anxiety and uncertainty about one's own capacity to sin. The debate of 'was so-and-so sane when he said such-and-such?' became 'was I sane when I said such-and-such?' No figure demonstrates more clearly the effects of an Inquisitional environment of enforced orthodoxy on a mind made incoherent by madness than Torquato Tasso, the Italian poet whose theories of the epic almost surely influenced Cervantes. Tasso, in addition to composing some of the most celebrated works in the Renaissance canon, spent seven years in a madhouse, and suffered for most of his life from delusions, paranoia, alternating melancholic and manic fits, and an unappeasable (even by assurances from the Inquisitors) fear of having unconsciously committed heresy. His story is particularly useful because Tasso was a poet and philosopher, and thus predisposed to put his fears and doubts into writing. We have over 1,500 of his letters, many written from the madhouse, in which he attempts to understand and represent his own unreason.[79] Tasso had a privileged language in which to work through his own crises of the self, but the Inquisition called to account many common folk, and they had to piece together their own strategies and narratives for reconciling perceived and reported realities.

This sort of psychological vigilance became particularly necessary after the Council of Trent. According to Gustav Henningsen and Jaime Contreras, beginning in the 1540s 'the Holy Office embarked on what would become its most important task: the consolidation of the dogmas and moral teachings of the Counter-Reformation'. These were prosecutions against old Christians for minor blasphemies and scandalous propositions, and almost always the accused confessed his offence (often mitigated by a plea of ignorance or a momentary lapse of judgement) and was given a relatively minor punishment (*abjure de levi*, exemplary lashes, spiritual penances, instruction). Between 1540 and 1700, by Henningsen and Contreras's count, these 'lesser crimes' constituted 57.8 per cent of the tribunal's caseload. The nature of the most commonly denounced propositions also has particular resonance with the error at the heart of *Don Quixote*. Particularly common were the expression of doubt about the virginity of the Virgin Mary before, during and after Jesus' birth, and the negation of the reality of transubstantiation.[80] At heart in both of these is the confrontation between a perceived reality and a belief to be taken on faith. Early modern Spaniards were constantly interrogating each other and themselves about the nature between perception and reality, between truth and the verisimilar. And in fact, when defendants refused to acknowledge doctrinal truth on these points after the Inquisitors repeatedly set it out for them and made clear the consequences of refusing to submit, the Inquisitors, rather than assuming this to be a sign of radical heresy, often initiated investigations into the accused's sanity. A sign of sanity in early modern Spain was the ability to recognise when to trust one's own eyes and experience, and when to cede to another authority. Shifted to a non-theological context, this is very much the debate and the criteria for diagnosis which guides much of the *Quixote*.

The person called to account for behaviours he could not control or remember faced a difficult choice. If he confessed his lack of control or command and could convince the accusing authorities of this, he faced possible stigmatisation and marginalisation as a *loco*. A determination of *locura* by any judicial or civil authority was grounds for economic dispossession, annulment of marriage and prohibition of exercise of a trade. The Inquisition felt safe in letting *locos* go free because they assumed that the stamp of *locura* would overshadow any heresy or scandal they might later cause; they would be treated as objects of pity or scorn but what they said and did would be treated as irrelevant. The accounts I have seen show that this did often occur, but also that early modern Spaniards were, in practice, accepting of ideas of partial or temporary madnesses. Family members, neighbours and customers often went about their daily dealings with the *loco* until he showed signs of an onset of his *locura,* at which point they would help subdue or isolate him, as their temperament and the situation required. This flexibility required the identification of specific behaviours or situations which signalled a shift from sanity to madness, and again led to personal and communal agreements about these symptoms and how best to respond to them.

The best evidence that we have that a determination of insanity was not the end of an individual's participation in society was that it was frequently invoked, even when the alternative might have been a fairly moderate punishment. Hence the Inquisition's dilemma: as much as the Inquisitor firmly believed that a 'true' madman could not sin and deserved no punishment, he was very suspicious of being tricked. The claim of mental incapacity, particularly temporary mental incapacity, was (and is) frustratingly difficult to prove. According to Hélène Tropé, 'the suspicion that madness was feigned ... was an obsession for the Inquisitors, and at the same time, it presented them with problems that were difficult to resolve. Without a doubt, that *no man's land* of presumably feigned madness ... [was] the Spanish canon lawyer's greatest concern.'[81] The Inquisitors devised all sorts of 'ingenious tricks and methods' to suss out fakers,[82] along with secret heretics, false mystics, feigned revelations, and a whole host of crimes of imposture which, in the late sixteenth century, 'become a fixture on the dockets of inquisition tribunals'.[83] Whereas medieval jurists would have judged principally between virtue and heresy, by the seventeenth century, 'the category of the natural expanded to encompass a wide range of purportedly miraculous events, and religious enthusiasm was increasingly described in medical terms, or as a psychological disorder, or dismissed as deliberate fraud'.[84] So it was now possible that visions and miracles were both false (in the sense that they were not true supernatural experiences) *and* real (in the sense that the subject believed them to be so, was not consciously faking them but was the innocent victim of a disease). Yet most of the 'tricks and methods' designed to determine between true, faked or mad were based on a dualist model.[85] They assumed that reason could ferret out the faker and affirm the true visionary – a faker would prove to be inconsistent, he would succumb to predictable and logical arguments and tricks. Inevitably, these strategies of reason failed and often led to circular and almost comical (at least from a distance of 400 years) results, when applied to the subject whose very problem was his inconsistency, illogic and unreason. Medical science was even less helpful, as the understanding of the human mind had changed little from Galen to Huarte de San Juan. The authorities often recognised the failure of their methods, but they had no other language or practice by which to attempt to diagnose unreason.

In the secular realm, everyday folk also sought to differentiate between malingerers and the truly ill, but since they did not have access to elaborate treatises on the matter, the 'clinical' terminology (such as it was) of vapours and humours do not generally figure in their accounts. Yet it is clear that they were facing the same problem as the 'experts,' being forced to make the same judgements and using the same criteria. On the streets, in churches and courts, they had to decide if the strange actors they witnessed were *sabios*, *bellacos* or *fuera de juicio* (wise men, rogues or out of their mind), to use the terms they most often offer, and which are so frequently offered as explanations for behaviour in *Don Quixote*.

Thus the Counter-Reformation led to a simultaneous increase in the preoccupation with knowing another's internal state and the recognition of its difficulty. Yet the dominant literary genres of the sixteenth century – the romance, the comedy, the epic, the satire – are all characterised by a narrative dominance that precludes gaps between what a narrator wishes to know and what he can, or which discourages multiple readings. When characters are mad, their madness has a known cause and consistent symptoms which support a final moral lesson. When characters are feigning madness, this is known to the reader from the beginning and revealed to the characters at the end. Even works which have been hailed as revealing the ambiguity of madness, such as Erasmus's *The Praise of Folly*, really do not;[86] they may explore multiple understandings of madness, but at the end the narrator steps in to reduce any *true* ambiguity and to fix the moral meaning behind all of these manifestations.

This morally clear reading of madness was, in various sectors of society, being displaced by a much more complex and confusing new madness, a madness which challenged society, ethics, knowledge and institutions. It will now be necessary to show that *this* madness is the one we find in *Don Quixote*.

Notes

1. In Ch. 1 of *El loco en el espejo*, published after this chapter was written, Belén Atienza provides a panorama of representations of madness in early modern Spain which coincides in many ways with the one presented here. In her chapter Atienza stresses the need to 'unearth' experiences of early madness that challenge the typical literary or historiographic narratives and in the interest of doing so she cites many of the same sources that I do in this chapter. Still, Atienza's principal interest, the theatricality of madness in Lope de Vega, inevitably leads her away from the non-theatrical examples she has 'unearthed' in her first chapter. The return to the idea of madness as spectacle reflects the fact that in his *plays* Lope is engaging a particular tradition of madness with roots in medieval *theatre* and theatricality. Nontheatrical, non-allegorical madnesses did, as Atienza documents, proliferate in Lope's time, but they are not relevant to his work in the way that they are for Cervantes.
2. Pseudonym given to the eponymous subject of *Sybil*, 'the true story of a woman possessed by sixteen separate personalities' (Schreiber).
3. In *On the Sacred Disease*, Hippocrates argues that madness is no 'more divine or sacred than any other disease' but acknowledges that 'it has been regarded as a divine visitation' (qtd in Hershkowitz: 2).
4. In *The Republic*, for example, Plato compares the soul to the state, and says that, in both, the domination by 'non-intellectual elements' is 'delusion, folly' and can only lead to 'loss of insight and tendency towards excess' (qtd in Hershkowitz: 9).
5. Saunders: 69.
6. Saunders: 73–4.
7. In Chapter 1, he offers a variety of allegorical meanings for medieval and Renaissance images and texts about madness, but it is only in Chapter 3, 'The Insane', that he retrospectively refers to the treatment of unreason in actual *people* in early modern Europe: Confinement 'signifies thereby an important change in the consciousness of *evil*. The Renaissance had freely allowed the forms of *unreason* to come out into the light of day; public outrage gave evil the powers of example and redemption.' The plurality of meanings from Chapter 1 disappears; here unreason is evil. Foucault, *Madness and Civilization*: 67.
8. Foucault, *Madness and Civilization*: 70.
9. Among the images and texts cited, Foucault mentions Cervantes, claiming that he and Shakespeare are the last figures of an age where 'madness still occupies an extreme place, in that it is beyond appeal', a reference point

against which 'we may decipher what is happening, at the beginning of the seventeenth century, in the *literary* experience of madness' (Foucault, *Madness and Civilization*: 31, italics mine). Nonetheless, the rest of the book will speak of societal experiences of madness, 'the *world* of the seventeenth century' etc. (Foucault, *Madness and Civilization*: 39).

10. Tropé.
11. López Alonso.
12. For example, James Iffland, in his summary of the readings of madness in *Don Quijote*, starts out noting that Foucault's 'Great Confinement' consists of 'practical measures that began to proliferate during the seventeenth century in Europe' but he then goes on to quote Foucault's discussion of this process at length, remarking that 'Seen as another representative of the underground danger of unreason, this threatening space of absolute liberty, madness turns into something that must be eradicated, something whose de-territorializing power should be neutralised through the reduction of the space in which it moves' (Iffland: 65). In a footnote he then cites Enrique González Duro's conclusions to the same effect about the Hospital of Innocents in Seville. González Duro's attitude toward the early modern period is shaped by his perspective as a modern day psychiatrist and by his reading of Foucault. Hélène Tropé, the historian who has worked most closely with the actual archives of the Hospital de Inocentes, comes to radically different conclusions.
13. Michael MacDonald's ground-breaking study of madness in early modern England suggests that many fewer madmen were institutionalised in seventeenth-century England than Foucault claims, and calls into question the applicability of many of Foucault's theses to England in general.
14. González Duro: 150.
15. Ibid.
16. Foucault, *Madness and Civilization*: 48–53.
17. According to González Duro, beginning in 1523 the *Cortes* regularly 'issue[d] successive pronouncements against the proliferation of beggars' (González Duro: 138). For more on early modern Spanish poverty and various reform projects (Soto and Robles; Vives; Cavillac), see Cruz, *Discourses of Poverty*, Ch. 1, 2; Soto and Robles.
18. González Duro: 139.
19. Ibid.
20. Ibid.: 141.
21. Salas Barbadillo.
22. Qtd in González Duro: 141.
23. See Cruz: Ch. 2; and Soto and Robles.
24. González Duro: 144.
25. Qtd in González Duro: 146.
26. Cavillac.
27. For an introduction, see Cohn; Emmerson and McGinn; Collins, McGinn and Stein.
28. Kagan: 99. The bibliography on individual prophet figures is immense. For more general works on popular prophesy movements in Spain, see Cueto Ruiz; Huerga.
29. This doctrine was clearly laid out by Jean Gerson in 'Discretio Spirituum'

and 'De Distinctione Verarum Visionum a Falsis' in the early fifteenth century, and the majority of early modern Spanish theologians continued to uphold his ideas regarding the relative weakness and susceptibility of women to demonic temptation. At the same time, we see that the most 'successful' (although most ending ultimately in prosecution) mystic movements in early modern Spain were led by women, e.g., Santa Teresa, Sor María de la Visitación, Lucrecia de León, Sor Luisa de la Ascención and Sor María de Agreda. There could never have been a *Doña Quixote*; female unreason was much less likely to be interpreted as a product of natural disease. See Giles; Sarrión Mora; Sluhovsky; van Deusen.

30. Zijderveld: 34, qtd in Iffland: 150.
31. Keitt, 'Religious Enthusiasm': 235; Keitt expands on these ideas in *Inventing the Sacred*.
32. Keitt, 'Religious Enthusiasm': 235.
33. Kagan: 38.
34. Ibid.: 36–7.
35. Lucrecia de León was a young woman in late-sixteenth century Madrid whose prophetic-apocalyptic dreams of the fall of Spain were transcribed and circulated among some of the most powerful members of the Church and Court. In addition to Kagan, see Jordán Arroyo; Blázquez Miguel.
36. Lucrecia was, by all accounts, one of the sanest participants in her story. Her sanity was never seriously questioned, as she seemed quite capable of caring for herself and, while awake, controlling her speech and body. However, many of the men who interacted with her (Juan de Dios, Domingo Navarro, Alonso Mendoza) were dismissed by acquaintances and authorities as mad.
37. Adán Carballo, AHN Inq. Leg. 200, Exp. 28.
38. López Alonso: 82.
39. For a full account, see Merenciano.
40. The founding constitutions for most of the hospitals have been preserved, but as far as records of daily operations, *ingresos* and *egresos*, the most complete preserved records are for the Valencia hospital. The Seville archives are fairly complete beginning in 1680, with some information for the earlier centuries.
41. Tropé: 372–5.
42. Baquero: 38.
43. González Duro: 153.
44. Tropé: 231.
45. Ibid.: 295.
46. Ibid.: 289.
47. Ibid.
48. Ibid.: 300.
49. Ibid.: 375.
50. Ibid.: 281.
51. López Alonso: 190.
52. The majority of the biographical information for Don Amaro comes from the 'Noticias de la vida de Don Amaro' which precedes the printed collection of his sermons. It is not clear who transcribed or edited the sermons, or who wrote these 'Noticias'. See Estepa.

53. López Alonso: 50–2.
54. Qtd in López Alonso: 82.
55. Ibid.: 290–4. For further documentation of the less than repressive treatment in Spanish asylums, see Ullersperger: 113–16.
56. For a general introduction to the history and sociology of carnival in early modern Spain, see Caro Baroja; Burke; Heers.
57. Redondo: 60.
58. Ibid.: 199.
59. Ibid.
60. The phrase comes from Bouza Álvarez.
61. Moreno Villa: 18. Lope recounts the same practice at the asylum in Valencia. Lope, *El peregrino en su patria*, and *Los locos de Valencia*.
62. Moreno Villa: 18.
63. Qtd in Bouza Álvarez: 120.
64. See Márquez Villanueva, 'Planteamiento'; Molho; Redondo; Iffland.
65. For a description of several such representations, see Bouza Álvarez: 71–2.
66. Bouza Álvarez: 142.
67. Eco.
68. The connections between forensics and theatre go back to classical times, but Hayden White is perhaps the founder of the modern turn towards reading law as narrative. The field is dominated by work on English literature (particularly theatre) and law. Important works outside the English context include Davis; Kahn and Hutson; Rabell; González Echevarría; Kallendorf.
69. For an introduction to the procedures of the Spanish Inquisition and the purpose and provenance of the texts in the individual files, see: Lea; Escandell Bonet and Pérez Villanueva; Kamen.
70. At the time of writing, my count is at approximately 150. There is no databank which notes the presence of madness in cases, so I have relied on secondary sources, hunches based on other information in catalogues, and a great deal of skimming. Given how much of the Inquisition archive has been lost, I am certain the actual number is much, much greater.
71. Derrida.
72. In their collection of nine criminal trials from seventeenth-century Rome, Thomas V. Cohen and Elizabeth Cohen remind us that even a lie, *especially* a lie, 'must bear verisimilitude' (Cohen and Cohen: 10). They consider many of the same issues discussed here and make a similar case for an informed credulity. The papal courts followed an inquisitorial model and thus most of their arguments and conclusions can be applied here.
73. Nalle: 5. For additional discussion of the possible uses and abuses of Inquisition documents, see Dedieu.
74. Nalle: 5.
75. Granted, we have many fewer remaining records of secular trials, but the extant records and the secondary literature about civil and criminal trials do not mention defences made on the grounds of insanity. For more on the classical and medieval history of the insanity defence see Midelfort: 182–96.
76. For the implications of public and private heresy, see Henningsen and Contreras.

77. Sacristán: 23–4.
78. Clearly most self-denunciations stemmed from a desire to take advantage of an edict of grace or, when this was not an option, to receive a milder penalty. However, there are numerous cases of suspects whose denunciations seem to – or at least in the Inquisition's judgement – correspond to imaginary 'crimes' or to 'crimes' possibly committed in a period of unconsciousness.
79. For the complete correspondence, see Tasso, *Le lettere di Torquato Tasso*. For biography and criticism on Tasso's madness, see Brand; Basile. I discuss Tasso in more depth in Chapter 5.
80. These came in second and third in terms of frequency. By far the most common denounced proposition was the denial that sex between consenting unmarried adults was a mortal sin. By Julio Sierra's calculation, a full 18 per cent of all the 1,554 cases heard by the tribunal of Toledo between 1575 and 1610 were for this 'offence' (Sierra: 166).
81. Tropé: 188–9.
82. Ibid.: 190.
83. Keitt, 'Religious enthusiasm': 235.
84. Ibid.: 233–4.
85. See Sluhovsky: Ch. 3.
86. As an example (just one of many) of this sort of reading of *The Praise of Folly*, see Iffland: 149–50.

Chapter 2

The Symptoms of Madness

Within the novel, there is no doubt about the origin and symptoms of Don Quixote's madness. The narrator unequivocally affirms that the gentleman read so many tales of chivalry that he took them to be real, and then cast himself as a knight errant and his present world as that of the epic. Quixote is not alone in his difficulties in judging the 'truth value' of texts; all of the characters in *Don Quixote* share a confusion between historical truth, poetic or moral truth, entertaining fiction and outright forgeries and lies,[1] yet only Don Quixote is considered mad because of it. Nor can his decision to participate in a fictional lifestyle be viewed as proof of madness per se; Don Quixote moves in a world of students and courtesans playing at shepherds, of dukes and duchesses playing at God. What symptom, or conjunction of symptoms, within the novel marks Don Quixote *as mad*, while others are merely opportunistic, gullible or bored? Do these symptoms resonate at all with those that similarly marked sixteenth-century historical subjects?

Quijano's movement from ingenuousness to true madness is found in his shift from a passive credulity about the past to an active imposition of that past world on the present and future, in situations where it is entirely out of context, and often when it will cause him harm. He assumes for himself not just a new identity but an *impossible* one: not just a modern-day knight but the greatest, noblest, bravest knight in history (or, more accurately, in literature), in love with a similarly superlative Dulcinea. He is obsessed with this grandiose identity and the feats he feels it compels him to accomplish, regardless of the obstacles in his way or the attempts to convince him otherwise. The more his friends and associates reject this identity, the more events conspire to (in the eyes of all those around him) render it ridiculous, the more he affirms its reality.[2]

This inability to determine between levels of representation, an obsession with a 'pet' idea that is in the eyes of society excessive, and delusions of grandeur are traits that Don Quixote shares with many early modern madmen. In both cases, these traits contribute to behaviour which, in the eyes of observers, is inconsistent with the context in which it is performed. Loss of physical control was another frequently cited symptom of madness. While other literary madmen (the inmates of the hospital in Lope's *Los locos de Valencia*, the title character of 'El licenciado Vidriera') are called 'crazy' by other characters for their mad *speech*, the majority of historical madmen also suffered from periodic inabilities to control their *actions*, particularly their own bodies. Most madness in the archives involved some form of violence, fits and/or periods of unconsciousness, what a doctor defined to the Inquisitors as 'hechos extraordinarios que no tienen por objeto algún hecho juicioso o razonable' ('extraordinary acts that do not have as their object any sensible or reasonable action').[3] In fact, the lack of any physical manifestation of madness was often cited as evidence that someone was faking. For example, a witness reporting on the mental state of Juan Egujo, a young man who wandered into a monastery and began spouting blasphemies, said he did not believe Egujo was mad because, as he explained it, 'su principal tema es *decir* que es Dios y que es Él que todo lo puede y que es el ángel San Gabriel y otras cosas deste género, pero no *haciendo* locura ninguna' ('his main theme is to *say* that he is God and He for whom all is possible and that he is the angel Gabriel and other things of this nature, but without *doing* anything crazy at all') (italics mine).[4] Years later, Egujo was finally released as mad, based on the testimony of jailers who reported that 'no *hace* acción alguna que no sea de loco' ('he *does* nothing that is not the action of a madman'). The key difference was the perception of physical, rather than verbal, symptoms.

Another common physical symptom was wanderlust; either because fits of violence made normal social relations impossible and necessitated a life of begging and theft, or because the madman chafed at the attempts of family and neighbours to control his symptoms, *locos* often lived a nomadic existence or, at least, periodically disappeared. The nomadism of Cervantes's protagonist also differentiates him from most literary *locos*, who are most commonly found in madhouses or royal courts. When found in literary madhouses, *locos* tend to be grouped according to the sources and signs of their delusions, each category providing the impetus for a moral lesson.[5] In literature of the Court, the madmen (or, as was more often the case, actors pretending to be mad or simple) were comic figures or, sometimes, voices of moral conscience. In Spain, court *locos* did exist, but they are entirely overrepresented in literature. The majority of historical *locos* were, like Quixote, on the roads and in the towns 'whose names we do not care to remember'; just as their bodies periodically escaped their own control, many escaped – at least periodically – the control of family, neighbours and institutions. The combination of physical and verbal symptoms, both uncontrolled speech and uncontrolled movement, is a key link between archive and novel.

Pet Projects and Obsessions

Don Quixote's love for books of chivalry becomes an obsession, and a sign of mental instability, when he pursues it at the expense of his social and economic well-being. He does not just read in his spare time, but rather so much that he neglects the administration of his estate, sells off his land to buy books, and finally 'by selling one thing, and pawning another, and undervaluing everything' (I, vii, 56), he collects enough to abandon family, land and fortune in pursuit of his fantasy. Several of the archival accounts tell similar tales. In true Cervantine spirit, let us listen to their stories (stories, just as in the *Quixote*, always mediated by the genres and institutions that elicited them).

One Giraldo París had been a wealthy and influential man in the Court of Felipe II, but after the king's death, according to a memorial he wrote and presented to the Inquisitors, he had for fifteen years 'apartado de los tráficos del mundo' ('separated himself from the traffic of the world').[6] During this period, when he must have been about Quixote's age (he was sixty-six when denounced to the Inquisition), he immersed himself in the study of alchemy for the same reasons Don Quixote turned to chivalric romances: 'por ocupar el entendimiento y para entretenerme' ('to occupy my mind and to entertain myself'). Like Quixote, who 'spent sleepless nights trying to understand [the books of chivalry] and extract their meaning' (I, i, 20) París became convinced he could, in his words, 'procura[r] poner todas las cosas en razón y equidad' ('manage to place all things in order and equity') through the study of a semi-science (like the chivalric romance's semi-history) which 'Aristotle himself . . . would not have been able to decipher or understand' (I, i, 20). And just as Quixote would have been considered obsessive, but would not have caused much trouble (or generated a novel) had he not decided to leave home and impose his misreadings upon the world, París's actions after emerging from his years of isolation were what got him into trouble. Like Quixote, having developed his own irrational ideas, he proceeded to insist on them in highly unfavourable contexts and to audiences who clearly were not receptive.

París was denounced to the Inquisition by several men who had heard his strange comments about alchemy. While the typical (and prudent) response of those denounced was to answer the Tribunal's questions and either repent or present a reasonable refutation to the charges presented, París took the opportunity of his first *audiencia* to spontaneously present his memorial, entitled 'Memoria de algunas cosas que he discurrido las cuales puedan haber escandalizado los oyentes por no saber a qué fin tendieron o la intención en que me fonde' ('Memorial of certain things on which I have discoursed, which may have scandalised listeners because they did not know to what end they tended or the intention in which they were anchored'), to the Inquisitors. It quickly became clear from the memorial that there had been many listeners (a note from a *familiar* mentions that 'su casa es frecuentada de mucha gente extranjera y Giraldo París es inclinado a disputar y argüir' ['his house is frequented by many foreigners and Giraldo París is given to dispute and argument']) – and that everyone he met got an earful of 'algunas cosas . . . [que] he sacado y me ha[n] servido de fundamento para hacer mis discursos' ('certain things . . . that I have worked out and which have served me as a basis for my speeches').

París shares with Don Quixote a seamless movement from humility to hyperbole. Like the would-be knight who alternately proclaims that he, 'unworthy and a sinner' (I, xxiv, 183), does 'not attempt to persuade anyone that I am clever when I am not' (II, i, 464), and then boasts that he is 'the most valiant knight who e'er girded on a sword!' (I, iii, 32), the would-be alchemist begins his speech modestly, reminding the Tribunal that 'no he estudiado ni sé letras, sino que todo lo que he discurrido ha salido del entendimiento' ('I have not studied nor am I a man of letters, but rather everything of which I have spoken has come from my understanding'), but he soon moves on to the revelation of a secret alchemic code for all of sacred and secular history, with glosses offering policy recommendations for Church and State.

His mission to right the wrongs he sees in the Spanish Empire through his alchemical conclusions has strong affinities with Quixote's professed goal of restoring justice and virtue 'as a service to the nation' (I, i, 21). As the barber mentions at the opening of Part II, there was no shortage of unsolicited *arbitristas* who claimed to have the solution for Spain's woes, but the difference between impertinence and madness lies in context: the correspondence between problem and proposed remedy, the audience to which it is offered. París crosses the line on all counts. While his arguments, like Quixote's lengthy diatribes on arms and letters or the ideal republic, have internal coherence and reveal scholarly erudition, he goes on and on and in the least propitious of venues. The Inquisitors read of his amazement that missionaries continue to have difficulty explaining Christianity to 'indios, moros y gentiles' ('Indians, Moors and Gentiles') when he 'con facilidad . . . a mi parecer [he] hallado ejemplos por donde se puede probar los mas oscuros artículos de nuestra fe cristiana' ('with ease . . . have found what seem to me examples with which one could prove the most obscure articles of the Christian faith'). He also has 'quedado maravillado' ('been left astonished') that Christians have disagreements among themselves, since he can explain the Trinity; the virginity of Mary before, during and after Jesus' birth; the existence of purgatory and hell; and the division of monarchic and papal powers, all according to alchemic principles. Alchemy, his *caballería andante,* is the solution to everything. The end result of his argumentation is a warning directly to the Pope about very specific policies and a Cassandra-like complaint of his frustrated past attempts to correct these abuses, neither the suggested strategy for ingratiating oneself with the Inquisition.

París's faith in alchemy is, like Don Quixote's faith in knight errantry, an anachronistic exaggeration of ideas that had been widespread centuries before.[7] Neither the codes of alchemy nor knight errantry are in themselves mad; París and Quixote's madness lies in the inability to recognise the historical and rhetorical frame in which the ideas were originally formulated, and to adapt the ideas to their own historical situation and rhetorical goals. Both misinterpret texts by reading at the wrong level of representation: taking the literal for the figurative and the figurative for the literal. Both embrace a framework which traditionally had been assumed to operate in a limited sphere of action, and apply it indiscriminately to grand political and moral problems as well as medical maladies and personal dilemmas.

The Inquisitors were concerned about just where París was getting his ideas, and ordered an investigation of his house. The results could practically be interchanged with the scene of the library inspection in Don Quixote. We do not have a record of the exact contents of París's library, but a note from the inspector gives a good general idea:[8]

Los papeles contenidos en esta arca son de diferentes cosas. Hay cartas tocantes a negocios y tratos de su dueño. Hay papeles tocantes a materias de estado. Hay de [papel roto] naturalezas y propiedades de [roto], piedras y metales, y algunas de estas cosas en orden a encantamientos [roto] el dueño está sospechoso. Otros papeles hay en francés que yo no entiendo. Ni he visto cosa que tenga más censura de oficio.

The papers contained in this chest are about different things. There are letters dealing with the owner's business and deals. There are papers dealing with matters of state. There are [torn] the nature and properties of [torn], stones and metals, and some of these things for the purpose of enchantments [torn] the owner is suspect. There are other papers in French which I do not understand. I haven't seen anything else which bears official censorship.

In a later note, he complained that 'el secuestro de Giraldo París es de mucho embarazo y se va continuando, que sólos los libros han de ocupar dos o tres días' ('the confiscation of Geraldo París's possessions is an overwhelming task and is still ongoing, the books alone should take two or three days').

Meanwhile, back in Toledo, París was apparently eager to *add* to what he had explained in his memorial, demanding an *audiencia* (again, a reversal of the usual order of operations) to offer more examples of his theories. He began by mentioning that various locals had come to him for training in the alchemic arts, and he had complied by explaining the parting of the Red Sea and most of Exodus in metallurgical principles. Given that the only thing the Inquisition was more strict with than heresy was the spreading of heresy, this was not a rational strategy, particularly as the Inquisitors had not asked him about any of this. In fact, he seemed to anticipate the Inquisitors' disapproval of his hobby, and hastened to assure them that alchemy was a perfectly honourable pastime, unfortunately digging himself even deeper in his reasoning. He recounted that 'cierto personaje le motejó de alquimista y respondióle que no se afrentaba por esto porque tenía entendido que el bendito Job había sido alquimista' ('a certain person had branded him an alchemist and he responded to him that he was not offended by this because he understood that blessed Job had been an alchemist'). He then proceeded to explain an entire hidden code of the book of Job through which he came to his conclusion. He assured the Inquisitors that similar codes were hidden in much of the Old Testament, in Homer and Virgil, which he would not go into, although he graciously promised 'que si fuere necesario las dirá' ('if it were necessary, he would tell them'). This secret understanding of widely read texts mirrors Quixote's privileged access to the personal lives of the *caballeros andantes*, including various episodes which even their chroniclers had never revealed (I, xiii, 90).[9]

The Inquisitors were not amused but, like the canon and other figures who censure but do not punish Quixote for his claims, nor were they particularly concerned. They concluded that 'todo este discurso es (al parecer) de hombre ignorante y flaco de cabeza, que tiene más peligro en el juicio que en faltarle la fee' ('all of this [it seems] is the speech of an ignorant and weak-minded man, whose sanity is more in danger than his faith'), and voted to have París secluded in a monastery for one year.[10] París took it in his stride. Just as Quixote proves to be an amiable guest in Don Diego's house and in the ducal palace, París was clearly a sociable character. During the first months of his seclusion, the prior of the monastery sent reports praising his conduct:

Habla en recato cuando habla con los religiosos y más con los letrados ...
y dícenos que antes no tenía afición a religiosos ni decía bien dellos, [pero]
ahora dice mucho bien de nosotros y dice que si fuera más mozo que tomara
el hábito en esta casa, y estos días pasados trataba de tomar una capilla para
su enterramiento ...

He speaks modestly when he speaks with the monks and even more so with
the scholars ... and he tells us that before he had no special liking for religious men nor did he speak well of them, [but] now he speaks very well of us
and says that if he were younger he would enter this monastery, and in these
past few days he has been trying to arrange a chapel for his burial.

His winning personality served him well, and he was released after
only three months. However, if the Inquisition was expecting París to be
a changed man, they had not listened to his testimonies very carefully.
From the beginning, he had insisted that his alchemic theories and the
Christian faith were compatible. Thus, it is not surprising that there is
a final note in the *proceso* with notes of a second sally of sorts. One
of París's new neighbours reported that he had 'tratado y comunicado
amigablemente con un hombre alemán, vecino de esta villa, que se llama
Giraldo París' ('dealt with and communicated amicably with a German
man, resident of this village, named Giraldo París') and was concerned
about some of his neighbour's ideas. París's new obsession seems to have
been a sort of animism:

que el hombre tiene alma, espíritu y cuerpo, y que los animales, árboles,
hierbas y piedras y minerales tienen también espíritu, y que la influencia de
los astros, árboles, piedras y minerales, juntándose a ellos su intención o
creencia, tenían virtud para hacer grandes curas.

that man has a soul, spirit and body, and that animals, trees, herbs, rocks and
minerals also have spirits, and that the influence of the stars, trees, rocks, and
minerals, when joined with his intention or thought, had the ability to effect
great cures.

Again, it is clear that the quirky París was good company, 'a gallant
madman' as Don Lorenzo describes Don Quixote (II, xviii, 571).[11] The
propositions had been proffered 'sobre mesa' ('around the table') after
various dinner parties to which the denouncer had invited his neighbour.
Had Don Quixote's *locuras* gone in a more religious direction, it is not
hard to imagine Don Diego sending the Inquisitors a similar note.

Perhaps the most famous example of an early modern Spaniard who
sacrificed position and fortune in pursuit of an obsession is Alonso
Mendoza, (another) canon of Toledo. Mendoza was, as Richard Kagan
writes, 'obsessed by dreams, visions, prophecy, and related spiritual

phenomena', and this obsession led him to involvement in several *causes célèbres* during the latter part of the sixteenth century. Like París, he was involved in mystical sciences: dream interpretation, divination and alchemy (the latter 'raised eyebrows' when it led him to seek out tin mines in Spain and England).[12] He publicly championed the prophetic credentials of the millennial 'soldier-prophet' Miguel de Piedrola, even after the Inquisition pronounced Piedrola a fraud, and he was Lucrecia de León's scribe and chief spiritual director. His work with Lucrecia landed him in the Inquisition jails, at which point he became entirely violent and irrational.[13] It is impossible to know for certain the motives behind Mendoza's involvement in the Piedrola and León affairs. Was he an astute, sinister politician taking advantage of a young girl and the discourses of prophecy and dreams to further his own interests? Was his total breakdown in jail a fake to secure his release? As Don Diego said of Quixote, Mendoza did 'things worthy of the greatest madman in the world and . . . things so intelligent they wipe out and undo his mad acts' (II, xviii, 569), making it nearly impossible to tell if he was mad, sane, or alternated between the two. His case is relevant because his mental state not only seems uncertain to us now but also was a cause of controversy among his contemporaries, a number of whom testified at his trial that he seemed thoroughly mad. His collaboration with (or manipulation of, depending on your point of view) Lucrecia de León gives insight into how unclear the line between socially acceptable zeal and irrational obsession was in the early modern period.

Mendoza's professed belief in Lucrecia's prophetic dreams would not have been sufficient to have him declared mad. No one seems to have questioned his sanity until he began demonstrating inappropriate behaviour in the jails and in his *audiencias*. As we see in all of these cases, madness requires that a purely intellectual error be accompanied by social errors: in this case, a seeming refusal or inability to preserve his own well-being. Both the quantity and quality of Mendoza's speech were entirely inappropriate to his audience and his plight. He would call his own *audiencias* and then declare he had nothing to say. Reprimanded, he threatened 'que cada día ha de pedir audiencia y que cuando se la diesen había de decir que le besasen en el culo' ('that he would call an *audiencia* every day and that, when they granted it to him, he would tell them to kiss his ass'). This seeming refusal to act in his own interest found its most extreme form in his violent attacks on the Inquisition jailers, property and even himself. He would sometimes erupt in violent fury, breaking down doors in the jail, attacking his doctors ('con el aceite que tenía en un boticón . . . [Mendoza] comenzó a hacer fieros . . . como mujer, y lo arrojó y derramó sobre [su doctor y su ayudante] y le ha hecho perder los vestidos' ['with the oil (the doctor) had in a medicine bag . . . (Mendoza) began to commit wild acts . . . like a woman, and he threw it and it spilled all over (the doctor and his assistant), ruining his clothes']). An Inquisition jurist testified that:

> casi todas las [veces] que con él ha estado en audiencia le ha visto dar tantas voces y con mucha descompostura, que entiende se oye en toda la casa . . . se prevenía y mandaba cerrar todas las puertas y que la gente [que] estaba afuera de la audiencia echarlos a la calle para que no le oyesen, y le ha oído decir cosas tan abominables, feas, y descompuestas que cualquier furioso por mucho que lo estuviera no dijera más.

> almost every time he has been in an *audiencia* with him he has seen him shout wildly, and he understands that it can be heard throughout the house . . . they took precautions and ordered all the doors to be closed and that the people outside the *audiencia* be tossed into the street so they would not hear him, and he has heard him say things so abominable, ugly, and disordered that a *furioso*, no matter how severe, could not have said more.

But just as Quixote could attack a group of friars or call an armed royal guard 'the cat, the rat, and the scoundrel' one minute (I, xxii, 170) and peacefully lecture the canon about *libros de caballería* the next, Mendoza would alternate between calling the Inquisitors 'tiranos bellacos' ('idiotic tyrants') and, for example, engaging them on the finer points of legal procedures. Mendoza's doctor remarked that Mendoza would mix 'con cosas de mucho enojo y pesadumbre cosas de risa y donaire, contando cuentos deshonestos' ('things that caused great anger and grief with graceful, laughable things, telling dirty stories'). The doctor had plenty of conversations with Mendoza, since one of the canon's obsessions was his health and, in particular, his intake and output. I will spare the reader the folios full of his problems in the jail with waste disposal (he alternated between complaining about it and making it urgently necessary), and his bizarre food and clothing requests. These preoccupations in themselves do not resonate with Quixote's renunciation of material luxury, but the insistence with which Mendoza returned to them and the contextual inappropriateness of his requests does match the pattern, if not the substance, of Quixote's madness.

Mendoza's preoccupation with excretion seems to have predated his time in jail. Pedro Salazar de Mendoza, councillor to the Archbishop of Toledo, testified that Mendoza spent excessive amounts of time at the home of the Dorias, a Genoese merchant family in Toledo, supervising the diet and purging of the whole family. The canon, it seemed, had arrived over two hours late to an Ecclesiastical Council where he was expected to say the opening mass, and 'entró excusándose con que estaba purgando [a] doña Jerónima Doria, soltera por casar, y que hasta que cesara no había querido dejarla' ('he entered, excusing himself saying that he was purging Doña Jerónima Doria, an unmarried woman, and that until it was finished he had not wanted to leave her'). Jerónima became a Dulcinea-like figure for Mendoza; amidst all the accusations of violence and irascibility, one of the charges against him was that he had requested paper in order to write Doña Jerónima a letter filled with 'coplas profanas y a lo divino . . . y sonetos y otras cosas'('secular and sacred couplets . . . and sonnets and other things') as well as 'un billete para la dicha Doña Jerónima que comienza "santa de mi corazón"' ('a note for the aforementioned Doña Jerónima which began "saint of my heart"'). While Mendoza's replies to the rest of the charges against him were alternately aggressive or evasive, his response to the charge of illicit poesy – '¿Qué mal haya en haber escrito unas coplas?' ('What wrong could there be in writing a few couplets?') – was almost sweet. They were the only means, he said 'con que entretenía su soledad' ('with which he filled his solitude'). While in the typical literary tale of love madness, including several of the intercalated stories of *Don Quixote*, the lover is driven to unreasonable acts by jealousy or frustrated passion, love and madness hold a more complicated relationship for Mendoza and Quixote. Love does impel the men to incoherent and violent acts (Quixote's demands at swordpoint that travellers affirm Dulcinea's incomparable beauty and Mendoza's demands that the Inquisition doctor send jewels and relics to Jerónima, 'amenazándole que si no se las daba y lo sabía le había de matar' ['threatening that if he did not give them to her and he were to find out, he would kill him']), but it also produces poetry and checks those same violent impulses. The 'mad' element of this love is precisely the unpredictability and incoherence of its manifestations: it drives Mendoza to violence, to poetry and to purging sessions.

Mendoza's obsession with Jerónima Doria is unusual in the archives because it was unrelated to the charges against him, and yet because it gave insight into his mental state, and thus his fitness to stand trial, it was considered worthy of documentation. In general, the Inquisition was not interested in recording the obsessions of early modern Spaniards except insofar as they could be construed as heretical. However, we should not assume, just because the obsessions that the archives record are – for reasons particular to the archive – largely of a religious nature, that early modern Spaniards' obsessions were purely religious. If we look at the obsessions that seem to recur in these cases, we can identify patterns which just as easily could have manifested themselves in secular forms.

Many of the obsessions were directly related to the insistence on a particular textual interpretation. Just as Don Quixote fixates on certain passages in the *libros de caballería,* clerics often developed obsessions with minor points of scriptural doctrine. Alonso Quijano's lack of social interaction and complete immersion in texts was, in fact, the typical lifestyle for a novice, and many priests and monks lost a sense of the boundaries between text and context.[14] 'Había leído mucho por cuya causa había estado como iluso' ('He had read a lot and for this reason had been as if possessed') was one priest's diagnosis of an ex-colleague, now reduced to alternate outbursts of blasphemy and prolonged spells of sitting and rubbing rocks together.[15] Although not so explicitly stated, this seems to have been the case in several other files. Juan Antonio Lázaro had made a personal mission out of correcting the translation of certain words of the Latin Bible.[16] He told witnesses that 'muchos lugares de la sagrada escritura estaban errados' ('many spots in the Holy Scripture were wrong'), citing as examples '*stabant iuxta crucem* . . . porque había de decir *stabat* y la razón que daba era que donde estaba la virgen no se había de nombrar otro' ('*stabant iuxta crucem . . .* because it ought to say *stabat*, and the reason he gave was that wherever the Virgin was present no one else should be named')[17] and that 'erra la Iglesia cuando . . . dice *Accipite, et bibi. te ex eo omnes* por [*sic*] debe decir *ex hoc*, que así lo dice San Matheo, y no *ex eo*' ('the Church is wrong when . . . it says *Accipite, et bibi. te ex eo omnes* because it should say *ex hoc*, as this is what Saint Matthew says, and not *ex eo*').[18] Translation of the Bible was a hot topic in post-Reformation Europe, and there was much heated rhetoric about the new Protestant Bible.[19] His other heretical statements also incorporated hot button topics of the day, but then distorted them or used them out of context. Clearly the individuals who denounced Lázaro to the Inquisition considered his statements to be threatening and heretical, but for others Lázaro's social errors – the insistence and length with which he argued about these few, relatively minor passages – raised suspicions that his problem was madness more than error. His loquacity and conjunction of seemingly randomly selected detailed examples or, as the canon described Don Quixote's speech, his 'reasoned nonsense' (I, l, 431) suggested to these listeners that something might not be right. Adding to this impression were Lázaro's actions. Like Quixote, he went out of his way to impose his opinions on the rest of the world. Lázaro had been known to call out from the *coro* during mass when the service was not being conducted according to his standards (yelling 'Cante el Prefacio, porque la Misa cantada sin Prefacio cantado es como la mesa sin pan' ['Sing the Preface, because a Mass sung without singing the Preface is like a table without bread']), and once, during a festival, he spontaneously ascended to the pulpit and blessed the entire town, assuring them that 'con esto quedan todos confesados y absueltos y pueden pasar a comulgar' ('with this you have all been blessed and absolved and can proceed to take communion'). The fundamental generosity of this blessing, despite the bestower's total lack of authority to deliver it, recalls Quixote's elevation of prostitutes to *damas* and his liberation of the *galeotes*. It should be noted that this extremely public outburst was not the episode for which Lázaro was denounced. While the archival examples all result from cases where someone was alarmed enough to alert authorities, testimony generally revealed years of public expounding on a pet topic without any official censure. Juan Egujo, who among his strange ideas had deeply held beliefs about the salubriousness of masturbation, told the Inquisitors that throughout his journeys, 'pensaba en las dichas proposiciones [his biblical defence of masturbation] y luego las preguntaba a cualquier hombre o mujer [con] que se encontraba'[20] ('he would think about the aforementioned propositions and then, whatever man or woman he met, he would ask them about them'). It is not hard to speculate that Cervantes might have at some point heard harangues similar to Egujo's and witnessed scenes similar to Lázaro's.

Critics have generally taken the mad Quixote's 'reasonable' criticisms and commentary about Spanish society and literature either as Cervantes's way of presenting his own critique without incurring censure,[21] or as an Erasmian satirical commentary of the state of 'truth' and 'madness' in his time.[22] Yet cases such as those of París and Lázaro suggest a third possibility, one not entirely incompatible with the other two. Craziness is not an ahistorical objective phenomenon; the basic operations of delusion and obsession take on particular shades and shapes according to the environment in which they are acted out. Real madmen, then and now, often take up topics and arguments from mainstream discourse. Men who voiced social criticism or theological disputes, but did so obsessively or in contexts where they did not seem appropriate (even as criticism or dispute), were often marked as mad.

Nostalgia

One topic from 'sane' discourse which often filtered into mad speech, and which is also one of Quixote's pet topics, was a nostalgia for the past. A series of military defeats, internal revolts and economic crises all contributed to what would become a 300-plus-year lament over the decline of the Spanish Empire. Medieval reform movements provided a model for critiquing the present by calling for a return to a Golden

Age of the early Church or prophesying an apocalyptic future. While most visionary-critics were not considered mad, such a public role of irrationality could not but influence those who were already predisposed to paranoia, delusions and other forms of unreason.[23] Nostalgia for a purer age of the Church or critique of current corruption was hardly irrational, but, for these predisposed individuals, the topic became an obsession, the cause or symptom of mental disorder. It was, again, the subject's lack of control or coherence in expressing it, or other external behaviours framing the expression, that signalled madness.

Juan Alexandro Pantalión, a Greek nomad in Valencia, had fairly typical Orthodox objections to the Western Church.[24] He said he was a Christian but that, since the Donation of Constantine, Christ had stopped entering the consecrated host and, as a result, he now only believed in Christ and the Apostles, not the Holy Roman Church. It was Pantalión's loquacity (in front of the highest tribunal of the Holy Roman Church, no less) and the 'nonsense' which he mixed in with it, which suggested mental instability: 'Aunque fue advertido perseveró en decir disparates . . . como dar al alcalde con un cántaro y no querer volver de las audiencias a su cárcel, diciendo que era príncipe de la tierra' ('Although he was warned, he persevered in speaking nonsense . . . such as hitting the *alcalde* with a pitcher and not wanting to return to his cell from the *audiencias,* saying that he was the Prince of the Earth').

A similar case, this one from New Spain, was that of Fernando Díaz.[25] His calls for 'a return to the purity of the primitive Apostolic church', and his rejection of the Catholic Church's temporal and economic power could have come straight from Luther or Wycliffe. However, unlike Díaz, neither Martin Luther nor John Wycliffe 'estuvo algunos días quieto y otros hacía cosas de loco o endemoniado' ('were calm some days and then on others behave like a madman or demoniac') nor did they, in the moment the priest was raising the Eucharist, burst from the pews 'para él arremetiéndole' ('launching themselves at him').[26]

Don Quixote's romantic evocation of the 'fortunate age and fortunate times called golden by the ancients' (I, xi, 76) is, like Pantalión's and Díaz's nostalgia, not inherently irrational. It could almost come from *Menosprecio de corte y alabanza de aldea*[27] or any other neostoic text. A closer look at the passages in which Don Quixote waxes nostalgic can show that 'literary' and 'historical' readings of madness in the work are not mutually exclusive, that in fact Cervantes uses verisimilar representation to rhetorical effect and vice versa. Don Quixote's praise of a communal era of rustic tranquillity, simplicity and communism is a criticism of the present day's excessive adornment, entanglement, avarice and falsity, and Cervantes's choice to voice this criticism, not strictly essential to the narrative, is clearly deliberate, but so too is his choice to connect the criticism with its speaker's dementia directly. Cervantes explains that the first nostalgic reverie 'could very easily have been excused' (I, xi, 77)[28] because it was the repast of acorns and wine that 'brought to mind the Golden Age, and with it the desire to make that foolish speech' (78). After the second similar monologue, Don Lorenzo, to whom Don Quixote has been speaking, seemingly invalidates the critique by immediately reminding us of the speaker's insanity: '"Our guest has gotten away from us," said Don Lorenzo to himself, "but even so, he is a gallant madman"' (II, xviii, 571).[29] This deliberate marginalisation of the protagonist's critiques in these moments may have been a way for Cervantes to voice his own criticisms of the present without facing censure. However, this does not presuppose a break with the verisimilar account of a madman's discourse. That is, we do not have to assume that Cervantes is 'using' or subverting his protagonist's mental instability to make his own social criticism. Real madmen often voiced acute social criticisms, and their madness did often allow them to escape censure; it was precisely madness that allowed their criticisms to 'easily [be] excused'.

Delusions of Grandeur

Spain was anything but a socially mobile society for 99 per cent of its inhabitants, but it specialised in the spectacular elevation of a few from the lowliest misery to the highest reaches of power. Again, Lucrecia de León's case is exemplary, but she was not alone. There were a few paths for a rags-to-riches transformation. The first was to live a life of such heroic simplicity or virtue that one became a national model. This was the posthumous story of many saints, but it was possible to gain such a reputation in one's own lifetime, as did Teresa de Ávila and Juan de Dios.[30] Another road was to profess access to a divinely revealed truth of supreme importance to the king: the proliferation of theories as to how to distinguish the true revelations from the false in this period suggests the frequency of such visions. For every Lucrecia de León, there were probably many Claudio Largiers;[31] this Frenchman living in Madrid, when arrested for a variety of heresies, told the arresting officers 'que tenía escritas treinta manos de papel en Medina del Campo en que se verán [sic] que muchas cosas que se hacen [sic] en España son mal hechas' ('in Medina del Campo he had written thirty quires of paper, in which it could be seen that many things being done in Spain are done badly'). Asked about this by the Inquisitors:

dijo que había residido seis años en Medina del Campo trabajando en muchos oficios a donde por su inclinación o por inspiración de Dios se puso a escribir treinta manos de papel de lo que causaba la Inquisición de España, y habiendo hecho esto vino a Aranjuez a buscar al Rey para darle memoriales de lo que había hecho, como se los dio.

he said he had lived in Medina del Campo for six years working in many trades, and there, either guided by his inclination or divine inspiration, he set about writing thirty quires of paper about what the Inquisition was causing in Spain, and, having done this, he came to Aranjuez to seek out the King to give him an account of what he had done, as indeed he did.

However, in Aranjuez he was accused of having been sent by the King of France. Largier would not be dissuaded, and took his 'treinta manos de papel . . . a tratar en el Escorial de lo que había escrito' ('thirty quires of paper . . . to discuss in El Escorial what he had written'). The Inquisitors demanded that he present his writings, but, according to the *proceso*, 'por no tener pies ni cabeza los discursos y la letra no poderse leer se dejaron' ('because they could make neither head nor tail out of them and the handwriting was illegible, they [the papers] were set aside').[32]

The dream of a heroic intervention to save Spain was not limited to the literate; in fact, the greater the social leap to be made, the more prominent these delusions seemed to be. Because of biblical examples of divine revelations made to the meek, aspiring prophets generally enjoyed public charity and respect far beyond their non-visionary peers and were permitted to make social criticisms that would have been immediately censored in most contexts. In his *Avisos históricos*, Josef Pellicer tells the story of a prophet who approached Felipe IV on a procession through Madrid and informed him that if he did not 'remedy' his policies, he would 'burn in hell'. The king, judging that he 'must be mad', merely moved him aside.[33] The narratives of vision, madness and criminality were constantly in conflict in this period; in this case, at least, the king decided to let ambiguous words lie (or perhaps to let lying words remain ambiguous).

Whether or not the anecdote is true, it testifies to the circulation of such stories of heroic interventions and social ascents, an atmosphere which no doubt provided a fruitful terrain for the cultivation of delusional identities in all sectors of society. In 1623, Antonia Núñez, a 33-year-old widow, was arrested for a variety of blasphemies.[34] From the very first testimonies (even before she presented a defence) the witnesses mentioned a probability of madness and/or perpetual inebriation. One of her main symptoms was a professed intimacy with an international panoply of celebrities; one witness claimed that Núñez 'decía que el Duque de Lerma era su amigo y otros disparates de que este testigo se reía' ('she said that the Duke of Lerma[35] was her friend and other nonsense which this witness laughed at'), while another 'la vio muchas veces borracha diciendo . . . que el Rey de Inglaterra era su hermano y que era cristiano y que también era su hermano el Rey de Francia y así a este modo decía otros disparates' ('had seen her many times when she was drunk saying . . . that the King of England was her brother and that he was Catholic, and also that her brother was the King of France, and in this vein she said other nonsense'). After her arrest, Núñez herself requested an audience with the Inquisitors to demand that 'pues no tiene culpa la despachen, y que todos dicen en la corte que su Majestad el Rey era su primo y que no sabe por dónde es el parentesco y que no le conoce' ('since she isn't guilty, they should dispatch her case, and that everyone in the Court says that His Majesty the King was her cousin and that she doesn't know how they are related and she doesn't know him').

Núñez imagined herself to be both royalty and divinity, with omniscience and omnipotence in divine realms. A neighbour of hers reported that:

> estando la dicha Antonia Núñez embriagada o loca la oyó decir muchos disparates y algunos decía contando historias de vidas ajenas, diciendo que su Majestad que está en el cielo estaría enhechizado y que ella le había de deshechizar y decía otras cosas de esta manera.

> he had heard the aforementioned Antonia Núñez say a lot of nonsense while in a state of drunkenness or madness, and sometimes telling gossip, saying that His Majesty in the heavens must be hexed, and that she could undo the hex, and other things of this sort.

Again, it is not hard to identify 'sane' components in this delusion: the Church did teach that the living could ease the path of the dead through Purgatory, there was a great deal of popular belief in sorcery and hexes, and we can be certain that in the sermons and iconography accompanying the king's funeral rites, the conflation of the royal and divine, a staple of Baroque political rhetoric at any time, had been particularly stressed. What made Antonia 'mad' was her insertion of herself as protagonist into a narrative officially reserved for others, and the incongruity between her grandiose narrative and her poverty, drunkenness and periods of physical and verbal incapacity.

Her claims were generally secular and thus not of particular interest to the tribunal; the scribe merely noted that she continued with 'otros disparates a este modo, por lo cual fue mandada volver a su cárcel' ('other nonsense of this sort, for which she was ordered to return to her prison'). The very next day, the Inquisitors voted to suspend the case and unanimously ordered her to be placed in an asylum for the mad.[36]

Another defendant with delusions of grandeur was Juan Egujo, the French vagabond, who first claimed royal descent and then switched to divine aspirations midway through his trial.[37] In the monastery, in fact, he was so concerned with his theological ideas that he seems to have mentioned the fact that he was 'hijo bastardo del Rey de Francia' ('the bastard son of the King of France') as an afterthought. As one monk told it:

> en todas las palabras que se trataron con el dicho peregrino cerca de la fe le parece que respondió con juicio cabal, salvo que después por vía de conversación dijo dicho peregrino que los que tenía por sus padres que le habían traído de Francia siendo chiquito, en una ocasión le dijeron que el dicho peregrino no sea [*sic*] hijo dellos sino que era hijo bastardo del Rey de Francia ... y que en conformidad desto él había ido a Francia a ver si le querían tener por su rey, porque si era voluntad de Dios que fuese Rey de Francia, las ciudades en viéndole le tendrían por tal rey. Pero esto lo dijo después de estar detenido en el dicho convento.

> in all the words they had with the said pilgrim regarding the faith he responded in his right mind, except that by way of conversation the aforementioned pilgrim said that the people he took to be his parents had brought him from France when he was very little, and on one occasion they told the said pilgrim that he was not their son but rather the bastard son of the King of France ... and in accordance with that he had gone to France to see if they wanted to have him as their King, since if it was God's will that he be King of France, the cities upon seeing him would accept him as that King. But he said all this after he had been detained in the said convent.

Later, Egujo switched to a delusion of divinity (a shift of which the Inquisitors were highly suspicious), although he was inconsistent about his exact identity. In one *audiencia*, in response to the formulaic inquiry as to whether he had recalled anything relevant to his case, he responded in the negative, but then casually continued, 'más de que piensa que es Dios *ab eterno* que creó todo el mundo' ('other than that he thinks he is God *ab eterno* who created the whole world') with the endearingly rationalist afterthought 'pero que no lo puede probar' ('but he can't prove it'). At other times he professed to be the archangel Gabriel. As the nurse at the Nuncio, to which he was transferred, summed it up, 'su principal tema es decir que es Dios y que es Él que todo lo puede y que es el ángel San Gabriel y otras cosas deste género' ('his main theme is to say he is God and He for whom all things are possible and that he is Saint Gabriel and other things of this sort'). Egujo's multiple claims follow a pattern; he identifies with the power of kings, angels and God to escape man-made limits. Quixote, trapped under his horse, claims to be 'the Twelve Peers of France as well, and even all the nine paragons of Fame' (I, v, 43), identifying not with their individual identities but with their ability to emerge from the jaws (or flanks) of defeat. As deliria go, this is a rational (or at least understandable) one. Juan Egujo, backed into a situation he could not escape, imagined himself extreme powers that would enable him to go free. Ironically (perhaps, unless we believe he was faking the whole thing), his fantasised powers had that very effect; he was, after a four-year ordeal, set free. Along very similar lines, Quixote's self-created adventures have been read as a 'rational' response of a *hidalgo menor* to the stratification and stagnation of sixteenth-century rural Spain. Like Egujo, who claimed that 'él era un cristo crucificado en *Zaragoza* y que de cien a cien años moría y resucitaba, y que ahora no había de morir en toda una eternidad' ('he was a Christ crucified in Zaragoza and who every hundred years died and was resurrected, and now he wasn't going to die in all eternity'), Quixote imagined himself a messianic hero, proclaiming that 'in him errant chivalry would be reborn' (I, vii, 55). He was no more a knight errant than Egujo was Christ, but like Egujo, who was actually sentenced to death but got a last-minute 'resurrection' for his crazy behaviour, Quixote ended up achieving his goal despite operating on delusional premises.

Did Egujo believe he was Christ because he believed he could be rescued from a certain death? Or did he believe he could be rescued from certain death because he believed he was Christ? The circularity of delusional narratives, their capacity to anticipate and refute their own counternarratives, is not purely a Quixotic fiction. The illiterate labourer Juan García[38] claimed the power to effect miracles ('haría venir a Nuestra Señora de la Iglesia Mayor de Toledo con la casulla de San Ildefonso' ['he would make Our Lady of the Great Church of Toledo come with the chasuble of Saint Ildefonso'])[39] and omniscience about activities in the Court. These same delusions of power and knowledge protected him from criticisms that his claims of power were heretical or delusional. Thus when fellow labourers threatened to report him to the Inquisition, he was not fased, as he claimed to know 'lo que hacen los señores Inquisidores, si es contra él o si es en su favor, y que otras veces le han llamado y han dado por bien lo que ha dicho' ('what the Inquisitors do, whether it is against him or in his favour, and that on other occasions they have called him and approved of what he had said'). In other exchanges, he made the same claim about royal authorities. His miraculous powers would protect him from prosecution for claiming false miraculous powers, since 'si él quiere se pondrá tres leguas en una hora sabiendo que le quieren prender' ('if he wants to he could go three leagues in an hour knowing that they [the Inquisition] wanted to arrest him').

The very nature of a delusion of grandeur explains why these madmen in particular came to the attention of public authorities and thus figure so prominently in the Inquisitional archives, and also why they are the sort of characters a wandering tax collector might come to know. The grandiosity of the delusion impels the afflicted to proclaim his identity publicly: one does not save humanity by sitting at home and quietly being the Messiah. García, for example, publicly threatened that God had revealed things to him such that 'si él quería entrar en hondura, haría andar a toda España en torbellino en poco tiempo' ('if he wanted to go into depth, he could put all of Spain in a whirlwind in a short time'), and, when listeners cautioned him to be wary of the Inquisition, he declared that 'se desea ver con los Inquisidores para que vea [*sic*] que no es cosa de burlar lo que él sabe sino que es gracia de Dios' ('he wants the Inquisitors to call him in so that they can see that what he knows is nothing to joke about but instead is the grace of God'). It is no surprise that he got his wish. Juan Antonio Lázaro is another example of a boaster who seemed to seek out the most public fora for his outrageous claims. He told congregants that 'sabía tales doctrinas, ni Lutero, ni Calvino los habían inventado' ('he knew doctrines that not even Luther and Calvin had invented') and that 'más vale una misa que él dice que todas las que le dicen en la Iglesia de Dios, porque él sabe cómo se ha de pedir a Dios, y los otros no' ('a mass he says is worth more than all the ones said in God's Church, because he knows how to ask things of God, and others don't'). His power of divine intercession affected souls and natural phenomena equally, as he also boasted 'que él tiene los candados del cielo; y que está en su mano el que llueva o no llueva' ('that he had the keys to the heavens; and that whether it rains or not is in his hands'). Lázaro was particularly confident of his intercessory powers with women, promising them that God had granted him special powers with the ladies, and even telling them that he was the Holy Spirit. Some witnesses saw such heresies as come-on lines rather than deliria, but others testified to a variety of 'acciones, y casos intempestivos y descompuestos que obraba' ('actions and unruly and untimely episodes that he elaborated') and concluded that the priest was insane. Like Don Quixote, Lázaro's is, on the face of it, a touchingly generous megalomania. As the Holy Spirit, he promises to use his powers to save souls, just as Alonso Quijano extends his knightly capabilities to elevate prostitutes and labourers to *doñas* and *damas*. The Messianic delusion lends itself to speculation about a madness caught between spirit and flesh; the desire to save and the will to power; and the role of self-definition and external affirmation in sustaining identity.

It is not surprising that fantasies of divinity or sainthood were predominant among the religious men called before the Tribunal. Yet Cervantes is clearly exploring these same tensions with his protagonist's (ostensibly) secular madness. One important connection between the Christological and the chivalric delusions is their inherent textuality. Don Quixote creates both himself and the world he inhabits from the books he spends day and night reading. Religious men spent their waking hours in biblical study, not reading *Amadís*; their confusions of text and reality would naturally take a scriptural form. It is not surprising that in those minds disposed to confuse text and reality, the historical immersion in texts set in a long-ago past and filled with miracles, metaphors and multiple layers would lead to confused fantasies of divinity similar to Don Quixote's secular imaginations. However, the textuality of priestly delusions was not limited to the imitation, continuation and correction of the Bible. Many of the would-be Messiahs were also very conscious of the need to leave written accounts of their unappreciated attempts at redemption (after all, Jesus spread the good news by his works, but someone else had to write the good news down). The record of the Inquisition's *audiencias*, which the defendant had to ratify at the end of each session, became a site of contested written accounts. The Inquisition was clearly the 'first narrator' and no defendant could take the scribe's place and write his own story. Still, in the act of signature, some defendants managed to make their own voices and self-narratives heard. The Portuguese priest Francisco Núñez Freitas was arrested in 1650 on charges of proclaiming himself to be 'hijo de Dios y consumador del nuevo testamento' ('the son of God and the consummation of the New Testament').[40] The record of his first *audiencia* reflects the Tribunal's dismissal of his claims to divinity; he had, the notary summarised, 'respondido según su tema' ('responded according to his theme') of being the son of God. Núñez Freitas sought to contradict the Tribunal's scepticism by signing his name '*spiritus xpo jesu consumator utriusque testamenti*'. Gaspar García Tenorio signed a letter in which he insisted on his own unfitness to stand trial 'Gaspar García, el loco' ('Gaspar García, the madman').[41] Vicente Clariana did not find it necessary to write his own gospel, but instead inscribed his narrator into his narrative.[42] Four days after Clariana was convicted of bigamy (in a trial with no mention of madness) and notified of his unusually harsh sentence,[43] the *alcalde* of the Inquisition jail came before the Tribunal to announce that the prisoner was behaving oddly. According to testimony from his cellmates and the jail officials, Clariana claimed 'que era el padre San Francisco, y que otras veces veía que estaba por la ventanilla del aposento la Virgen Santísima con ángeles, con antorchas encendidas, que le bajaba la comida' ('that he was Father Saint Francis, and other times he said that through the window of his cell he could see the Holy Virgin with angels with lit torches, and that she brought food down to him'). After an *audiencia* in which he spoke 'inconsecuentemente' ('incoherently') and claimed to see 'el Padre Santo, y Dios' ('the Holy Father, and God') in the *sala,* the schoolteacher could only sign 'dos malos rasgos' ('two rough scratches') but he pronounced that 'San Francisco bien sabe escribir . . . y a él se le ha de remitir' ('Saint Francis knows how to write . . . and he will defer to him').

Was Clariana, perhaps, imagining this version for posterity, as Don Quixote does upon setting out on his first sally, speculating on how 'whoever thou mayest be, whose task it will be to chronicle this wondrous history' (I, ii, 25) will word things?

Dreams and Visions

Lázaro, Egujo and the others who claimed divinity never explain how they came to know their identities. The divine are omniscient: they do not need to come to know that they are. The Bible, however, offers many examples of divine revelation to mere mortals. In the Old and the New Testament, as well as classical tradition and popular lore, God (or gods) reveals truth to men in revelations or dreams.[44] It is not surprising that many sleeping or hallucinating men assimilated narratives of divine revelation into their own dreams, and this, combined with a tradition of belief that dreams could reveal truth, made claims of grandeur particularly common, and particularly credible, when explained as the result of dreamed revelation. Let us look specifically at the oneiric narratives of two men eventually judged to be mad, to see the form they take and to consider the connections with those of Don Quixote.

Juan García, the labourer with claims to omniscience, said he received his insights in dreams. He bragged to fellow labourers that:

en los sueños que sueña sabe más que todos los letrados del mundo ni que los inquisidores, y que ensueña que ha de ser el mayor señor que ha habido de trescientos años a esta parte y que ha de hacer cosas que nunca los nacidos las hiciesen y Dios se las muestra a él más que a hombre ninguno de cuantos han nacido de trescientos años a esta parte, aunque sean justicias ni letrados ni la clerecía.

in the dreams he dreams he knows more than all the scholars in the world and all the Inquisitors, and he dreams that he is to be the greatest gentleman there has been in 300 years preceding and that he is to do things that no one born had ever done and that God shows more to him than to anyone born in 300 years prior, not even judges, scholars or clerics.

God revealed to him events on Earth ('lo que se hacía entre reyes y grandes señores y . . . lo que hacía el Gran Turco y en qué día y año y en qué hora' ['what was done between kings and great lords . . . and what the Gran Turco was doing and on what day and year and at what time']) and, even more scandalously, in Heaven ('él sabe en la tierra lo que hace Dios en el cielo' ['he knows on earth what God does in the heavens']). We can sense the influence of specific biblical episodes – episodes García would have been familiar with through sermons and iconography (and as a labourer on a cathedral he would have heard and seen his share) – on particular dreams. We sense Noah behind his insight into connections between natural disturbance, earthly sin and divine anger ('los nublados que hace cuando llueve es por las injusticias que hacen los que tienen cargo de la justicia' ['the clouds that form when it rains are due to the injustices committed by those in charge of justice']) and his particular obsession with Saint Ildefonso's chasuble reflected the popularity of that miracle in post-Tridentine teachings.

Other dreams had more earthly referents and reflected more immediate desires. The most detailed vision García recounted was the vision he had of God descending from the heavens to warn his parents not to touch 200 *ducados* he claimed they had 'encerrados en un palacio' ('locked in a palace'). He explained that:

> dos o tres veces quisieron entrar dentro y que abajó Nuestro Señor del cielo y dijo 'tente, no abráis ese palacio hasta que Juan García venga', y que le dijo Nuestro Señor después a Juan García, 'mira Juan lo que te dije, no se te olvide, a dondequiera que vayas yo iré contigo'.

> two or three times they wanted to go inside and Our Father came down from the heavens and said 'hold it, don't open that palace until Juan García comes', and that Our Father later said to Juan García, 'pay attention, Juan, to what I told you, don't forget, wherever you go, I will go with you'.

García combines elements of scriptural doctrine,[45] popular legend[46] and personal history (García had – before his arrest – claimed that an Inquisitor had 'tomádole mas de diez mil ducados de hacienda y alzádose con ellos' ['taken more than 10,000 *ducados* from his estate and made away with them']). It is not necessary here to speculate as to the precise psychic mechanisms through which these diverse elements come to form an oneiric narrative; what is important to note is that Cervantes's countrymen were publicly claiming to have such dreams, that they announced these dreams in order to convince others of the truth of their own narratives, but that in practice such announcements only lead to further doubt about the sanity of the narrator.

Even more strikingly Quixotic than García is one Andrés Hernández Tejero. Hernández was a fifty-year-old labourer in the village of San Silvestre, who by all accounts except his own had been for the last twenty years the town *loco,* causing minor property damage and civic disruption. When his outbursts ventured into the territory of minor blasphemy in a dispute with the Duke of Maqueda, he was brought before the Inquisition.[47] In the *audiencia,* however, it became clear that his version of his past would follow a different narrative. As in every *audiencia*, the Inquisitors began by asking his genealogy and life history, including if he had ever travelled outside Spain. The illiterate Hernández had clearly already been thinking about his own textual legacy; he replied that for this the Inquisitors should really refer to the testimonial he had given to a scribe and neighbour in his home town of Noves. Yet, like Quixote, he was more than willing to tell the story himself, and he proceeded to launch into the account of his intervention in the coronation of the Emperor in Rome.[48] It is worth quoting his account at length because the connections between Hernández's dream and Quixote's Montesinos vision cannot be reduced to specific plot points. The two narrators share a style characterised by shifts in scale and scope, a mix of action-packed narrative and ironic commentary, and, most of all, a clear enthusiasm for the act of storytelling itself. Given that the Inquisitors let Hernández go on in so much detail, one can even imagine that his interlocutors, like the canon of Toledo in *Don Quixote*, set aside their official condemnations for a moment to be seduced by narrative. To the extent that the Inquisition allowed it, let us have Hernández tell his story.[49]

On the day of the coronation of the Emperor, he began, he had gone from his house:

> [para] ver un [¿?] suyo frontero de la fuente . . . y junto a la fuente le vino [un] temor de carnes y arrojó el [¿?] en el suelo y salió a lo alto y al saltar tuvo temor pero después iba como un pájaro y [se] vio en la iglesia de San Pedro de Roma, y allí estaba el Emperador con dos pajes.

> to see a [?] of his in front of the fountain, and when he was by the fountain, he was overcome by a bodily fear and he threw the [?] on the ground and rose through the air and upon jumping he was afraid but afterwards he went like a bird and he found himself in the church of Saint Peter's in Rome, and there was the Emperor with two pages.

The pages held the Emperor's sword, while the Emperor, dressed in 'un sayo pardo' ('a brown cape') held his 'varuelo' ('little papal staff'). Suddenly, a conflict arose between the Pope and the Emperor, when the former told the latter that 'si no sabía letras no le daría la coronación' ('if he wasn't lettered,[50] he wouldn't crown him') and also demanded a lock of the Emperor's hair, which he refused to give. At this moment, Hernández shifted from being a passive to an active participant, this seeming to be his 'feat reserved only for thy invincible heart' (II, xxiii, 606). Just as Quixote recalled that Montesinos recognised him and called upon him for help:

> el Emperador conoció a este declarante y el mismo Papa y dijo al Emperador que se llamaba Tejero y como el Emperador no quiso dar [los cabellos] por él y este declarante y el emperador, pidieron al Papa que les dijese las palabras de la consagración de la hostia y que la consumiese en su cuerpo, y el Papa lo prometió y se quería entrar a vestir el Papa y no le dejaron y el Papa dijo *domino vobiscum* y este declarante sin saber leer dijo la epístola a los Hebreos y luego se quedó el libro en blanco que no quedaron más de once letras escritas en el.

> [T]he Emperor recognised this declarant, and the Pope himself, and he said to the Emperor that he was named Tejero, and as the Emperor refused to give [his hair] for him and this declarant and the Emperor, they asked the Pope to say the words of the consecration of the host and to consume it in his body, and the Pope promised to do so. And the Pope wanted to enter to get dressed and they didn't let him and the Pope said *domino vobiscum* and this declarant, without knowing how to read, said the epistle to the Hebrews and then the book went blank and there were not more than eleven letters left written on it.

The *audiencia* with Hernández ended here. Several days later, the Inquisitors – seemingly provoking Hernández to continue his story – asked why, if he had done all he said, the Emperor had not rewarded him. Hernández responded that there had been some difference of opinion over his remuneration: 'Salieron algo desconformes este declarante [y] el Emperador, y el Emperador le dijo que le había hecho una [merced] y no fue así' ('This declarant and the Emperor left with something of a disagreement, and the Emperor said he had granted him an indulgence and this was not the case'). However, Hernández was not discouraged:

> le dijo 'ni vos sin mi ni yo sin vos. ¡Allá nos veremos en España!' y desafiaron dos por dos, el emperador y este declarante, a quienquiera que quisiese impedir la coronación, y el Papa dio unos dineros a este declarante . . . habían hecho eso, subido el emperador arriba para recibir la comunión y este declarante preguntó al emperador . . . si prometía defensión de la fe y de hacer

justicia en su reino, que a ambas cosas dijo que no, y entonces este declarante saltó dichas maravedís abajo y dijo 'echa paja a ese asno' y se abajaron.

[H]e told him 'neither you without me, nor me without you. We'll see each other in Spain!' and then he and the Emperor challenged two by two whoever wished to impede the coronation, and the Pope gave this declarant some coins . . . they had done this, the Emperor having gone up to receive communion and he asked the Emperor . . . if he promised to defend the faith and spread justice through his kingdom, and to both things he said no, and then he threw the aforementioned *maravedís* down and said 'send this ass out to pasture' and they descended.

The Pope sent a page for the key to the altar, but this proved unnecessary, as Hernández magically produced his own and took charge of the ceremony, even having to explain to the head of the Catholic Church that he had already taken communion and 'no cabía una comunión sobre otra' ('you couldn't pile one communion on top of another'). The Pope asked Hernández to break the wafers, but the Spaniard resisted. Hernández 'suplicó al santo sacramento que le subiese al cielo, que él le prometía de irle a ver allá y el sacramento no quiso subir ni moverse de las manos' ('begged the Holy Sacrament to raise him to the heavens and he promised to go and see it there, and the sacrament refused to rise or move from his hands'). Just then, 'habló uno en lo alto de la iglesia y dijo que le partiría con él y le dijeron que era el rey de Francia y dijo este declarante, "otro asno tenemos que rebuzna ya"' ('someone spoke from high up in the church and he said he would break [the host] with him, and they told him it was the King of France and this declarant said, "now we've got another ass braying!"'). Having put the King of France back in his place, Hernández approached his grand finale. 'De allí se salieron el Papa y el Emperador y este declarante iba en medio dellos' ('From there the Pope and the Emperor went forth, and this declarant went between them'), but just when we might expect some spectacle with even greater transcendental import the fantasy twisted back to the trivial and the real. Suddenly all of the local authorities from San Silvestre showed up in the vision, like Dulcinea and her peasant friends in the Cave of Montesinos, and they interrupted the Pope's attempt to grant Hernández a permanent absolution for eating meat. Poor Hernández 'se vio sin dineros y tenía pena' ('found himself without money and troubled') thanks to the untimely intervention of the Duke of Maqueda – the very man who had (or was about to, depending on whose timeline we are following) denounced him to the Inquisition. Hernández 'subió en lo alto y vino a la fuente del Emperador aquel día en acabando de comer y halló allí su [¿?] donde lo había dejado' ('rose into the air and came to the fountain of the Emperor that day just finishing his meal and there he found his [?] just where he had left it'). Quixote, of course, also left the cave down four *reales*, and returned exactly to his point of departure, with scarcely any time having passed. The perfect ironic touch came with Hernández's confident citation that, if perhaps the Inquisitors were disinclined to believe him, 'en prueba de su intención nombra por testigos al emperador y aquellos dos pajes' ('in proof of his intention he names as witnesses the Emperor and those two pages').

The appeal to the imaginary as proof of its own reality is only one of the parallels between Hernández's story and Quixote's experience in the Cave of Montesinos. A change in altitude (albeit in the opposite direction) marks an impossible journey to a place outside of time, a composite of historical and literary antecedents, in which the subject appears *in medias res* as a figure who can change the course of history. The miracles and magical events are clearly shaped by referents in the real world. The Counter-Reformation insistence on the miracle of the transubstantiation, controversies surrounding the coronation of Carlos V, rivalries between France and Spain, Hernández's personal difficulties with the Duke of Maqueda: all enter and recombine in Hernández's fantasy. Just as in Quixote's vision, the space created as an escape-from-reality is suffused with reality recombined. The fantastic space fulfils a desire/delusion of heroism, but also ultimately denies it; the narrator curiously incorporates obstacles and failures into a story whose very purpose and possibility would seem to be to deny them.[51]

Hernández's conversation with the host rests on a misunderstanding which for many *locos,* and certainly for Don Quixote, became a point of obsession and delusion. Many of the specific points of dissent between Protestantism and Catholicism, and thus the foci of the Counter-Reformation Church's education campaigns, had to do with the proper understanding of levels of metaphor. It was essential to understand that the consecrated host *was* the body of Christ, that a cross or an icon was sacred but not a *verum corpus*. In several archival accounts, the accused's fury was either set off by or manifested itself against a cross, statue or other representation of divinity. Juan de Larrea was charged with having 'con grande escándalo' ('with a great deal of scandal') thrown a rock at a statue of Christ at the door of the Anton Martín Hospital, the very hospital where he had earlier been treated for 'enfermedad de loco' ('madman's disease').[52] He was also suspected of having 'ensuciado una imagen de Nuestra Señora' ('dirtied an image of Our Lady'), stealing the supply of unconsecrated wafers from the sacristy, and throwing a hat onto the St Sebastian image in the *cabildo*.[53] Blas Aguilar was accused of refusing to take off his hat when a procession of the Holy Sacrament passed by, and then removing one from a relic in a church.[54] Bartolomé Sánchez questioned the divine presence in the host, reasoning that 'en la hostia que alzaban los clérigos no venía Dios porque una vez que había venido, tal lo habían tratado, ¿para qué tornase a venir?' ('God didn't come into the wafer that the priests raised because the one time he had come, they had treated him like they did – why would he come back?')[55] and smashed all of the icons in his Inquisitional cell. The criticism of Catholic attitudes toward sacred images was hardly proof of madness, but among the mad (and Larrea, Aguilar and Sánchez were all found to be so) the literality of the host and the metaphoricity of sacred images seemed particularly prone to provoke excesses. Confusions about levels of metaphor and the frontier between reasonable and mad (in)credulity are, of course, recurring themes in *Don Quixote*.

Another important element of Hernández Tejero's story, one that we have seen in previous cases, is its obsessive textuality. The illiterate Hernández dreamt that he miraculously recited the book of Hebrews from a blank page, and pulled off the coronation despite the obstacle of the Emperor not knowing 'letras'. He also refers the Inquisitors to the account he had dictated to a scribe; inside and outside of his fantasy, he imagined writing as his salvation. París and Clariana also referred the Inquisitors to textual accounts – one real, one imagined; Mendoza delayed his own trial for years bickering with the Inquisitors over the words and format of the trial record; Claudio Largier could not stop writing;[56] and one Andrés Martínez had been spied in his room burning and tearing papers and then running to the river 'con mucha oscuridad y vuelto al cabo de una hora con muchos papeles viejos que había hallado por el camino' ('in great darkness and returning an hour later with a lot of old papers that he had found along the way'). Martínez explained that he burnt the papers 'pareciéndole que alivia la enfermedad y terror que ha dicho padece' ('because it seemed to him to alleviate his illness and the terror he has said he suffers from'). Writing could inspire unreason and alleviate it, and even do both at the same time.

If we think about the power of scribes and *letrados* in bureaucratic Spain, we can again see a socio-historical reason for this obsession. In any sort of legal procedure, from a wedding to an Inquisitional trial, the illiterate Spaniard was required to put his fate and wallet in the hands of infamously corrupt notaries. He could visibly see his experience being turned into a script which would both shape and become the 'truth' of his story. His future depended on this mysterious and mistrusted encoding of his experience. Thus it is to be expected that an early modern Spaniard predisposed to anxiety and obsession might turn his worries to his own textual representation, and that an early modern Spaniard predisposed to escapist fantasies and grandiose delusions might imagine a fantastic textual redemption. In a society where letters were such a source of power, it is not surprising that delusions of grandeur would involve the pen and the sword, *armas y letras*.

Yet while Hernández, like others, had an obsessively *textual* madness, it is important to recognise its non-*literary* elements. Hernández's dream was an episode embedded in a real, and sad, life. He was married, with four adolescent children. During his trial, his wife came before the Inquisition both to testify that her husband 'de más de diez años a esta parte es loco . . . y no sab[e] lo que hace ni dice' ('for the last ten years has been mad . . . and he doesn't know what he does or says') and also to plead for the Inquisitors to return enough from what they had confiscated to support herself and her children. Hernández Tejero's madness did not consist solely of peaceful raptures; he also was given to violence and fury. He had previously been arrested for killing a bird belonging to a prominent townswoman, 'descalabrar a un capellán' ('splitting a chaplain's head open') and 'dar de *cuchilladas* a unos [?] diciendo que aquellos eran los que mataron a su padre' ('attacking some [?] with a knife saying that they were the ones who had killed his father'). This violence affected strangers and loved ones alike; a neighbour of Hernández said 'le ha visto muchas veces estar muy loco y sus hijos irse huyendo de su casa' ('he has seen him many times be completely mad and his children run fleeing from his house').

Literary authors (Cicero, Dante, Quevedo) create dream narratives full of meaning, but their dreamers, when awake, are never plagued by this meaningless unreason, the violence and suffering that was present in almost every archival account of madness. The combination of senseless violence and sensational fantasy is essential in *Don Quixote*. Scholars have long debated whether *Don Quixote* is or is not principally a 'funny book' and whether Quixote is a 'hero or fool';[57] the archival record, in some sense, renders this debate unnecessary. There is no more 'proper' way to read Don Quixote than there is a 'proper' way to read Hernández Tejero, or any of the other *locos* whose lives take on tragic and comic turns depending on the perspective you assume. For Hernández, his vision was both important and real, yet to various outsiders, it would seem ridiculous, empowering and pathetic. Cervantes's narrative innovation is to allow the reader to choose which eyes to see through. What the archival tales make clear is that an argument as to whether Quixote's madness is predominantly exalted or abased misses the fact that, in madness, the fantastic and the sordid are fundamentally intertwined; delusions beget violence *and* paradox, suffering *and* escape.

Madness Between Literature and the Archive

Clearly literary and 'historical' madness did not operate entirely independently of each other. If they did not have points of contact, the literary designation would make no sense. It is impossible to demarcate a line where literary representations of madness depart from historical referents. There are undeniably fictional texts (e.g., Lope's *Los locos de Valencia*) in which the representation of madness may still draw from historical referents (patients and practices of the Valencia asylum), and there are texts in which it is impossible to say even whether the characters and events are fictional, historical or some combination of the two. Alonso Jerónimo Salas Barbadillo opens his collection of Italianate novellas with a prologue in the first person, in which he describes his visit to the Nuncio in Toledo and his discovery there of an 'unfortunate soul' who had been labelled as mad because he said he was Don Ferdinand, the Catholic king.[58] Juan Huarte de San Juan presents 'clinical studies' of uneducated men who, when suffering from mania, speak in Latin with the elegance of Cicero, a description it would seem difficult to accept as purely historical.

Yet this does not mean we should assume that across epochs, genres and individual works, madness in literature always bears the same relationship to madness in society.[59] The Inquisition testimonies, which were not written primarily to educate or delight, can help us understand how much of what we see in other textual accounts is, in fact, literary invention. It is immaterial here that some defendants may have been inventing their delusions; we can make a distinction between fictional characters and the fictional inventions of historical actors (inventions designed precisely to convince judges of their veracity). My purpose in placing Inquisitional accounts alongside *Don Quixote* is not to go through the novel and 'rate' each of Don Quixote's symptoms or experiences as 'realistic' or 'fictional'. What the Inquisitional accounts allow us to explore is the way that a fictional text reflects, refracts, engages, negates and otherwise transforms a historical phenomenon. This engagement goes far beyond the level of symptoms; in fact, I will argue, it is the novel's concern for non-symptomatic aspects of madness, the movement into the questions of ethics, philosophy and language that madness in the archives raises, that differentiates Cervantes's treatment of the theme from that of his contemporaries. This remains to be shown, however; for now, the historical parallels need only justify reading Cervantine madness as something more than an abstract allegorical state. They allow us to read Cervantine madness in dialogue with a lived experience, but in no way do they tell us how that dialogue will go. The historical parallels are our jumping off point to ask how Cervantes uses the tools of fiction to explore madness as lived experience, and how he uses madness as lived experience to create – and to meditate on the nature of – literature.

Notes

1. We could make the exact same claim about our present day, surrounded as we are by 'reality' TV shows, partisan media, conspiracy theories, spin doctors and staged events.
2. This is not true of Don Quixote throughout the two volumes, of course. In Chapter 5 I will return to examine in more detail the narrative progression of the symptoms which we may here establish as his 'baseline' condition.
3. Sor Antonia Teresa de San Joseph, ADC Leg. 547, No. 6880–1.
4. Juan Egujo, AHN Inq. Leg. 99, Exp. 6.
5. See, for example, Garzoni, Beys, Vélez de Guevara.
6. Giraldo Paris, AHN Inq. Leg. 100, Exp. 21 (*proceso*); Leg. 2106 Exp. 3 (*sumario*).
7. Giraldo París may well have been immersing himself (with a Quixotic lack of critical distance) in the many texts dedicated to alchemy by or falsely attributed to the thirteenth-century philosopher Ramón Llull.
8. The tears in the *proceso* are small, each corresponding to one or two missing words.
9. Don Quixote claims to know that Amadís de Gaul's brother, Don Galaor, was 'secretly very much in love' despite this never being mentioned in the text (I, xiii, 154).
10. The full sentence was '*abjure de vehementi, sea gravemente reprehendido, y recluido en el monasterio por un año*' ('*abjure de vehementi*, gravely reprehended, and confined in a monastery for a year'). Although the Inquisitors do not give their reasoning, it seems to me almost certainly a compromise sentence, in which doubts about insanity led to a moderate or expedient verdict, when in theory it should have offered either a total absolution or been discounted.
11. The original is 'bizarro', which can be 'gallant', but also can mean 'odd', 'bizarre'.
12. Kagan: 102–3.
13. Alonzo de Mendoza, AHN Inq. Leg. 3713, 8° pieza.
14. Belén Atienza notes that 'melancholy among religious men was a frequent topic in literature' (120). The theories to explain this varied from excessive solitude (Leon Alberti) to willfulness or a demonic ruse (Teresa de Ávila). Whatever the cause, what interests us here is the particularly textual manifestation of symptoms.
15. Juan Calvo de Illescas, AHN Inq. Leg. 103, Exp. 1.
16. Juan Antonio Lázaro, AHN, Inq. Lib. 944, fols 261–6.
17. John 19.26.
18. A phrase in the canon of the mass.
19. One of the principal outcomes of the Council of Trent was the affirma-

tion of the Vulgate as the sole authorised Latin text of the Bible, and the commission of a single standardised version. The first result, published in 1590, was notoriously full of errors and mistranslations and was almost immediately replaced. Although Lázaro is not arrested until 1688, it is possible that the 'errors' he is referring to reflect actual points of contention during this controversy. However, it is equally likely – and in fact more in concert with the Inquisitors' belief in his insanity – that he was assimilating an atmosphere of heated debate and applying his own personal obsessions. I did not find historical referents for the specific examples of Papal error or mistranslation that he mentions.

20. Juan Egujo, AHN Inq. Leg. 99, Exp. 6.
21. 'Through the metaphor of madness Cervantes incorporates marginality, authenticity, and the transgression of conventions into life and literature. He is transgressing societal norms by suggesting that self-imposed madness is the only valid response to the institutionalised madness of society; at the same time his new "novel" transgresses current literary norms' (Martín: 79).
22. This reading can be found in works across the spectrum of Cervantine interpretation. The 'soft' readers who emphasise the influence of Erasmus (or liberal humanism à la Erasmus) unsurprisingly take this view: Castro and Bataillon are the foundational texts for this reading. For more contemporary examples, see Forcione, *Cervantes and the Humanist Vision*, and Márquez Villanueva, 'Erasmo y Cervantes una vez más'. 'Hard' critics such as Anthony Close ('Algunas reflexiones sobre la sátira en Cervantes') also read Quixote's madness as a literary device facilitating satire, only they reject the idea that Cervantes's satire is principally ideological or political.
23. Kagan shows how political and religious reform projects intertwined, and how non-rational experience, be it dream or prophetic vision, could enhance the truth of a social criticism and be used to protect the critic. For further bibliography on Lucrecia, see Blázquez Miguel and Jordán Arroyo. For a later example of dreaming being used to protect prophet(esse)s from accusations of heresy or treason, see Cueto Ruiz.
24. Juan Alexandro Pantalión, AHN, Inq. Lib. 939, fol. 140.
25. Fernando Díaz, AGN, Inq. vol. 366, exp. 42, fols 443–55. Qtd in Sacristán: 104.
26. Sacristán: 104.
27. Guevara.
28. Grossman translates 'escusar' as 'omit', but it could just as easily be to 'excuse' in the sense of 'pardon.'
29. See note 11 regarding the polysemy of 'bizarro'.
30. Juan de Dios was a sixteenth-century Spanish cleric responsible for founding hospitals and caring for the sick in Granada. Ironically, according to his hagiography, his moment of conversion was so overwhelming that he went running into the street crying for repentance and was interned in the Hospital Real (the madhouse) in Granada. He was canonised in 1690.
31. Claudio Largier, BUH, Fol. 365r. En Sierra, #1161.
32. Because of a variety of heretical propositions Largier made in the *audiencias*, he did not get off scot free (he received fifty lashes and ten years

of exile). I had only the *sumario* in this case, so I cannot tell what the Inquisitors' reasoning was for this moderate punishment.

33. Pellicer de Ossau y Tovar: 81–2.
34. Antonia Núñez, AHN, Inq. Leg. 206, Exp. 43 (*proceso*); Leg. 2106, Exp. 24 #25 (*sumario*).
35. Francisco de Sandoval y Rojas, Felipe III's *valido*. From 1599 to 1618 he was behind most of the king's decisions. Antonia's comment was made sometime between 1619 and 1623; given that Lerma's fall from grace occurred in 1618, her willingness to profess friendship with him would have raised eyebrows.
36. They first tried to remit her to the Hospital Nuncio in Toledo, but were told that there was no space available, further evidence of the 'abundance' of *locos* and the inadequacy of institutions to care for them (and hence the irrelevance of the Foucauldian idea of a mass confinement). She was eventually sent to the Hospital de la Misericordia.
37. Juan Egujo, AHN Inq. Leg. 99, Exp. 6.
38. Juan García, AHN Inq. Leg. 114, Exp. 7. The case is discussed in Nalle: 149–52.
39. Saint Ildefonso was a seventh-century Visigothic monk and then abbot who, according to hagiographies, received the gift of a chasuble from the Virgin Mary. Many 'unofficial' versions circulated among commoners. John Longhurst records the 1529 trial of Diego de Uceda for, among other things, claiming that 'Our Lady had brought a chasuble to Saint Ildefonso and that an archbishop who had insisted on wearing it had blown up. The accused had replied that this was a joke' (Longhurst: 76).
40. Francisco Núñez Freitas, AHN Inq. Lib. 931, fol. 380 and Lib. 932, fol. 27r. He was arrested in 1650 and in the account of pending cases, dated 25 October 1677, there is still no final sentence, although it seems the Tribunal had decided to reject an insanity defence. The delay was caused in part because in each *audiencia* he kept committing new heresies and thus generating new charges every time they attempted to close the case, and in part because the Tribunal could not decide on his mental competence.
41. Gaspar García Tenorio, AHN Leg. 35, Exp. 25. In this case, his narrative became the official account; he was in fact released as mad.
42. Vicente Clariana, AHN, Inq. Lib. 944, fols 155–60.
43. *Abjurase de levi*, two hundred lashes, ten-year exile from Valencia and five years of unpaid service in the *galeras*.
44. See Jordán Arroyo: Ch. 2; Egido, for a more detailed discussion of Old Testament, classical and New Testament ideas about dreams and revelation.
45. Besides the obvious referent of voices of divine warning, the phrase 'vayas donde vayas, iré contigo' is repeated exactly or near-exactly in several biblical stories (Ruth 8.1; 2 Kings 2) and is a direct quote from Villegas.
46. The rumours of treasures buried by various populations as they fled Spain (Goths, Arabs, Jews, *moriscos*), were so prevalent that they funded en entire *sacatesoros* industry.
47. Andrés Hernández Tejero, AHN Inq. Leg. 38, Exp. 6.
48. Hernández never names the participants in his vision, but the last imperial coronation had been that of Carlos V, in 1530 (by Pope Clement VII).

Given Carlos's role as Spanish monarch, this would have been a public event marked indelibly in the memory of every Spaniard of the period. The identification, later in the transcript, of the fountain as the 'Fountain of the Emperor' gives further evidence of a mnemonic chain connecting reality and vision. The actual coronation of Carlos V occurred in Bologna, but it is not hard to imagine that popular rumour would have transposed the events to St Peter's and the traditional seat of papal power.

49. The handwriting and ink bleed was particularly difficult in this case. Working with the various tellings of the story in the *proceso* and English transcription of part of Hernández Tejero's testimony by Dedieu, I have done my best. I have included in brackets my best estimates for illegible portions. In no case does the illegibility affect overall sense or meaning.

50. To 'saber letras' could refer to being erudite (*letrado*) or simply literate.

51. Montesinos tells Quixote that he is 'the great knight about whom the wise Merlin has made so many prophecies' (II, xxiii, 608), but even in his own fantasy Quixote does not disenchant anyone and cannot produce the six *reales* Dulcinea's friend requests to rescue his love from a 'great difficulty' (613).

52. Juan de Larrea, AHN Leg. 2106, Exp. 28 (*sumario*); Leg. 225, Exp. 21 (*proceso*).

53. The centre of civil government of the city.

54. Blas de Aguilar, AHN Inq. Leg. 31, Exp. 5.

55. Bartolomé Sánchez, ADC, Inq. Leg. 186, Exp. 2216, fol. 6r. Sánchez's case is the subject of Nalle's *Mad for God*. Because Nalle does not cite all of the testimony I am including, and because in her own translations she adapts the depositions to first-person, I have chosen to do my own translations from the archival documents. When the quoted material is discussed or translated in the book, I have included page numbers. All transcriptions have been done by Sara Nalle, to whom I am deeply indebted for her work on this case and for giving me her transcription of the 164 folio file.

56. See note 31.

57. Titles of works by P. E. Russell and John Jay Allen, respectively.

58. Qtd in Bouza Álvarez: 142.

59. For further discussion of a critical tendency to equate literary and historical madness, see Shuger.

Chapter 3

The Madman on the Road

I spent the whole of Chapter 1 mapping out the particularly ambiguous nature of madness in this period and the high stakes of choosing one interpretation over another, because both account for the tentative or multiple reactions of characters to madness. It is no coincidence that, in his creation of Don Quixote and his adventures, Cervantes emphasises exactly what I take to be the defining characteristic of madness at this time: the confusing and contradictory outward signs. In this chapter I will concentrate on how persons from various strata of Spanish society, when presented with persons about whom they had limited information, came to diagnose the irrational actors in their midst; how those diagnoses (or the resistance to diagnose) affected the ethical choices they made; and how Cervantes builds upon these dilemmas and decisions in the episodic encounters among strangers, mad and sane, found (primarily) in the first part of *Don Quixote*.

Faced with a spectacle of apparent unreason, the early modern Spaniard had to choose between many possible interpretations. What is perhaps most remarkable in the Inquisitional testimonies of witnesses of irrational behaviour is the general reluctance to make definitive judgements. Since the nature of the judgement almost always would determine a particular course of action with the irrational actor in question, the suspension of diagnosis could lead to one of two outcomes. Either the person attempting to judge withdrew from interaction altogether, having been unable to decide the proper way to respond, or he/she adopted multiple courses of action and pursued them simultaneously. Often early modern Spaniards did not, in the presence of someone they suspected of madness, feel it necessary to choose between ridiculing and caring for this ambiguous subject. Sometimes an individual would alternate between actions that appear to rest on incompatible judgements, and sometimes a social group would divide the different reactions, but without this causing conflict or suggesting contradiction among its members. It will be useful to examine a single case in detail in order to see how early modern Spaniards did (or did not) diagnose madness, and how their judgements affected their behaviours, as a starting point from which to think about how Cervantes has his characters negotiate the ethical choices that the confrontation with the unreasonable Quixote forces them to make (or studiously avoid): between charity and cruelty, laughter and pity, self-sacrifice and self-defence. I have chosen the case of Bartolomé Íñiguez[1] because it is particularly rich in accounts from a wide variety of communal actors about their judgements and actions toward a man who might be mad. The case, like every story that emerges from the archives, is unique, but the communal reactions in this file are also representative of the dynamics found in many others.

Bartolomé Íñiguez

Íñiguez was tried for blasphemy in 1562,[2] but this charge came from his behaviour while already in the custody of the local jail, where he was being held for public disturbance. According to Íñiguez's account to the Inquisitors, his problems began during the festival of Corpus Christi, when he got stuck atop a roof which he had climbed to see the running of a bull. He claimed that the overexposure to the sun had caused him to lose his mind, to say and do things he was not responsible for and could not now remember. These included a collection of some rather creative and eclectic heresies, in which Íñiguez not only denied his belief in most of the key figures of the Christian Bible but also to various visitors declared himself to be Lutheran, Jewish, Muslim, a priest, and possessed by Satan. When the Inquisitors went back to interview townspeople to confirm Íñiguez's account of the bull-running, most confirmed the basic facts of the rooftop episode, but saw it as one more action in a history of madness, not the immediate cause. (Ironically, then, their contradiction of his defence helped defend him.)

While the basic facts of Íñiguez's life before this arrest were agreed upon, the various witnesses had different opinions about the mental state of their neighbour. All confirmed that Íñiguez had, around ten years ago, been separated from his wife and denied the administration of his estate, but one witness chalked up the divorce to Íñiguez's 'falto de juicio'('madness') while another said it was because 'trataba mal a la dicha su mujer y desperdiciaba su hacienda' ('he mistreated his aforementioned wife and wasted his estate'). Íñiguez remained in his house, while his wife moved to an inn in which she worked. She continued to serve Íñiguez his meals, and at least on the night before his arrest gave him a room to sleep in when he was too disturbed to stay alone.

In the community, we find a variety of opinions and reactions to Íñiguez. One neighbour 'confirma que lo tienen en el pueblo por loco [porque] afrentaba a muchas personas y les decía algunas tachas . . . y las tales personas no hacían caso de sus dichos por que les parecía era loco' ('confirms that in the town he is considered to be mad because he insulted and slandered many people . . . and these people didn't pay attention to what he said because he seemed to them to be mad'). Still, this did not mean that the townspeople unanimously absolved him of guilt for his actions or pitied him as an afflicted innocent. They often left open various possibilities which today we would consider incompatible. One neighbour's report that 'del lugar más comúnmente le tiene por hombre de sin seso . . . que lo más de ello lo dice de bellaco y de mal hombre' ('in the town he is commonly held to be out of his wits . . . but he says most of what he does because he is a rogue and a bad man') is a typical example. Nor did his neighbours see an incompatibility between affirming Íñiguez's lack of reason and attempting to reason with him. The local sacristan said that 'le ha comunicado muchas veces y procurado de decirle algunas cosas en razón y en seso y que no hiciese los desatinos que hacía y decía' ('he had communicated with him many times and tried to talk to him reasonably and sensibly and that he should not do the nonsense he did and said'). It is telling that, while almost all of the witnesses knew of his dispossession and divorce and could cite years of aberrant behaviours, none of them would officially rule out the overexposure to the sun as the cause of his madness. Asked specifically to validate that the sun had caused Íñiguez to be 'del todo sin juicio y sentido y loco' ('completely out of his mind and his senses and mad'),[3] almost all replied something to the effect that 'no sabe si le vino por estar al sol ni por qué le vino' ('he doesn't know if [the madness] came over him for being exposed to the sun or why it came over him'). In general, they seemed uninterested in assigning a cause-effect narrative to his madness, preferring to deal with the symptoms as they presented themselves.

One of the responses to his symptoms had been an economic embargo. Several witnesses confirmed that in the town it was prohibited to enter into economic transactions with him 'porque no valdría cosa lo que hiciere' ('because nothing he did would be worth anything'), from which we can intuit past conflicts over labour or payment. This boycott is typical of the complicated relations between society and the *loco*, since the community remedied the very poverty they had imposed by supporting Íñiguez with charity. In particular, his ex-wife (who, from the witness's comments cited above, we can imagine as having plenty of motive for ill will toward Íñiguez) made sure he was fed, and gave him a place to stay when he was unsafe on his own.

The ambiguity of the town's relations with Íñiguez are particularly evident in the accounts of the day of his arrest. The townspeople, gathered in the plaza to see the running of the bulls, were called to go see 'el loco de Íñiguez en el tejado' ('Íñiguez the madman on the roof') and at least some of the crowd did decide that a *corrida de Íñiguez* was a worthier spectacle than the *corrida de toros*. Still, we should not assume that everyone who gathered did so for entertainment. The town mayor reported that he was called to the plaza to get Íñiguez to come down from the roof because 'tiraba tejas a unos y a otros como loco' ('he was throwing tiles at one and all like a madman'). Upon arriving, the mayor said, he found Íñiguez naked on top of the roof, saying 'tantas locuras a unos y a otros y disparates' ('so many crazy things and nonsense to one and all'). These 'disparates' were purely secular, mostly insults of the townspeople and passersby. Even those with the most charitable of motives in helping Íñiguez down might have been provoked to anger or retribution seeing themselves publicly insulted. The mayor himself, calling up peaceably to Íñiguez and asking '¿conocéisme?' ('Do you know me?') received in reply, 'Sí, que os conozco por un gran bellaco' ('Yes, I know you to be a great rogue'). Still, the mayor testified that after getting him down, he returned Íñiguez to his home, and it was only after seeing that 'allí no estaba seguro' ('he wasn't safe there') that he ordered his wife to take him in, 'porque le pareció que estando solo en la casa en que él vivía haría algun desatino o pegaría fuego a la casa' ('because it seemed to him that alone in the house he lived in he would do something ridiculous or set fire to the house').

Íñiguez remembered things differently. In his version, his role was more passive, with his fate being determined by the increasingly repressive and unprovoked whims of his neighbours and local authorities. With no mention of his own stone-throwing or insults, he said that the owner of the house upon whose roof he was perched 'le quiso echar de allí abajo [del tejado] y sobrevinieron las otras personas y le abajaron y le querría llevar a la cárcel' ('wanted to kick him down [from the roof] and then other people appeared and they took him down and he [the owner] wanted to take him to jail'). Yet Íñiguez also recognised that the mayor had stepped in and taken him home instead, and that the mayor's motive for subsequently removing him to his wife's inn was Íñiguez's own protection. Once the mayor had placed him in the inn, 'le echó la llave y mandó que la señora suya le sirviese y así estuvo aquella noche y no durmió en toda ella' ('[the Mayor] locked the door from the outside and ordered [Íñiguez's] wife to serve him and he was there that whole night and he didn't sleep at all'). Íñiguez clearly sees himself as the object of the actions of others, but it is ambiguous as to whether he considers himself to have been the object of abuse or charity. From a modern perspective, the removal of the key seems to be an act of confinement, while the order to tend to him seems an act of charity, yet Íñiguez merely links them with 'and', not giving the slightest hint that he sees them as stemming from contradictory or even different impulses.

Notwithstanding his recognition that 'tenía la cabeza alterada' ('his head was disturbed'), by the next morning Íñiguez wanted out. As his wife could not open the door (the mayor had taken the key), he knocked it down with a stone and went into the street. There he met up with a priest and relative of his wife. At this point, Íñiguez's version of events takes an undeniably Foucauldian turn. As he tells it, this priest then demanded that:

> le llevasen a la cárcel al loco y le echase en el cepo y allí le dio con el puño cerrado en el carrillo que le hinchó la boca de sangre, y se llegó gente y le tomaron para llevarle a la cárcel y este que testifica decía muchas cosas contra todos ellos de que no se acuerda y le llevaron a la cárcel y le echaron en el cepo en el cual estuvo quince días . . . entre los otras personas estaban muchachos y mujeres que le decía[n] 'al loco' y unos a otros decían 'entra y veréis al loco' y que estaba abierta la puerta del corral y de la casa donde le tenía[n] y podía[n] entrar todos los que querrían y como él estaba de día al sol y de noche al sereno en el dicho corral donde estuvo dos días y dos noches no se acuerda de más . . . y después le sacaron y le echaron una cadena, la cual tuvo hasta que fueron por él de este santo oficio.

> they take the loco to jail and toss him in a cell and right there he was punched in the cheek making his mouth fill up with blood, and people arrived and they took hold of him to take him to jail and this witness said many things against all of them that he doesn't remember and they took him to jail and they threw him in a cell where he stayed for fifteen days . . . among the other people there were young boys and women who said 'have at the madman' and some of them said to the others 'come in and see the madman' and the door to the said corral and the house where they were holding him was open and anyone who wanted could enter, and as he was exposed to the sun during the day and the open air at night during the two days and nights he was in the corral, he doesn't remember anything more . . . and later they took him out and put a chain on him, which he wore until the men from the Holy Office came for him.

From the townspeople and authorities, however, we get different accounts. The sheer number of witnesses confirms that Bartolomé had become a local attraction, and the versions of his progressively fantastic blasphemies make it understandable.[4] He certainly responded to provocation and provided material for his audience. Considering the insults

Íñiguez had been offering all day, plus the past insults and inconveniences we can imagine, it is not hard to see the town's reaction as affirming the cynical observations about laughter made by Henri Bergson and oft cited by Foucauldian critics analysing the dynamics of laughter in *Don Quixote*.[5] Bergson defines laughter as 'above all, a corrective . . . intended to humiliate', through which 'society avenges itself for the liberties taken with it'.[6] The town sacristan attributed Íñiguez's popularity to this motive, reporting that 'le iban allí a ver todos los que querían, a cuya causa cree este testigo que le hacían decir desatinos . . . provocándole a ello' ('everyone who wanted to went to see him, which is why this witness thinks they made him say nonsense . . . provoking him to it'). This created a vicious cycle: Íñiguez refused to be corrected by the laughter, instead becoming more offensive and thus provoking a greater response of correction and humiliation.

By all accounts, those most guilty of provoking Íñiguez purely for the purpose of humiliating him further were the *muchachos* who threw things at him and the jailers who left him in a corral, exposed to the elements and with the door open so that 'anyone who wanted could enter'. This suggests a relation between power and reactions to madness, one we see again in *Don Quixote*. The children free to run in and out of the local jail were probably street urchins, and thus themselves victims of degradation and marginalisation, so it is understandable why they would be the most likely to close ranks in the humiliation of one even more degraded than themselves. As children, they also had not reached the stage of psychological development essential for empathy. The jailers, in contrast, seem to be acting on more insidious human impulses. (Still, their cruelty seems oddly un-Foucauldian; Íñiguez was, literally and figuratively, *over*-exposed and given *too much* freedom and contact. One witness testified to witnessing the guards *remove* the rope that the prisoner had been tied with, as he was 'tirando della como quien se quiere ahogar' ['pulling on it like someone who wanted to strangle himself'].)

The majority of the visitors to the jail, however, evince more complex motives, in which punishment and humiliation were mixed with charity and kindness. One witness reported that he told the chained Íñiguez, 'los locos por la pena son cuerdos', ('punishment makes the crazy sane'), a gloating recitation of a popular refrain which indicated little sympathy for Íñiguez or belief in his lack of control over his own speech and behaviour. Still, after hearing Íñiguez's extraordinarily blasphemous response, this certainty was shaken, and the witness concluded that 'en estas palabras y desatinos lo tiene por hombre fuera de seso y loco pero que no sabe si lo está o no' ('based on these words and nonsense, he considers him to be out of his mind and mad but he doesn't know if he is or not'). Some visitors spared the adages and took the disciplinary cure into their own hands. One witness hit him with a rope, but this only seemed to incite Íñiguez further. He welcomed the punishment, crying 'dadme dadme en este cuarto indio' ('hit me, hit me, on my Indian quarter'),[7] and, in this instance, his interlocutor adapted to the failure of force by switching to a gentler tack. In general, admonishment and reasoned argument was the preferred response of the visitors. While the *muchachos* threw things at Íñiguez from outside, and others peeked in through cracks in the walls, a neighbour reported that 'los que entraban de dentro, personas del pueblo, a verle, lo reprehendían que no dijese tantas blasfemias' ('those who went inside, people from the town, to see him, reprehended him and said he should not say such blasphemies'). Íñiguez was more than willing to engage his visitors and propose his own questions, inviting them along with him on infernal visits. The visitors spent a fair amount of time trying to make him see his mistakes. They wanted to steer him back to the proper belief but, when this seemed hopeless, they sought to warn him to at least keep his heresies to himself: a witness reminded him that people had been burned for saying similar things. When this too failed to intimidate or quiet Íñiguez, his conversant gave up. As he put it, 'no quiso más esperar sino santiguarse y salirse por no oírle mas blasfemias . . . que no tornó más a verle por no oírle' ('he didn't want to wait for more, but just to cross himself and leave so he wouldn't hear any more blasphemies . . . and he didn't go back to see him so he wouldn't hear him'). We know that others in the town resisted the spectacle from the beginning; perhaps the least Foucauldian response was that of the neighbour to the jailhouse who could not answer the Inquisitors' questions because 'no lo quiso pasar a ver aunque estaba cerca' ('he didn't want to go by to see even though he was close').

Some of those who tried to correct Íñiguez's mental deviance also tried to ease his physical suffering. A neighbour said that he had gone to see and talk to the delusional Íñiguez 'para ver si le aprovechara en algo' ('to see if he could be of help to him in any way'), and his wife came with him and brought him something to eat. The husband's typical non-diagnosis that Íñiguez was either 'loco o endiablado' ('mad or possessed') seems to have had no effect on the couple's charitable activities, and even when Íñiguez threw and broke the dishes they had brought him, he and his wife persisted and 'por ruegos y halagos se lo hicieron comer' ('through begging and flattery they made him eat'). Finally, we should not forget that, even when their own accounts of their actions suggest little charity, almost all of the witnesses end up opining that

Íñiguez was at least intermittently mad, knowing this would release him from any legal culpability. The same actors who enjoyed Íñiguez's subjugation and confinement thus achieved his release. For their part, the Inquisitors, despite their harsh and intimidating questions of Íñiguez in the *audiencias*, were exceedingly diligent in tracking down the defence witnesses and they finally ruled that Íñiguez had indeed been mad. Thus even the facile association of power with cruelty does not hold in this case. When the Inquisitors informed Íñiguez of his liberty, they asked him if he had a way to get from Toledo back to his home. He said no, but that he had faith that some generous towns-people – the very same population that he had recently characterised as his enemies and persecutors – would give him enough alms to get home.

I have lingered on this case because it contains so many instances of different practical and ethical responses toward one madman, and is thus a useful reference point for diverse episodes of *Don Quixote*, but I will bring in details of other cases as they apply. The relations between Don Quixote and society change significantly from Part I to Part II: most of the encounters in Part I are on the open road and the actors are predominantly tradesman, farmers and *pícaros*, while the second half is dominated by the aristocracy and clergy. In the novel and in the archival material, the social status and degree of familiarity of the participants in an interaction greatly affected the nature of that interaction. In this chapter, I wish to focus on the ways in which strangers from all rungs of the social ladder reacted to a madman in their midst. An understanding of the ethics of their responses is, I argue, important to a reading of *Don Quixote*, not only because such scenes make up much of Part I (and some of Part II) but also because it provides insight into the more central and complex ethical relationships in the work: between Quixote and Pero Pérez the priest and Maese Nicolás the barber, and between Quixote and Sancho. As I move in this direction – from fleeting encounters on the road to the central relationship of the text – I rely less on direct archival comparisons, as the depth of Sancho and Quixote's relation transcends anything found in a judicial file. By highlighting the ample archival parallels in the descriptions of more transient encounters, I hope to map out the ethical landscape of early modern dealings with the mad and show that this landscape is where Don Quixote resides. This, in turn, justifies the application of these ethical criteria to the more central relationships of the text, in an attempt to read these relations beyond Erasmian, Romantic, Freudian, Foucauldian or Bakhtinian filters.

Laughter and Status

During his three stays at an inn in Part I, Don Quixote comes into contact with men and women, strangers and acquaintances, authorities and the destitute. Furthermore, it is in these inns (the inn where he is 'knighted' and then that of Juan Palomeque) that Cervantes has characters speak about Don Quixote. Quixote's first night at an inn brings him into contact with total strangers: two prostitutes, an innkeeper and several mule drivers. They do not know him, and they do not know what and how he has been reading. Cervantes has not kept his readers similarly in the dark; in the first chapters, an omniscient (or seemingly omniscient) narrator has entered into Don Quixote's mind and confirmed that 'everything [he] thought, saw, or imagined seemed to happen according to what he had read' (I, ii, 26). We need not even speculate as to how Quixote applies his readings to his reality, as the narrator translates point by point how Don Quixote interprets the inn (a 'castle complete with four towers and spires of gleaming silver' [Ibid.]), the two prostitutes at the door ('two fair damsels or two gracious ladies' [Ibid.]), and the innkeeper ('the steward of the castle-fortress, which is what he thought the innkeeper and the inn were' [27]). Cervantes is setting the reader up to observe, but not share, the experience of a stranger observing and judging how best to deal with an utterly incomprehensible individual. Thus the reader will, at least initially, be able to partake in the double consciousness that fiction allows – to know and yet to share the perspective of those who do not know. The verisimilitude of the encounters encourages identification, while the fictionality of the same exchange allows the reader to experience multiple points of view and to contemplate social and ethical dynamics that would have been lost in the 'real' encounter.

The first people to see Don Quixote are two prostitutes, figures whose gender, class and occupation place them at the bottom of the social ladder and beyond the protections of the law. It is no surprise that, upon seeing 'a man armed in that fashion' approach the inn, they are 'filled with fear' (26)[8] and attempt to flee. Their first response then is not diagnostic but practical. Their instinct is to avoid possible danger. The mysterious armed man, however, engages them with 'a gallant manner and reassuring voice' and, in bizarrely archaic language, he promises not to hurt 'highborn maidens such as yourselves' (Ibid.). The promise of passivity combined with the bizarre misreading of the women's social status defuses the women's terror: 'They could not control their laughter, which offended Don Quixote' (Ibid.). James Iffland identifies this as the first of many moments of 'top-down laughter' in the novel, a pattern which, he argues, 'we can consider destabilising . . . and even more so if we take into account that the person that these two marginalised women are laughing at is trying to embody the qualities of that cultural icon of the traditional aristocracy'.[9] Iffland's reading of the drastic inversion of social roles depends on the women's laughter being of the humiliating, corrective, Bergsonian sort, but the freedom to humiliate and correct depends on a confidence in one's own superior position, and Cervantes tells us that the women's laughter increases with their confusion and nervous fear: 'The language, which the ladies did not understand, and bizarre appearance of our knight intensified their laughter' (I, ii, 27). This is a laughter not accounted for by Bergson – a nervous laughter which signals not disapproval but confusion, a reaction placeholder until the women can better determine an appropriate response. Don Quixote, unaware of the bizarreness of his speech and of the women's incomprehension, interprets the laughter exactly as Bergson would, and responds angrily. This is one of the first moments in which we see the disjunction of interpretations based on each character's limited grasp of the others' condition.

At this point the innkeeper enters and quickly takes stock of the situation, or as much as he can know of it. Cervantes tells us that the innkeeper's natural reaction to 'that grotesque figure' (27) is to accompany the prostitutes in their laughter. In the section 'De la comedia' in his *Filosofía antigua poética*, Alonso Pinciano identifies the source of the laughable in exactly these terms: 'A naturally ugly or grotesque body or face' is a 'ridiculous thing', and such things 'naturally cause laughter'.[10] There is certainly an element of disapproval in the judgement of something as 'ugly or grotesque' but the response is natural, instinctive and not incompatible with less cruel conscious responses. In this case, the innkeeper is unsure of which aspect of Don Quixote to respond to – his ridiculous style and dress, or his anger and weapons. The apprehension of mixed signals from Don Quixote's speech and action, his words and appearance, or his words on one topic versus those on another, is a pattern that is repeated in almost every new encounter the *hidalgo* has, and it is also a defining feature of madness. As discussed in the previous chapter, in almost all of the diagnoses of madness from this period, the key identifying symptom boils down to an incongruity among different aspects of a person's conduct – whether it be between his words and action, or the action and its context, or from one moment to the next.

Don Quixote, over the course of the novel, manifests all these, and the ways the other characters respond to such inconsistencies in large part determines their interactions. The innkeeper, in keeping with his 'very peacable' (I, ii, 27) character decides to err on the side of safety: it was better to be respectful of a harmless loony than offend a *furioso* (mad or not). 'Fearing the countless difficulties that might ensue, he decided to speak to him politely' (Ibid.). The strategy works: Don Quixote, 'seeing the humility' (Ibid.) of the innkeeper, responds in kind and the tension is temporarily defused. Cervantes's insistence on the precariousness of the situation and the uncertainty of diagnosis show us that, as humorous and boisterous as some of these scenes may be, they occur outside a carnival framework. Carnival is a festival with specific rules and limits known to all the participants. (The fact that the predominant rule is a disobedience of rules only makes the shared understanding of the limits more important.)[11] By highlighting the vacillation between fear and amusement of both the prostitutes and the innkeeper, Cervantes is telling us that the rules of this game are not clear to either party, and that the stakes of misinterpretation are potentially high. The prostitutes and the innkeeper are in the presence of a figure who may look like 'someone escaped from a Carnival parade',[12] but because it is not carnival they have no clear idea of how to react, and, since he is armed, they have real fear of making the wrong choice. Iffland reads Quixote's elevation of the two prostitutes to ladies-in-waiting as 'perhaps even more radically carnivalesque than converting Aldonza into Dulcinea'.[13] But Cervantes goes out of his way to show that none of the characters seems to consider this a burlesque atmosphere. Don Quixote is completely unaware of any game or inversion. The innkeeper must test the waters before he feels secure enough to begin to introduce burlesque elements. Cervantes gives the episode a peaceful and humorous resolution, but by foregrounding the characters' process of determining the spaces in which it was safe to play he also reminds us that, outside the official demarcation of carnival, such a resolution was hardly guaranteed. It is precisely when madness presented itself outside a space where it could be easily interpreted that it became a social problem – and a source of narrative tension.

How did women and innkeepers negotiate this tension on the days between Lent and Mardi Gras? A close reading of archival accounts offers clues about early modern ethics of ridicule, an ethics which does not necessarily mirror our own. We saw in Bartolomé Íñiguez's case that early modern Spaniards were able to garner pleasure from another's degradation at the same time that they helped to relieve it. Other cases show how relations of power and status could determine, but could also be inverted by, judgements about another's sanity. One Pedro Salinas approached a convent and, speaking through the barred windows, told the assembled novices and nuns that he would identify among their ranks one person with an 'espíritu muy perfecto' ('a very perfect spirit'). He eventually pointed out a woman who was not a nun but only a visiting singing teacher. One of the nuns said she determined that Salinas was not 'en sí' ('in his right mind') because she had heard that 'había tenido algunas lesiones' ('he had suffered certain lesions') and because, when he spoke, 'daba unas risadas con descompostura' ('he would laugh in a disturbed manner'). She reported that one group of nuns, 'por hacer experiencia dél y como riéndosele' ('to test him and as if laughing at him'), pointed out others who, from a distance, looked somewhat like his singing teacher, questioning him if each was the 'perfect spirit'. As he said yes about anyone with a similar hairstyle, the nuns 'coligieron que todo era locura' ('gathered that it was all madness'). Still, they did not openly ridicule him and it was only after confirming his madness with the abbess, who in turn had made inquiries with church officials, that they dared to have some fun.[14]

In the trial of a 'nest' of *beatas* in Toledo in the 1570s, we find a secondary story concerning the appearance of a wandering apocalyptic prophet who, like Alonso Quijano, had assumed an identity based on popular legends: in this case, the popular saint Juan de Dios. He arrived with farfetched stories of prophetic visions and magical powers. When he first proclaimed to the *beata* Francisca de Aguilar that he knew of a special water that would cure her ailing niece, she, like the women at the inn, gave his words a commonsense interpretation, assuming that he referred to 'algún agua [que] haya en la botica' ('some water in the dispensary'). However, once she found out that he was referring to his saliva, or, in other words, when the logical inference was no longer tenable, 'la echó ésta a mal y [se] ri[ó] delante del dicho Juan de Dios' ('it sounded wrong to her and she laugh[ed] in front of the aforementioned Juan de Dios').[15] Juan de Dios reacts just as Don Quixote did to the laughing *mozas*, chastising her for her laughter and defending his own claims. The wandering prophet – showing his awareness of both Bergsonian and Erasmian responses to madness – retorted, 'No me espanto de que se ría porque soy loco, más soy loco de Dios' ('I'm not surprised that you're laughing because I'm mad, but I am mad for God'), and then proceeded to tout the benefits of his saliva 'color de cielo porque ... tengo a Dios conmigo' ('the colour of the heavens because ... I have God with me'). The still-suspicious Francisca did not challenge him directly, limiting herself to a repetition of his words, although she hastened to clarify, 'no porque lo creyese sino porque le pareció cosa muy fuera de camino' ('not because she believed him but because it seemed very strange to her'). She was not the only one to find Juan de Dios suspicious; a number of the *beatas* reported scepticism, but as women they were insufficiently confident in their own judgements of sanity and insanity, or heresy and orthodoxy, to confront him directly.

The entire Church hierarchy was set up to make sure that these judgements were made 'properly', by those with the authority to do so. These *beatas* knew that the proper way to check the accuracy of their initial perceptions was to consult a male authority. Another *beata*, Luisa de los Ángeles, went to her confessor and reported Juan de Dios's claims, 'pareciéndole mal a ésta estas cosas' ('these things seeming wrong to her'). Her confessor responded that Juan de Dios had been before the Inquisition three or four times and 'pues ellos le había[n] soltado, que no había qué tratar' ('since they had let him go, there was nothing to talk about'). The women accepted his authority and treated Juan de Dios with a wary respect. Only in his absence did some of them tentatively voice their doubts. Francisca Aguilar said to Luisa de los Ángeles 'como por baldón, que había creído lo que había dicho Juan de Dios y . . . ella dijo que sí . . . [pero] lo había dicho haciendo burla' ('as if in reproach that she had believed what Juan de Dios had said . . . and she said yes . . . [but] that she had been joking'). However, they never confronted Juan de Dios directly, just as the *mozas* at the inn, however suspicious they might have been about their guest's behaviour, follow the cues of their social superior, the innkeeper.

The innkeeper's apparent recognition of the validity of Don Quixote's claims, like the confessor's guarded approval of Juan de Dios, determines the women's further actions. As the innkeeper is conducting the knighthood ceremony, he orders one of the women to gird Don Quixote with his sword, and she does so, albeit struggling not to 'burst into laughter at each moment of the ceremony' (I, iii, 34). The women suppress their giggles in the light of their superior's opinion and their own fear, since 'the feats they had seen performed by the new knight kept their laughter in check' (Ibid.).[16] Just as Francisca de Aguilar reprovingly repeated Juan de Dios's words to him without her sarcasm registering, one of the women wishes the newly-made knight, 'May God make your grace a very fortunate knight and give you good fortune in your fights' (Ibid.). This is a safe commendation, neither affirming her own faith in his identity nor openly demonstrating her doubt. The rest of the encounter continues in this vein, with Don Quixote asking the questions and offering to elevate the women to aristocracy, just as Juan de Dios promised to bring the Toledan women to Rome and the site of the Second Coming; as the Toledan women go along with their guest without committing themselves to future action, so the prostitutes listen to Don Quixote's flowery sonnets but, because they are 'unaccustomed to hearing such high-flown rhetoric', they do not respond (I, ii, 29). To assume the role of humiliator requires a conviction that the balance of power is overwhelmingly in one's favour, and because the women cannot comprehend Don Quixote's strange speech and ways, they are either unwilling or unable to take this risk. Thus they continue to serve the knight, and although the narrator comments that 'it was a cause for great laughter to see him eat' he does not indicate that the women do any laughing (Ibid.). Instead, it seems that their non-satiric participation in the scene, feeding the knight through his helmet and visor, is a key component of the scene's risibility for the reader, who *has* been prepared to hear 'such high-flown rhetoric'. Only the narrator and reader, who know for certain who is crazy and who is uneducated, can find in the situation 'cause for great laughter'.

The innkeeper is a higher status figure than the prostitutes but initially he is as baffled as they by Don Quixote's behaviour; when Don Quixote first throws himself at his feet and addresses him as 'valiant knight', the innkeeper is left 'perplexed, not knowing what to do or say' (I, iii, 29–30). He, like the women, tries to extricate himself from the immediate difficulty, which he is only able to do by promising 'that he would grant the boon asked of him' (30). Initially, then, the innkeeper's adoption of Don Quixote's logic and language is pragmatic, not mocking. However, because he is better-read than the prostitutes, he has an idea of where the knight's 'high-flown rhetoric' is coming from, and thus he is able to move from his initial 'inkling of his guest's madness' (Ibid.) to a relatively certain diagnosis. This diagnosis rearranges the social hierarchy and, consequently, the ethical landscape. The innkeeper is *not* a madman's social inferior. Iffland's conclusions about the radical social implications of 'bottom-up' laughter in 'a rigidly differentiated society'[17] ignores the fact that a diagnosis of madness was an immediate ticket out of the entire social hierarchy. It is a reflection of the innkeeper's more secure social position and exposure to literature that he has the confidence to make his diagnosis, while the prostitutes do not. But his verdict that Don Quixote is mad empties his laughter at the knight of any social transgression; he is laughing at a *loco,* not a social superior. Whether he chooses to mock or protect Don Quixote reflects only the tug in his nature between compassion and *schadenfreude.*

The way the innkeeper responds to this tug is characteristic of the way real people responded to those they assumed to be mad. He is neither wholly generous nor wholly cruel; it is not so much that he strikes a middle ground as that he concludes that a little fun at a madman's expense is acceptable as long as it is compatible with a reasonably charitable outcome. As Cervantes (or Cide Hamete) states near the end of Part II, 'jests that cause pain are not jests, and entertainments are not worthwhile if they injure another', but a *true* jest, one which did not cause harm, was not only ethically uncompromised but its practitioner could be judged 'seemly and benign' (II, lxii, 865). When laughter was aimed at a 'butt' it threatened his honour, dignity and/or social standing. But the madman had already lost all of these; laughing at him, therefore, did no harm. The risk of cruelty lay only then in a laughter that took the place of the alleviation of suffering mandated by the precepts of Christian charity. The fact that none of the witnesses in these Inquisition cases, including nuns, shows any compunction about his or her laughter nor criticises others for laughing strongly implies that, as long as the madman left the interaction more helped than hurt, no one saw any reason why the interaction should not be enjoyable for the sane participants. If it offered the opportunity for a generally marginalised group to enjoy the upper hand and even flaunt it for a while, then both sides benefited from the interaction. Unlike the role inversion in carnival, however, the 'success' of this exchange (the extent to which both laugher and laugh-ee ended up better off) was in no way guaranteed or scripted. At the inn and in so many other scenes in which characters attempt to deal with Don Quixote, the line between cruelty, compassion and conflict is constantly being probed and adjusted.

The innkeeper's actions throughout the first inn-scene exemplify this negotiation of a space of ridicule. Cervantes would seem to give mixed messages about his ethics in dealing with Don Quixote:

> The innkeeper, as we have said, was rather sly and already had some inkling of his guest's madness, which was confirmed when he heard him say these words, and so in order to have something to laugh about that night, he proposed to humor him. (I, iii, 30)[18]

He characterises him as 'sly', and the movement from 'confirmation' of madness to a desire for entertainment seems insensitive. Yet he will achieve this entertainment by 'humoring him', by indulging the desires of the laugh-ee (the Spanish 'seguirle el humor' makes his submission to Quixote's narrative clearer). The fact that he waited until he was certain of Quixote's madness could reveal a cruel impulse to take advantage of a newly discovered social superiority, or it could show that he did not want to laugh at his guest until he knew how his jokes would be interpreted and felt by their object. Once he understands that Don Quixote is mad, and thinks he understands the logic behind his madness, he can set up a joke that, far from causing Don Quixote to suffer, will follow the rules ('seguirle el humor') the knight himself sets out. The Inquisition archives suggest that what may seem to a modern reader to be at best a contradictory attitude and at worst outright cruelty would not have been seen as such in the period. The goal of most people who came into contact with a madman was to get the maximum personal gain (amusement, social cohesion, the moral high ground) while minimising damage (moral and physical) both to self and *loco*. This is the moral compass guiding the innkeeper's actions.

It is a compass that requires continual calibration. The initial discussion between the innkeeper and Don Quixote regarding the proper exercise of the knightly profession suggests that the innkeeper has found an ethical balance. It is truly a dialogue, with Don Quixote successfully getting what he wants – a place to stand vigil over his arms and the promise of an official knighting ceremony – and what he enjoys – discussion of proper knight errant etiquette – and the innkeeper likewise achieving his goal of procuring entertainment, all the while enjoying his own ironic superiority. This superiority depends on Don Quixote's total ignorance of the sincerity differential, but as long as he is ignorant or unconcerned about it he cannot suffer humiliation. Thus he heartily thanks the innkeeper for his advice and promises 'to do as he had advised with great alacrity' (I, iii, 31).

As Henri Bergson notes, laughter is a social phenomenon, and, since to this point the innkeeper has only been amusing himself, his natural next step is to inform everyone in the inn of the 'lunacy of his guest' and to invite them to share in the sure-to-be entertaining events to come (32). This initiates the first destabilisation of the mad–sane interaction. A ready and willing audience, like that which assembled around the roof-bound and later the imprisoned Íñiguez, gathers to observe 'so strange a form of madness' (Ibid.). The majority of the spectators are content to watch from afar, but practical necessity, ambiguously tinged with (or not considered as incompatible with) a desire to provoke, leads to a more intense confrontation. This was exactly the situation in Íñiguez's case; the word spread of his imprisonment and there was a call to come and see 'el loco'. Many did, but their motives did not fall into easy categories of charity or cruelty; they attempted to save him from his own blasphemies but in doing so incited him to further blasphemy. The muleteer's motive for approaching Quixote is equally opaque. Cervantes says only that 'it occurred to one of the mule drivers in the inn to water his pack of mules, and for this it was necessary to move Don Quixote's armour' (Ibid.). He does not indicate that there is a contradiction between the whimsical 'occurred' and the necessity of watering one's oxen, just as the residents of Yunquera felt no moral ambivalence about their more-enthusiastic-than-necessary fervour for getting Íñiguez off the roof. The results of the two confrontations are also similar; the madman, who might have gone on providing his laughable spectacle indefinitely, becomes violent when a member of the audience attempts to rewrite his 'show'. The response goes beyond the bounds of comedy and brings the interaction to crisis, implicating other members of the (ex-)audience, and finally necessitating the intervention of an authority figure. The mule-driver does not heed Quixote's threats and throws the knight's arms away from the water trough. (Again, Cervantes's prose emphasises the blend of provocation and normal conduct. The mule-driver adds his own theatre to the necessary removal of the armour, 'thr[owing] it a good distance away' [I, iii, 32]). The response of the madman to something that to an objective observer would seem to be a mildly provocative action – disregard of a warning to let him stay on the roof, disregard of a threat to leave his arms alone – is entirely disproportionate and irrational. Íñiguez responds to the affront to his liberty not just by fighting with the mayor or, later, by threatening the visitors to the jail but rather by railing against God, to a degree that was, in seventeenth-century Spain, akin to a physical assault. Don Quixote does not respond to the muleteer's affront with an escalating war of words, but rather he nearly kills the muledriver with a blow to the head from his lance. When another muleteer, unaware of Quixote and his mania, again moves the arms to get access to the trough, there are neither threats nor warnings; Quixote cracks his head into three pieces. What might have begun as a carnival-like farce has exploded into serious violence. The entire 'audience' is forced to step into a situation with no clear guidelines.

Outside the carnival frame, reactions to unreason, at the same time that they become more uncertain, become more ethically ambiguous. Cervantes certainly intends for Don Quixote to seem silly in the reader's eyes, but he also takes pains to show us that the reader's perspective is at odds with the various characters' own understanding of the knight's behaviour. With the entrance of each new element on the scene, Cervantes gives the reader specific details – through both the narrator's voice and Don Quixote's speech – of his protagonist's misperceptions and, up until his imitation of Amadís in the Sierra Morena, in none of them do we see the possibility of either play or irony. Those scenes that are most frequently and persistently characterised as carnivalesque, such as the episodes at the first inn, show a dynamic which is much closer to humiliation and abuse, a social dynamic operative year round. Insofar as Quixote becomes the butt of violence or humiliation, it is not carnival-violence (without injury, without consequences) *to him*. To recognise this does not entail accepting the Romantic reading of the knight as a tragic figure abused by an unfeeling society. Instead, it shows us how Cervantes is exploring ethics of human interaction from multiple perspectives, using fiction to juxtapose the perspective of the butt of the joke with that of the joker. Readers are forced into the uncomfortable position of deciding whether to laugh or take offence.[19] If they have been, like the innkeeper and guests, passively enjoying the spectacle, they must, like the innkeeper, recalibrate their response.

Rules of Non-Engagement

Unlike the reader, few of the characters in Part I have a chance to recalibrate. We cannot say whether they are cruel or charitable in their treatment of the *madman* because their response to Don Quixote's irrationality is to avoid diagnosing him at all. Don Quixote's nomadism in Part I may reflect the madman's characteristic wanderlust or his inability to remain in static situations that demand conformity. Once the madman has left home, however, this pattern of fleeting encounters perpetuates itself, not because of any intrinsic quality of madness but because of the early modern Spaniard's reaction to unexplained unreason. In novel and archive, the most common reaction to the spectacle of unreason (possibly heretical, possibly mad, possibly malicious), particularly when coming from someone from a higher social class, was either to suspend judgement, to avoid contact or to maintain an interaction that was as normal as possible and leave more profound diagnoses (heresy, madness, malice) for others. Francisco del Vado and his brother had a lifelong history of killing, stealing and/or eating other people's provisions and livestock.[20] Ana Muñóz, who had known them since childhood, described the common town reaction: since it was public knowledge that they stole provisions, 'en este pueblo la gente ordinariamente vivían con recato con ellos y les herraban las puertas por las calles donde iban' ('in this town people usually treated them with caution and locked the doors on the streets they passed through'). Like the townspeople of Yunquera who declined the opportunity to see Íñiguez, these locals evidenced neither cruelty nor charity, just self-protection.

In the majority of the scenes in Part I, Don Quixote has a conflict or perplexing encounter with a figure on the road who has no knowledge of his past troubles or current thoughts, although he has an immediate glimpse at some very bizarre behaviour. After the encounter, the figure attempts to recoup his losses and does his best to get as far away from the potentially dangerous Quixote as possible. We have no idea how these strangers feel about the ethics of treating the mad because they do not stick around long enough to make a diagnosis. Those of a more timid nature – the friars, barbers, shepherds, *bachilleres* and ladies – head off 'without considering what Don Quixote was demanding' (I, ix, 70), 'without further inquiry' (I, xviii, 130), and never able to 'understand the meaning of Don Quixote's words and questions to them'

(I, xxix, 652). The more generous types, such as the shepherds who set out food for Cardenio even after he raids their supplies, accept their losses with stoicism. And those of a more aggressive nature – *mozos, vizcaínos* – defend themselves, but they too skip off when their immediate anger (at a legitimate offence) passes or when a more conflict-averse third party takes them away.

Because wandering madmen were often at the mercy of strangers for their lodging, *locos'* most sustained contacts were with the *venteros* and strangers who offered them beds for the night. When investigating an insanity defence, the Inquisitors often went straight to these figures, as they would seem to have had a privileged opportunity to judge the behaviour of their guest. Yet many of the house and innkeepers deliberately avoided judgement. After Francisco del Vado's insanity plea, the Inquisitors went to his home town and interviewed Francisco Roldán, owner of a boarding house in which del Vado had occasionally stayed. Roldán reported that del Vado would flog himself to the point of bleeding and 'algunas veces le oía decir azotándose "alberi alberi" y muchas veces le preguntó este testigo que qué quería decir en aquellas palabras, el cual respondía que quería decir cuitado de mí y que era lenguaje de moros' ('sometimes he heard him say as he flogged himself "alberi alberi" and many times he asked [del Vado] what those words meant, and he responded that it meant poor me and that it was the Moorish language'). Roldán did not pursue the matter further. Alonso Hernández de Villarubia, a *familiar* in the town, said that 'no le entendían' ('they didn't understand him') or his words 'de morisco o de arábigo' ('in *morisco* or Arabic'), and, while he added that 'antes se escandalizaban' ('but rather they were scandalised'), he did not take the matter further. It seemed easier, even for a *familiar*, to let unintelligible words alone rather than start trouble with a man clearly capable of causing problems.

Women seemed particularly disposed to step in and offer shelter to a helpless stranger, even if he happened to seem crazy. A lady named Juana del Río Mayor testified in the trial of Juan de Larrea that she saw Larrea being chased down her street by citizens 'amenazándole con un palo' ('threatening him with a stick').[21] As she recalled it:

> vino aquí un mozo que dice es medio loco y tiró un sombrero a Nuestra Señora . . . ésta lo recogió en su casa y durmió allí hasta el amanecer y luego le dio un poco de pan . . . y con esto se fue.

> a young man they say is half mad came by here and he threw a hat at Our Lady . . . she took him into her home and he slept there until daybreak and then she gave him a little bread . . . and with that, he left.

She does not say that she gave Larrea a bed *because* he was mad. Her judgement of his mental state is doubly displaced – it is others who say that Larrea is mad, and only half mad at that – and this backstory prefaces her own actions without a causative conjunction ('and' and not 'because'). She was charitable because it is her nature to comfort those in need. When asked by the Inquisitors as to her opinion of Larrea's sanity, she replied that 'le tiene por loco a lo que ha visto y entendido' ('from what she saw and understood, she took him to be mad') so we know that she did register his irrationality, but this conclusion does not seem to have been the guiding force behind her actions. She did for him what she would have done for any poor wayfaring stranger, although noting along the way that this stranger was a bit stranger than most.

In each of the inn-scenes, Cervantes connects the behaviour of the staff with their degree of comprehension of Don Quixote. As we saw with the prostitutes, non-comprehension (the norm for the passing irrational guest) led to limited engagement. At Juan Palomeque's inn, the innkeeper's wife and the 'Asturian girl' Maritornes are bewildered by Don Quixote's bizarrely archaic words: 'they understood no more of them than if he had been speaking Greek' (I, xvi, 111) (or 'the Moorish language' or Arabic). Cervantes does not tell us whether they conclude that Don Quixote is speaking irrationally or that their own comprehensive faculties are at fault. He records that they register an incongruity ('he seemed to them a different kind of man from the ones they were used to') and wonder at it ('they looked at him in astonishment') (Ibid.). The attitude of *admiratio* precedes judgement – it is the initial registering of a phenomenon that is out of the ordinary. The women do not proceed from wonder to critical judgement; on the contrary, they decide to proceed *as if* there were nothing to wonder at. In order to respond to Don Quixote as if he had spoken normally they do their best to grasp the main idea of his monologue and, once reasonably certain that it tends toward 'compliments and flattery', they gamely thank him and leave him alone before they get in deeper than they can manage (Ibid.). The innkeeper's wife, like Juana de Añomayor, continues to behave according to her duty as a hostess and her nature, a woman who was 'naturally charitable and took pity on the calamities of others' (109). The only change in her behaviour is perhaps an increased desire to shorten the interaction, to leave Don Quixote to his recovery and return to safer, more comprehensible ground.

Even many of the characters who harm Don Quixote are acting out of a similar refusal to pass judgement on his mental state; they too proceed as they would normally, but they happen to be generally aggressive or uncharitable. The morning after the bed-and-switch debacle which leaves the tryst between Maritornes and her muleteer unconsummated and Sancho and Don Quixote unconscious, the officer who had broken up the fracas the night before comes in to inspect the damages. Finding Don Quixote flat on his back and unable to move, he asks him how he is doing, at which Don Quixote takes offence and protests, 'Is it the custom in this land to speak in that manner to knights errant, you dolt?' (I, xvii, 118). The officer notes an incongruity between the aggression of the words and the 'sorry look'[22] of the speaker, but he does not step back to reflect upon the causes of the disparity or the irrationality of the words themselves. He seizes upon the affront and literally returns fire, tossing the oil-filled candle at Quixote's head. Even the officer, however, is more hot-tempered than malicious. Soon after, Sancho goes in search of first aid, he comes upon the officer and, echoing Quixote's irrational words but not his aggressive tone, asks for the necessary ingredients to cure 'one of the best knights errant on the face of the earth' (118–19). His judgement no longer clouded by a perceived insult, the officer makes the diagnosis that 'Sancho was out of his mind' (Ibid.). Once he has determined he is dealing with a madman, he obligingly calls for the innkeeper and relays the request.

The only characters in Part I who interact with Don Quixote long enough to conclude that he is mad, and then seize the opportunity to do him greater physical harm, are Maritornes (I, xlii) and the *galeotes*, led by Ginés de Pasamonte (I, xxii). There certainly were criminals and violent types in early modern Spain who, upon realising that someone 'was not very sane' as Pasamonte puts it (I, xxii, 172), saw a chance to humiliate or steal with impunity. Maritornes, when she lures Don Quixote to her window and literally leaves him hanging, acts as the *muchachos* in Bartolomé Íñiguez's case, finding enjoyment in a madman's suffering. Francisco del Vado ran into a citizens' arresting squad that he recalled as saying that 'se habían de hacer y ejecutar muy ejemplares castigos, como decían que me habían de cortar las orejas, manos y otros miembros' ('they were going to do and exact very exemplary punishments, such as saying they were going to cut my ears, hands and other limbs'). Still, this might-makes-right attitude, which, if we were to read the picaresque tales as historical documents,[23] would seem to be nearly omnipresent in early modern Spain, is the exception, both in the Inquisition archives and in the novel. Hardened criminals might bite the hand that freed them, but your typical working man seemed more likely to flee the hand that hit him. This was not because he was a coward or a prophet of nonviolence; on the contrary, in many of the Inquisition files, his initial response to a physical threat was violent. However, very few became violent if they had time or evidence to conclude that the offender was mad (and many explicitly said that they restrained themselves),[24] and almost none indulged violent impulses *because* a victim was mad.

Frequently the victim of violence himself recognised the lack of cruelty in the physical intervention. Juan de Herreria, from Valhermosa, vaguely recalled neighbours tying him up during his fits, but knew that they did it 'porque no hiciese mal' ('so he wouldn't do any damage').[25] When Hernando de Madrigal fell to the ground, foaming at the mouth, those present restrained him 'porque no se hiriese' ('so he wouldn't hurt himself') and one said that 'le favoreció en tenerlo en las manos' (he 'protected him holding him in his hands').[26] Generally, once the attack had passed, the participants resumed their normal daily relations. María Sacristán gives us the example of Alonso Hernández Marín, a surgeon in Mexico and, most of the time, a respected and popular member of his community. Occasionally, however, he would suffer fits of incoherence and violence. One neighbour recalled:

> se embravecía de manera que no eran poderosos cuatro o cinco hombres a tenerle, para atarle las manos y pies . . . y quebraba los vasos en que le llevan la comida y bebida . . . y todo lo que podía haber a las manos lo hacía pedazos.

> he became enraged to the point that four or five people weren't enough to restrain him, to tie his hands and feet . . . and he broke the glasses in which they bring him food and drink . . . and he broke into pieces everything he could get his hands on.[27]

We can imagine, given the description above, that such an intervention required a fair amount of force. Yet this was not a repressive or vindictive violence. During his spells, Hernández would refuse to eat, and one neighbour described how, after he had gone seven days without eating, the neighbours 'le pusieron en la boca un closé de maíz para abrírsela y le dieron muchos azotes para que tomase unos caldos' ('put a corn cob in his mouth to open it and gave him many lashes so that he would drink some broth').[28] Yet as soon as his fits had passed, these same neighbours seemed willing to integrate Hernández once again into regular community life. The day after he had recovered from his attack, 'he went back to being a "good surgeon" and there were patients who came to him to be bled'.[29] As Sacristán writes, 'his case demonstrates . . . the integration of a madman into everyday life once he had recovered his sanity . . . at no point was he an outcast'.[30] While Hernández's violence was a threat to self and others, his neighbours stepped in with violence *and* charity. Yet, as soon as it was socially possible to do so, the community preferred to return to a basic, sustainable pattern of daily life.

Restoring Order

Sometimes, however, in novel and archive, violence spins out of control, and characters not only react in kind to Don Quixote's violence but provoke it further. For instance, once Don Quixote splits the head of the first muleteer, his friends begin to throw rocks, more interested in avenging their injured colleagues than understanding the aggressor's mental state. At this point, it becomes the responsibility of figures of relatively higher social status to step in. The innkeeper, despite Don Quixote's unprovoked violence against his paying customers, intervenes to stop the stone-throwers, reminding them that that 'he had already told them he was crazy, and that being crazy he would be absolved even if he killed them all' (I, iii, 33). As in the archival accounts, the intervention is specifically justified in terms that blur modern ideas of charity and cruelty. The innkeeper's argument is practical, not moral; he does not order the stone-throwers to desist because Quixote was unaware of his actions but because the revenge sought by the stone-throwers will be ultimately thwarted by the law. He certainly does not express any remorse for having arranged the entire spectacle. Moral calculations are left aside in the name of a more immediately pressing cause: the restoration of order.

When Francisco del Vado ('alberi, alberi') was arrested by a group of angry citizens after a series of livestock thefts, he spouted off a variety of blasphemies.[31] The mayor's lieutenant, despite having organised and led the civilian justice force, was also responsible for reining it in, and he even went as far as defending the victim before the Inquisition. The lieutenant reported that he doubted that del Vado truly meant everything he had said,[32] telling the Inquisitors that 'algunas de las dichas palabras me parece las debía de decir porque mucha gente le apretaba con malos tratamientos por ver las herejías que decía' ('it seems to me that he must have said some of the aforementioned words because many people were pushing him with ill treatment to see what heresies he would say'). As with Íñiguez and the objects of his libellous accusations, and as in the scene at the inn, a group eager for revenge for offences to their honour and property responded violently and, in doing so, provoked the madman to further offences, which the group then sought to punish with further violence, and so on in a vicious cycle. Again, the figure of relative authority, who had a broader understanding of the issues and interactions at play, stepped in to defuse the violence that he had set in motion: 'Y visto que estaba de aquella forma y mal pensamiento el dicho Francisco del Vado, porque no le hiciesen decir más malas palabras, hizo le dejasen la gente' ('And seeing that the said Francisco del Vado was in this state and bad frame of mind, he made the people leave him alone, so that they wouldn't make him say any more evil words'). Again the appeal to calm is made not in moral terms but as a practical, expedient way to avoid further damage.

Even an Inquisition *familiar* might defend law and order at the cost of the enforcement of doctrinal orthodoxy. Juan Arias Dávila, a defrocked Augustinian monk, installed himself in the street and began to yell at some local boys, asking them whether a crucifix made out of gold should be worshipped. When one of the boys said yes, Arias contradicted him, and the whole group followed Arias to the main square, where 'juntó mucha gente con grande ruido tratando de la dicha materia' ('many people assembled and made a lot of noise talking about the said matter').[33] An Inquisition notary who had seen the episode ran and found the local *familiar*, and the two of them found Arias in the Plaza Mayor, 'rodeado de mucha gente, y le sacaron de allí y le llevaron a casa deste testigo, donde estuvo un rato y le dio de comer' ('surrounded by a crowd, and they took him out of there and to this witness's house, where he stayed a while and he gave him something to eat'). When questioned by the Inquisitors as to whether Arias continued with his blasphemies in the house, the *familiar* replied that he could not say, as he was dedicating all of his attention to dispersing the mob and thus 'no le oyó cosa alguna' ('he didn't hear him say anything'). The authority figure's first duty was to restore the public order that had been disrupted by irrational behaviour, although both in this case and in that of Cervantes's innkeeper doing so required a temporary neglect of his official responsibilities. The innkeeper insults his own paying guests in order to placate Don Quixote, and the *familiar*, agent of the tribunal against heresy, ignored the heresies being spouted in his own house.

Because these authorities see their main ethical duty as the maintenance of calm, they often proceed uncharitably once they have defused the immediate threat of violence. The innkeeper, having kept the muleteers at bay, decides to give Quixote 'the accursed order of chivalry then and there' (Ibid.). In order not to provoke the testy guest, he assumes a false humility and apologises for the muleteers, and then proceeds to invent the arrangements for the farcical knighting ceremony. At first he acts out of fear for the safety of his person and his guests but, as the immediate physical danger passes, he also gives in to his more 'socarrón' side, investing the ceremony with more theatre than strictly necessary. The impulses – to humour Don Quixote and to turn him into the butt of humour – are in constant tension. As long as Don Quixote is present, he must keep his 'laughter in check' but, once the new knight departs, the innkeeper, judging himself out of danger, gives mockery free rein, matching the departing Quixote's bizarre language with his own 'no less rhetorical' words (35). The moral imperative he obeys does not require him to respect an inherent and inalienable human dignity but to maximise his own enjoyment without increasing another's suffering.

This dynamic is replayed towards the end of Part I in the debate over the identity of the *bacía-yelmo*. Cervantes not only gives us each character's perspective on the 'identity' of the basin/helmet, but he extends the ontological and linguistic perspectivism to an interpretation of Quixote's behaviour. Cervantes shows us how each character judges Don Quixote, and how that judgement affects his reaction. The barber initially decides to prolong the debate because 'as he knew Don Quixote's madness so well . . . he wanted to encourage his lunacies and, by carrying the joke even further, give everyone a good reason to laugh' (I, xlv, 391). The barber's familiarity with Don Quixote's delusions and his ability to anticipate his reactions gives him the security to play, to derive amusement for himself and the others in the know, without the situation threatening to erupt into violence. The guests at the inn who are aware of Quixote's history join in the laughter and further the joke, because they too enjoy the same security in its safety and harmlessness. Although Don Quixote is the source of the laughter, he too benefits from the joke, insofar as he sees his own world-view affirmed. The joke fails – ceases to produce laughter or be harmless – when the officers, who do not know Quixote's history, step in and provoke the knight. Once the situation, whose whole purpose was to produce laughter, veers into the tragic, the jokers recognise that they are responsible for restoring calm. 'Persuaded by the judge and the priest', both of whom had earlier helped further the joke, the officers 'ma[ke] peace' (395).

Both the priest and the officers, representatives respectively of ecclesiastical and secular authority, seek to prevent disorder, but they understand this responsibility differently; the priest gives priority to restoring order at the inn and avoiding violence, while the officers are willing to use violence against the individual in order to defend the republic against disorderly criminals and their would-be liberators. There are archival cases where secular and ecclesiastical authorities split along similar lines. Juan de Larrea entered a church, according to a witness, 'desarrapado, con alboroto, al parecer de hombre desatentado' ('raggedly dressed and agitated, seemingly a man out of control') and began sticking his fingers in the hanging lamps. When asked to leave, he replied, 'déjenme, que yo digo la verdad de aquella misa' ('leave me alone, I am saying the truth about that mass').[34] We should not underestimate what a scandal this would have presented in the middle of a mass, and yet the acolyte (who was also an Inquisition scribe) very charitably:

se levantó y llegó a él ofreciéndole limosna de dos quartos porque le saliese de la capilla, y el dicho mozo mirando muy atento a este testigo dijo 'déjeme déjeme que yo me estaré quedo' y este testigo le dejó.

got up and came to him, offering him in charity two *cuartos* so that he would leave the chapel, and the aforementioned young man, looking at him very carefully, said 'leave me alone, leave me alone, I will be quiet,' and so he left him alone.

Larrea did not keep his promise, unfortunately, and ended up throwing a rock and hitting a crucifix. A local *alguacil* arrived and although, according to another witness, 'decían allí muchos de los que allí estaban presentes que era loco el dicho mozo y como a tal no había que hacer caso dél' ('many of the people present there said the aforementioned young man was crazy and as such they shouldn't pay attention to him'), the officer replied that 'aunque fuese loco le había de hacer azotar' ('mad or not, he ought to be whipped'). In this scene, everyone witnessed the same behaviour and noted its irrationality, but they responded differently. As in the inn, the religious authority offered his own money, the secular authority insisted on punishment, and the parishioners recommended marginalisation. Rather than judging one group as more charitable than the other, we should recognise different strategies for restoring stability.

Madness and Social Cohesion

Over the course of Part I, Cervantes transforms the social space of the inn. When Juan Palomeque and his family first meet Don Quixote, they do not know that he will become a recurring fixture in their life, and so they do not initially take much time to analyse or interrogate him, nor does Cervantes give much insight into their thoughts about Don Quixote. This is an extension of the early encounters on the road, characterised by episodic action rather than psychological speculation. With the convergence on the inn of characters from home and from previous episodes, we exit the linear, episodic structure and enter an intermediate space – neither home nor the road. As the inn's space in the narrative economy changes, so too will the nature of interactions with the madman that occur there. When the priest and barber, and then Sancho, pass through the inn, they inform the staff of the whole history of Don Quixote's madness and the plot to bring him back home. This marks an important turning point in the narrative and ethical determinants of Quixote's encounters. Up to this point, as we have seen, the other characters' response to the knight is largely determined by his *inexplicable* behaviour. The (seemingly) omniscient narrator provides the reader with the information needed to grasp the dynamics of the situation, but no single character perceives reality, or other characters' reality, fully. Up to this point, then, the reader is the only one who has been forced to make the ethical decision as to whether or not to laugh at a *madman*, since he/she is the only one who can confirm and comprehend Don Quixote's madness. Beginning with the second stay at the inn, the characters come to share the reader's ethical space. They are not privy to the voice of the narrator, of course, but, increasingly, neither is the reader – or at least not to a narrator who can in any way be counted on to provide 'omniscient' or objective analysis. The episodic structure will give way to an exploration of community and psychology; the characters will sit at a table and try to 'read' Don Quixote, making diagnoses and responses based on an interrogation of the past and present. They will still try to return Don Quixote to sanity, but now they can plan ahead and anticipate responses, employing reason rather than violence. At the same time, their understanding, their ability to consult with each other and the time they have to plan their responses, all give their interactions an ethical dimension that shepherds saving their sheep from a sword-wielding lunatic did not have. They have the time and information to consider what they *should* do, what the *right* course of action would be. This shift from episodic reaction to sustained discussion and diagnosis will change the nature of the text, moving it definitively away from previous models (or even a parody of those models) and into new terrain.

The community at the inn builds in layers, and the connection between each successive layer is Don Quixote's madness. When the priest passes through the inn, he explains 'briefly . . . Don Quixote's madness' to the innkeeper's wife (I, xxvii, 212). When priest and barber return with Quixote in tow, the assembled guests sit down with the inn's staff to discuss in more depth 'the strange madness of Don Quixote' (I, xxxii, 267). The innkeeper adds his piece of the story – the night of musical beds with the muleteer. The exchange of information is important, but there is clearly an element of entertainment in these discussions. Don Quixote's actions and sanity become a *tertulia* topic to which everyone can add a new anecdote and insert his/her own opinion. The *tertulia* is resumed each time someone new comes to the inn. The newcomers are informed of 'the madness of Don Quixote' and are both awed and amused (it 'both astonished them and made them laugh' [I, xxxvii, 323]), and then they offer their own opinions and proposals for getting Don Quixote home. The *tema* of the madman creates a socially cohesive community among the sane but not *via* a simple dynamic of ostracism and exclusion. Each return to the *tema* is an opportunity to laugh, to inform, to marvel, to understand and to invent. In the arduous and solitary life of rural Spain, it is no wonder that such an opportunity for communal enjoyment would be seized upon.

Indeed, madmen who came from outside the community often did serve as the catalysts of enthusiastic public speculation. When Juan Egujo wandered into a monastery, the doorman engaged him in conversation and was surprised to hear the visitor spontaneously announce his belief that Abraham was Adam's firstborn son.[35] The doorman corrected him and summoned Padre Gregorio. Padre Gregorio came over and, after hearing a few more strange propositions (see Chapter 2), Gregorio ran to 'dar cuenta de lo que pasaba al Padre Fray Luis de Laredo ... [de] los disparates que decía dicho peregrino' ('inform Father Fray Luis de Laredo of what was happening ... of the nonsense that the aforementioned pilgrim was saying'). As Egujo became more bizarrely heretical, his audience increased in number and stature, until the monks made the decision to lock him in the monastery library while they alerted the Inquisition. While they awaited a response from the Tribunal, they could not resist the temptation to probe the nature and degree of Egujo's heresy or madness. Each visitor emerged to share his observations with his fellow monks and to plan the next emissary's strategy. Fray Buenaventura de Sevilla explained that, 'habiendo sabido que otros religiosos del convento habían conversado sobre los dichos errores con el dicho peregrino' ('having learned that other religious men of the monastery had conversed with the said pilgrim about the said errors'), he decided to go in and chat him up about the Holy Sacrament. Judging from the number of monks who testified, it seems that half of the monastery found an excuse to engage the unexpected guest and then report back. Some of the anecdotes surely got exaggerated or confused in successive retellings – Fray Buenaventura admitted not being sure about something 'el dicho portero le dijo que el dicho peregrino había dicho' ('the aforementioned doorman told him that the aforementioned pilgrim had said'). These deeply religious men were concerned about heresy, but they were also intrigued. In the austere, unchanging routine of life in a rural convent, this was probably the most exciting event that had happened in some time, and nobody wanted to miss the chance to play a part.

The discussion and speculation about Don Quixote's mental state was most entertaining when Don Quixote himself was an active participant. The scene at Don Diego's house is one of many examples. Don Diego specifically invites Quixote to dinner because he is intrigued by his questionable sanity and wishes to share his own diversion/confusion with others who will also appreciate it. He knows his family well; wife and son are similarly bemused and amused. While Quixote is away disarming, father and son confer, with the father commissioning his son to 'speak to him, and explore what he knows', so he can 'make a reasonable judgement regarding his cleverness or foolishness' (II, xviii, 569). This charge determines the tenor of the entire evening's conversation. Don Quixote takes command of the dialogue, while the reader hears the son comment 'to himself . . . "So far . . . I can't call you crazy; let's move on." And to Don Quixote he said: "It seems to me that your grace has spent time in school: what science have you studied?"'(Ibid.) and so forth, constantly questioning and then making conclusions, but all the while engaging in a spirited and entertaining conversation. Cervantes uses the power of the omniscient narrator to emphasise the disjunction between Don Diego and son's outward 'compliments and courtesies' and their private reactions: 'once again father and son were astonished by the mixed speech of Don Quixote, sometimes intelligent and sometimes utterly foolish' (575). Still, Don Diego's parting offer to his guest to 'take from their house and estate everything he wished' (574) and Quixote's reply that if he could he would take Don Lorenzo himself testify to a spirit of generosity and mutual goodwill. The family's pleasure is a social phenomenon, but this social component does not necessarily involve censure and cruelty. Amusement could be compatible with charity.

The fusion of mirth and mercy in dealing with a *loco* is not an isolated Cervantine moment. The couple drawn in by tales of Bartolomé Íñiguez's madness also brought him food. When Juan Calvo, wearing a priest's robes, appeared in the town of Almadén and began making some decidedly unpriestlike declarations, mixed in with 'muchas palabras sin concordancia' ('many unconnected words') and 'voces entre sí' ('talking to himself'), word travelled quickly.[36] All who heard Calvo expressed shock and a fascinated horror, but opinions varied as to whether he was crazy, possessed or a heretic. Like Don Quixote, Calvo had conflicting symptoms, prompting much discussion and debate in the town. Because he was causing such a scandal, Calvo was locked in a citizen's home while local priests and officials contacted outside authorities. From the numerous testimonies of locals to the Inquisition, it is clear that many in town were intrigued by the case. While some are simply identified as 'vecinos' ('townspeople'), many are clerics or noblemen. Just as the characters in *Don Quixote* who have read chivalric epics are the ones most curious about the mad knight, here too those of higher standing and wider reading had greater interest in and confidence to opine about Calvo's mental state. Did they come to save his soul, to punish him or just to be able to participate in the town conversation? Their testimonies indicate all three. One said he went 'llevado de la curiosidad y recelo' ('driven by curiosity and suspicion'), another 'le fue a visitar y consolar por verle en el estado referido' ('went to visit and console him, upon seeing him in the aforementioned state'). Whatever their motives, they were not content to sit back and observe. Like Lorenzo and Don Diego or the canon, they used their own knowledge to engage Calvo in debate and dialogue, sometimes seeming to provoke him, but also asking with genuine curiosity about his past and his opinions, and at other times offering him solace, 'exhortándole a que llevase con paciencia sus trabajos' ('exhorting him to bear his trials with patience').

Just as clerics are capable of having sophisticated discussions about the possible sources and ramifications of Calvo's statements because they had dedicated the greater part of their lives to the study of Catholic doctrine, the residents of the inn turn out to be dedicated readers of *libros de caballería*, and thus equipped to have long and lively discussions about the genre and its role in Quixote's deliria. Their obvious enjoyment in exchanging opinions and experiences about the crazy would-be knight in no way, for them, contradicts their view that Quixote's madness is a pitiable affliction from which he ought to be cured, and their commitment to effecting this cure. When Don Quixote attacks a roomful of wine casks in the mad delusion that they are giants, the group which had just hours ago been regaling each other with tales Quixotic springs into protective action. The dynamic immediately shifts from calm conversation to active intervention, with each character responding according to his interests and his character. Dorotea, afraid, hangs back. The innkeeper attacks Don Quixote and demands payment for the lost value of his wine casks. The barber resuscitates him and 'the priest was holding Don Quixote by the hands . . . [and] with no small effort, the barber, Cardenio, and the priest, returned Don Quixote to the bed' (I, xxxv, 307). All of the men's responses involve violence, but the innkeeper means to injure, while the others use violence to protect.

The moment the threat of violence is neutralised, the chaos is recycled into material for laughter and group cohesion. When Don Quixote, awake, continues to confuse his friends with characters from his dream (and the gullible Sancho goes along), the author/narrator suddenly enters to give his own judgement of the scene. 'Who would not have laughed at the foolishness of both master and servant?' (I, xxxv, 307). In fact, the only character who does not laugh is the innkeeper, too angry about his material losses to find anything funny. If all of the characters, *except* the one who wishes the knight harm, respond with laughter, it is difficult to accept that laughter here is malicious or censorious.

The laughter in fact defuses even the innkeeper's ire; outnumbered, he saves his protests for later, when the butt of his wrath is not present to suffer from it. After the innkeeper has delivered his catalogue of Don Quixote's offences, the priest 'restored calm' by promising to do 'everything in his power' to repay the damages (308). In contrast to the readings of Miguel de Unamuno and many others who have seen the priest and barber as the epitome of a materialist, heartless world,[37] the priest shows here that he values human relations (both the well-being of Don Quixote and the restoration of the friendly community that had been established at the inn) above material ones. The similarities with the arrest scene of Juan de Larrea, cited above, are obvious, except here the 'parishioner' who offers his own money prevails over the 'officer' who insists on beating the troublemaker 'aunque fuese loco' ('mad or not').

We must suspend modern assumptions about laughter and violence when we look at the scenes in *Don Quixote* in which strangers and acquaintances laugh at or harm the main character. The diversity of reactions to the same behaviour and the way that Cervantes connects these actions to the thoughts and interests of the characters involved show us that we are not in a space of Bergsonian allegory, of actions that fall neatly into binaries of Cruel and Kind, nor are we in an extra-moral carnivalesque space where anything goes. Cervantes's characters, like the characters we find in archival scenes of public madness, have multiple, complex and conflicting interpretations of disorder and multiple, complex and conflicting ethical priorities. Cervantes is not principally a moralist or a satirist, using madness to teach a lesson or tell a joke; he is a novelist using madness to explore the relationship between the individual and society.

If many of these individual reactions are verisimilar, the opportunity Cervantes provides to see all of them together creates a viewpoint for the reader that is only possible within literature. Cervantes's juxtaposition of conflicting dynamics can produce an emotional and intellectual impact that no early modern Spaniard would get in real life, limited as he probably would be to a fleeting intervention in the life of the *loco*. The individual reading an archival case sees the doubts and opacities caused by the interaction with the unreasonable – doubts that arise from practical limitations (limited interactions) and existential limitations (the impossibility of judging an individual's *true* motives) – and also confronts the power of authors/authority in creating or clarifying those doubts. The reader cannot know what the defendants truly thought, and cannot know what the Inquisitors did not ask. In the inn-scenes, we find Cervantes manipulating the revelation of events and thoughts, and directly stepping in via his power as all-knowing author (or through his somewhat-knowing narrators), sometimes to fill in these gaps and sometimes to insist on them. Because the archival material has allowed us to see the determinant dynamics – the competing and contextual ideas about order – at work in scenes of irrational disorder, we can then be sensitive to which elements of this dynamic Cervantes chooses to alter, the particular reactions he juxtaposes against each other, and the way he uses his narrator to enhance or obscure the reader's identification with the various actors. The degree of narrative manipulation and the departure from the archive becomes more pronounced in the encounters discussed in Chapter 4: the exchanges between Sancho and Quixote, or between Quixote and characters who have read *Don Quixote*. Yet our attention to the ways Cervantes begins to draw character out of differential perceptions of and reactions to madness will continue to serve us in our reading of these more complex, more continuously calibrated relationships.

Notes

1. Bartolomé Íñiguez, AHN Inq. Leg. 38, Exp. 35.
2. See Shuger for a discussion of the case in a different context.
3. The Inquisitors themselves seem to leave open the possibility of various versions of Íñiguez's madness. Note the differences between the suggestion of a long-term condition posited in the first *repregunta*, a second round of questioning of initial witnesses, and the sudden-onset account proposed in the final question. '1. Si saben que el dicho Bartolomé Íñiguez en todo este año de 1562 y antes y siempre le conocen por un hombre mentecato y falto de juicio y sentido y como tal le han quitado la mujer y la administración de su hacienda y es tenido por hombre sin juicio y seso y que ninguna cosa habla que tenga tiento en lo que dice . . . 7. si saben o entienden que el susodicho Bartolomé Íñiguez el domingo después de Corpus Cristi por el sol que le dio en el tejado y los días siguientes estuvo del todo sin juicio y sentido y loco y los testigos así lo sintieron y conocieron dél' ('1. If they know that the said Bartolomé Íñiguez in all of this year of 1562 and before and always they know him to be an idiot and out of his mind and senses and as such they have taken away his wife and the administration of his estate and he is held to be out of his mind and wits and that nothing he says makes any sense . . . 7. if they know or understand that the aforesaid Bartolomé Íñiguez on the Sunday after Corpus Christi due to the sun he was exposed to on the roof and on the following days was completely out of his mind and senses and mad and that witnesses felt this was so and knew about it').
4. Among these: 'si Dios no le llevaba con Él imperialmente vestido y calzado con Él al cielo que no creía en Él y renegaba dél y que él se volvería a la ley de Mahoma y de Moisén' ('if God didn't take him with Him dressed and shod imperially with Him [*sic*] to the heavens he renounced Him and he would return to the law of Mohammed and Moses'), 'dicen que Santa

María parió virgen, voto a Dios que parió por cabo el culo' ('they say Saint Mary gave birth a virgin, I swear to God that she gave birth through her ass') and strange stories – 'que de noche veía un perro negro que decía que era el diablo o diablos y que se había de ir con ellos y que estando comiendo dos huevos *crudos* decía que en el uno *quebrado* que se habían entrado en él Barrabás y Satanás y Bierzebul y se sorbió el huevo *crudo* como estaba y que se había sorbido con él tres diablos y que los tenía en el cuerpo' ('that at night he saw a black dog who said he was the devil or devils and that he [Íñiguez] had to go with them and that while he was eating two raw eggs he [the dog?] told him that Barrabás and Satan and Beelzebub had entered into the broken one and he drank up the raw egg just as it was and that he had drunken with it three devils and he had them inside his body').

5. E.g. Iffland.
6. Bergson: 87.
7. Several times during his days in jail, Íñiguez makes reference to varying proportions of Indian blood, but in the first audience with the Inquisitors, when they solicited the accused's genealogy, he gave a full account of his ancestors, and all were old Christians.
8. Grossman has 'became frightened'.
9. Iffland: 43.
10. Qtd in Bouza Álvarez: 92.
11. See the discussion of carnival in Chapter 1.
12. Iffland: 63.
13. Ibid.
14. Pedro Salinas, ADC Leg. 400, No. 5675.
15. Juan de Dios (*proceso* of Francisca de los Apóstoles), AHN Inq. Leg. 113, Exp. 5. Covarrubias confirms, in his *Tesoro*, the existence of *saludadores* who claimed to heal with their saliva (he jokingly claims they ought to be called 'salivadores'), but the women's reactions to Juan de Dios prove that the would-be prophet had (like Don Quixote) taken a rather archaic practice and, by offering it out of context, made it ridiculous.
16. Grossman has 'great feats' but the sarcasm she draws out here is not clear in the original.
17. Iffland: 43.
18. In addition to 'sly', 'snide' or 'sarcastic' are also possible translations for 'socarrón' – the connotations are generally negative.
19. The contextual ethics of jokes is foregrounded in II, i, when Cervantes shows the effect of a simple joke, such as one might find in a *Libro de chistes*, when it is told and understood as veiled ridicule. The best-known such book was Luís de Pinedo's, written sometime in the late sixteenth century. Many of the jokes are collected in A. Paz y Maliá. See See Chapter 4 for further discussion of this scene.
20. Francisco Ramírez del Vado, AHN Leg. 101, Exp. 3.
21. Juan de Larrea, AHN Ing. Leg. 2106, Exp. 28 (*sumario*); 225, Exp. 21 (*proceso*).
22. Grossman has 'unprepossessing appearance'.
23. As many historians and literary scholars do. See, for example, Maravall.
24. E.g. a priest, after a conversation with a blasphemous parishioner, 'viendo que aquellas palabras y acciones eran do hombre loco no le fueron a la

mano' ('seeing that those words and acts were those of a crazy man, they didn't strike him') (qtd in Sacristán: 104).

25. Juan de Herreria, ADC Leg. 141, No. 1730.
26. Hernando de Madrigal, ADC Leg. 229, No. 2879.
27. Qtd in Sacristán: 39–40.
28. Ibid.
29. Ibid.: 76.
30. Ibid.: 75.
31. Francisco Ramírez del Vado, AHN Inq. Leg. 2106, Exp. 3 (*sumario*), Leg. 101, Exp. 3 (*proceso*).
32. Among other things, that he was Jewish, Turkish, Muslim, and 'espía de moros' ('a Moorish spy'), and demanding that 'le trujesen un familiar [de la Inquisición], que tenía otras cosas porque le quemasen' ('they bring him a *familiar* to him, that he had other reasons for them to burn him').
33. Juan Arias Dávila, AHN Inq. Leg. 213, Exp. 5.
34. Juan de Larrea, AHN Inq. Leg. 2106, Exp. 28 (*sumario*). Leg. 225, Exp. 21 (*proceso*).
35. Juan Egujo, AHN Inq. Leg. 99, Exp. 6.
36. Juan Calvo de Illescas, AHN Inq. Leg. 103, Exp. 1. There are three trials here, but madness is only raised as a defence in the third.
37. This is a commonplace of the Romantic reading, beginning with Schelling, reaching perhaps its maximum expression in Unamuno, but still alive and well, for example, in Iffland.

Chapter 4

The Madman at Home and among Friends

Ciriaco Morón Arroyo, writing on the development of the novel after Cervantes, remarks that 'with psychologism truth was lost. There was again one protagonist, or at most two. The people were lost; those thirty harvesters who gave life to Juan Palomeque's inn; the local judge, the damsel, the pícaro, the charitable young girl.'[1] I would argue that Cervantes gives us both *pueblo* and, rather than psychologism, an unprecedented insight into psychology. In the previous chapter I examined the role of madness in the actions of the *pueblo*; in this one, I turn to how Cervantes uses madness in his development of the recurring characters, and the way the priest, barber, housekeeper and niece connect *pueblo* and *psicología*.

The subjects of Chapter 3 are meeting Don Quixote for the first time. Both because they have only partial knowledge of his past and little stake in his future, their response to him is fundamentally different from that of his friends and family. María Sacristán argues that the degree of familiarity between mad and sane was the key factor in determining the nature of the interaction.[2] She divides the madman's interactions into three types: with friends and family, with officials and institutions, and with those figures (*familiares*, local priests, *alcaldes, tenientes* et al.) who often mediated between the first two groups, their identification with one or the other generally depending on their intimacy with the purported *loco*. Sacristán goes on to show the surprisingly small role that the second group – the agents of Church and State – had in the lives of most *locos*. Because these institutions were the ones that left written records, theirs has been assumed to be the *societal* attitude towards unreason. In truth, the care for the *loco* almost always fell to friends and neighbours, and it was only when the *loco* left his community, when a stranger to the community misinterpreted the *loco*'s words or actions, or when the loco was so uncontrollably violent that friends and family could not protect him and themselves, that his diagnosis and care was turned over to State or Church.

The trajectory of Don Quixote's wanderings fits this pattern. James Iffland argues that Quixote is a threatening figure chiefly because a *hidalgo* who abandoned his land and renounced traditional aristocratic values was, by his very presence, a visible threat to that society itself.[3] However, the archival material shows that a *loco*'s nomadism was a problem for more immediate reasons: on the road, the *loco* was bound to meet strangers who, not knowing his history, would misunderstand and misinterpret his behaviour, bringing him into conflict with his compatriots and/or the law. Nomadism was also problematic because it was the family's responsibility to 'restore the madman to sanity . . . [to] convince him to return to true belief and to recognise the value of solidarity in daily life' and, where this was impossible, 'at the very least make his existence more comfortable'.[4] When the family failed in this, the community stepped in, and together they 'collectively faced up to his madness', helping the *loco*'s family 'make life more bearable and more bearable for him'.[5] If the *loco* became too much for the neighbours to handle, they sought help from lower-level officials: doctors, policemen, priests.

Don Quixote's 'case' passes through this hierarchy, and it is important to think in these terms when we look at the actions of his housekeeper and niece; the peasant who brings Don Quixote home the first time; and finally the priest and barber. The housekeeper and niece cannot travel across Castile: the priest and barber are the intermediate figures, professional men with responsibilities in society, who are from home but can leave it. From the moment they meet up with Don Quixote in the Sierra Morena, they translate their neighbour's odd behaviours for the sane world and, at the same time, strive to bring Don Quixote back into that world. Their actions in the inn are best understood if we see them not only as figures who belong both to the familial, domestic sphere and the public, institutional one but also as the characters whose duty it is to coordinate the interaction of those two worlds. At times they act more as representatives of Society, and at times they act more as representatives of Home. The way niece, housekeeper, priest and barber negotiate these spheres is fundamental to their characterisation and to the ethical space of the novel.

The Inner Circle: The Madman and his Family

While there was variation in the way lower-level representatives of society (lower-ranking justice and church officials, property owners et al.) interacted with the mad, the common thread in the archival accounts is their desire to fulfil the responsibilities of their job without causing unnecessary conflict. They were generally reluctant to involve themselves in a madman's case further than necessary and this reticence, combined with the similar reticence of strangers, meant that madmen who left home typically had a nomadic, 'episodic' lifestyle; it was not just a literary convention. The primary goal of the madman's family, in the archives and in the novel, was to counteract this nomadism: to keep the madman in one place, to have knowledge of and responsibility for his behaviour and well-being. In general, the stories of families' care for *locos* reveal compassion, sacrifice, endurance and an assumption of responsibility. They also reveal a continuous struggle, as the madmen (at least the ones whose stories made it into writing) were rarely content to sit at home and be cared for. Families were constantly chasing after their charges, getting them out of predicaments, and trying themselves to understand what was wrong with their relative and how it could be treated and controlled. The caretakers were usually women, which posed additional problems. A woman was less able to defend herself from a violent relative or restrain one who wanted to leave her care. If the madman had, before his illness, been the family breadwinner, she was suddenly without income and, at the same time, even less able to leave the house to take on work or beg for alms. If the madman had temporary or partial attacks of unreason, or if he did not see himself as insane, the women caring for him would have almost no authority to restrict his behaviours or limit his movement. Their only hope was to reason with the sufferer on the subject of his own unreason, or to appeal to male community members for assistance.

Sara Nalle's extensive study of the case of Bartolomé Sánchez, a (possibly) mad Spaniard, provides a remarkable account of how a hierarchy of social actors interacted with a madman. The primary responsibility for controlling and caring for Sánchez fell to his wife Catalina, who also had five young children on her hands. Although more desperate and pathetic, Catalina's attempts to care for and control Sánchez resonate with the housekeeper and niece's trials with Don Quixote. Catalina told the Inquisitors of her ordeal at Sánchez's second trial:

Ha hablado con su marido muchas veces y reprendiéndole de las cosas que decía y oía a otras decir dél . . . que le decía '¿habéis hablado con berzebu?' y que el segundo día de Pascua de Resurrección se fue dos horas antes del día y que le dijo, 'volveos y decid a donde vais,' y que le respondió, 'tornaos a acostar y encomendaos en Dios' . . . y que estuvo allá ocho semanas y que vino muy flaco y perdido y que le dijo, 'en alguna cueva habéis estado metido pues venís tan flaco y perdido,' y que le respondió '. . . no tengáis pena que luego me tengo de ir porque mis pasos no son sin misterio y no puedo dejar de irme' . . . y que decía tantas cosas que no se acuerda y que nunca le vio hacer cosa ninguna en su casa ni ceremonia más de andar ablegado . . . y que nunca dormía de noche.

She had spoken with her husband many times, and reprimanding him for the things he said and what she heard other people say about him . . . she said to him 'You've talked to Beezelbub?' And on the second day of Easter he left two hours before daybreak and she said to him, 'Come back here and tell me where you're going,' and that he answered her, 'Go back to bed and entrust yourself to God . . .' and that he was away for eight weeks, and he came back very thin and lost, and she said to him, 'you must have been stuck in some cave you've come back so thin and lost' and he answered, '. . . don't be sad, that later I must go, because my steps are not without mystery and I cannot help but go' . . . He said so many things that she didn't remember and she never saw him do anything at home or any ceremony besides walking around as if he were on a special mission . . . and he never slept at night.[6]

Catalina, like the housekeeper and niece, was bewildered and frustrated by her husband's strange speech. She had some idea of the source of his delusion – her assumption regarding Beezelbub's influence is about as precise as the housekeeper's condemnation of all secular literature – but she did not enter into theological arguments and, when he began to speak irrationally, she did not try to refute his ideas. Instead, she focused on controlling the external symptom which directly threatened her well-being and his: his wanderlust. (Almost all of his previous run-ins with the law had come while he was on the road, and after his first trial he had been ordered not to leave Cuenca.) Bartolomé's admission that, having decided to make a penitential journey to a nearby monastery, he had to hide the articles of penance 'porque su mujer no las viese' ('so his wife would not see them') shows that she was committed to keeping him at home.[7] Catalina did not refrain from her wifely duties, fixing him supper after she reprimanded him, but neither did she acquiesce silently to his madness. Her reprimand upon his return is very similar to the housekeeper's in its joint evocation of frustration and pity.

Don Quixote's housekeeper and niece, like Catalina, have neither the authority nor the strength to keep their mad relative at home. The first time Quixote escapes, the niece recalls her uncle's past behaviours – his two-day reading sprees, after which 'he would toss away the book and pick up his sword and slash at the walls' (I, v, 44). A teenage girl, who could not have known that Quixote's violence was limited to a delirious re-enactment of *Amadís de Grecia* and would not be directed toward her, could do nothing but observe with worry and try to get outside help. The niece blames herself for her failure, lamenting to the priest and barber that she didn't advise them sooner 'so that you could help him before it went this far' (Ibid.). This assumption of responsibility is a key difference between the responses of family and strangers to the *loco*. Strangers might act charitably, but they generally sought to limit their interactions to the absolute minimum, particularly when the irrational subject was violent. The family, in contrast, sought to increase their engagement with the *loco*, to keep him at home or under observation. When he escaped, they, like the housekeeper and niece, often went to great trouble to bring him back, even when their lives would have been easier without such a charge.

Don Quixote's housekeeper and niece may play relatively small roles in the narrative as a whole, but because they are among the first characters we meet and because their actions set in motion all of the adventures that follow, the way we 'read' them has great consequences. To see them as symbols of anti-intellectual conformity is to see Don Quixote's quest as liberating and admirable. To see them as comic but fundamentally commonsensical is to read Don Quixote as comically but undeniably insane. Either reading requires ignoring, or interpreting as purely ironic, one aspect of their characters: either their obvious concern for Don Quixote or their clear role in limiting his freedom.[8] The archival accounts of caretakers and family of *locos* show that the dilemma between care and control is at the heart of the family narrative of madness and, perhaps more importantly, these parallels between archive and novel from the very outset suggest to us that for the rest of the novel we will be travelling in a complex social world. The humour *and* the pathos of this world (for its complexity consists precisely in their uneasy coexistence) is lost when characters are forced into absolute, allegorical types.

Reading the niece and housekeeper as repressive requires ignoring that, throughout the novel, they act as loving, concerned caretakers. When Quixote returns home after his first aborted sally, their first response is to run to embrace him. The housekeeper declares her commitment to cure the bruised would-be knight, taking him directly to bed, searching for wounds to tend, and bringing him food (I, v, 81–2). When he returns the second time, pitifully mounted on a bale of hay, the response is the same (I, lii, 445). This scene continues at the opening of Part II, with Cide Hamete telling us that for almost a month niece and housekeeper were 'pamper[ing] him and giv[ing] him food to eat that would strengthen and fortify his heart and brain' (II, i, 459). And when Don Quixote returns for good, they take him to bed for the last time 'where they fed him and pampered him as much as possible' (II, lxiii, 933). After each of Don Quixote's returns, the women, once they have tended to his immediate physical needs, try to reason with him. It is only after Quixote refuses to anwer the housekeeper's 'thousand questions' (I, v, 45) that she resorts to the sack of the library. To a modern *reader*, the bonfire of the Don's library might seem narrow-minded and mean-spirited. In the housekeeper's mind, however, the books have harmed someone she loves and feels responsible for, and it is necessary to get rid of them before they harm again. Burning a vast library is no different to her than exhorting Quixote's visitors not to mention knight errantry (II, i, 459) or keeping away Sancho Panza, whom she accuses of being responsible for 'lead[ing] our master astray' (II, ii, 468). Burning books, controlling conversation and limiting dangerous visitors are all prongs of the same strategy: to protect Don Quixote's sanity without directly provoking or confronting him. The women see this as a gentler, more humane strategy than physical restriction. Rather than make Don Quixote do something he does not wish to, they will help him wish to do what social norms dictate.

After Quixote's final return, the housekeeper's tone as she tries once more to reason with her employer suggests not censure but a heartfelt plea. Instead of launching into her usual attacks on the tales of chivalry, she asks simply that Don Quixote 'take my advice; . . . stay in your house, tend to your estate, go to confession often, favor the poor, and let it be on my soul if that does you any harm' (II, lxxiii, 933). Far from eschewing involvement in Don Quixote's present and future health, she invests the most precious thing any early modern Spaniard could offer – her own soul – in Quixote's cure. She shows no anger or blame except that which she offers to take upon herself if her advice does not prove beneficial. Cervantes[9] seems to go out of his way here to insist upon the fundamental sincerity of the housekeeper and niece. He not only describes the pair as 'good women', but he then interrupts this narrative to confirm, as if to dispel any possible ironic readings, that 'the housekeeper and niece undoubtedly were' (Ibid.). A similar narrative insertion comes a few pages later. When the priest announces that Don Quixote has recovered his reason and is ready to make his will, housekeeper, niece and squire are overcome with tears and 'a thousand deep sighs'. But as if to distinguish this from all the examples of feigned tears and satiric sighs in the preceding thousand pages, Cervantes steps in to assure the reader that 'the truth is . . . [Don Quixote] was dearly loved not only by those in his household, but by everyone who knew him' (II, lxxiv, 937).

Erasmian and Romantic readings of *Don Quixote* foreground the positive aspects of Don Quixote's *locura*: what it allows him to escape from, what it allows him to believe in.[10] Such a reading inevitably paints all who try to impede his realisation of 'the impossible dream' as villains.[11] However, in no archival account I consulted did anyone express doubt about the desirability of a return to social conformity or its connection to the restoration of mental health. The Spanish populace had generally learned to associate dissidence with heresy, or at the very least, to view it as a recipe for trouble. In fact, the risk of any sort of social nonconformity was so great that it was commonly taken as evidence of irrationality. Conversely, the return to the social fold was both the proof and the goal of a cure. The housekeeper and niece, with their insistence that Don Quixote stay at home, tend to his land, confess and give alms, are not neglecting their master's health – mental, spiritual or physical – in an obsession with outward conformity. They want health and happiness for him, and the seventeenth-century Spanish commoner simply did not conceive of a disjunction between social stability and felicity.

The desire to keep the *loco* at home did not necessarily stem from purely disinterested charity and love. The female caregivers in the novel and in the archives want their relative at home because they believe he is spiritually and physically safest acting out his socially prescribed role, because they can best observe and care for him there, and because their own economic and social status is dependent on his. Archival accounts show family members going to great lengths to keep *locos* at home for all of these reasons. In her study of the Seville asylum records, Carmen López Alonso notes that the percentage of *locos* sent to the hospital by family members remained low until the eighteenth century.[12] In the seventeenth-century records, she finds cases such as that of Juana de Páez, whose family came to claim her four days after she was transferred from the secular prisons.[13]

Family members were usually the ones to step in when a *loco*'s case became critical. In several Inquisition cases, family members who had lost track of their loved ones appeared midway through the *proceso* to explain the accused's condition and request that they be returned to their care. Joseph Valles was arrested for causing disturbances in church.[14] His brother tracked him down, requested an audience before the Inquisitors and explained that:

> está demente . . . y que como a tal podría haber hecho o dicho algunas acciones o palabras en que algunas hayan notado o reparado. Y porque a este Tribunal constase de la falta de juicio que dicho su hermano padece, ha hecho hacer los instrumentos que presentaba (y con efecto presentó cuatro instrumentos en prueba de ello)[15] para lo que puedan concluir.

> he is demented . . . and as such he might have done or said some words or actions which some people may have noticed or taken note of. And in order

that this Tribunal certify the madness from which his aforementioned brother suffers, he has ordered the instruments he was presenting to be drawn up [and in effect he presented four instruments in proof of the matter] so that they might conclude.

In another case, one Pedro Rodríguez had been living for several years apparently as 'hombre de bien y cuerdo' ('a good and sane man') but when he moved to a new town, he began to have problems and one day, by his own account, 'le dio cierta enfermedad de locura, que estaba atronado, que no sabía parte de sí y que si no le quitaron que le iba un día al río' ('he was struck by a certain disease of madness, and he was out of control, and he was out of his wits, and if they had not stopped him one day he would have gone to the river [to drown himself]').[16] His brother, who lived nearby, sent for him and brought him to his home. Rodríguez's case also reveals the helplessness of family members. The brother's widow recalled the episode:

> lo trujo a casa desta declarante adonde lo tuviere algunos días y allí estuvo el dicho Pedro Rodríguez malo y fuera de seso que le andaba caído por dondequiera, que iba haciendo meneos con la cabeza y nunca estaba el dicho Pedro Rodríguez sino pellizcando los ojos y las barbas y nunca estaba quedo con las manos.

> They brought him to the house of this witness where he could stay a few days and while he was there the said Pedro Rodríguez was ill and out of his mind and he wandered all about depressed, shaking his head as he went, and said Pedro Rodríguez was always scratching his eyes and his whiskers, and his hands were never still.

Seeing that Pedro 'nunca estuvo bueno, antes empeoraba' ('was never well, in fact he was getting worse'), Pablo instructed his son to accompany his uncle home. It is not clear whether the nephew stayed with Pedro, but his situation must have improved somewhat, as another two years passed without incident. A later episode in the case shows that caretakers' compassionate acts often served their own economic needs as well, although there is no indication that they, or anyone else, felt this as a moral contradiction. Towards the end of the file, there appears a note from a neighbour of Pedro's wife, pleading that the Inquisition let Rodríguez out on bail because 'su mujer y hijos a falta suya pasan muy mal' ('his wife and children are suffering greatly due to his absence') and offering the 'fianzas como Vuestras Mercedes mandaron' ('bail as Your Honours ordered'). We do not learn the source of the bail money, but given the family's poverty, we can imagine a network of family and/or community collaboration and sacrifice. Andrés Hernández Tejero's wife made a similar plea,[17] first assuring the Inquisitors that her imprisoned husband was innocent, as 'demás de diez años a esta parte es loco' ('he has been mad for more than ten years now') and then asserting that the goods they had confiscated actually belonged to her and thus should be returned. Bartolomé Íñiguez's marital situation is another case that shows that self-protection and selfless charity were not incompatible motives.[18] For both physical and economic protection, 'porque trataba mal a la dicha su mujer y desperdiciaba su hacienda' ('because he mistreated his aforementioned wife and wasted his estate'), his wife obtained an annulment and moved out of the house, but she also continued to serve him food and, when he was unable to stay by himself, to provide him with a room in her boarding house. Once Bartolomé broke out of the *mesón*, however, she could no longer protect or control him. As in the *Quixote*, the female caregiver's sphere of direct influence was limited to the home.

Up the Chain of Command: Madmen and their Neighbours

Just because their influence stopped at the front door did not, however, mean that women gave up or wrote off their responsibility for the *loco* once he had left. More often, they turned to male family members or neighbours for help in returning the *loco* to the domestic sphere. These men performed various functions that the women could not: neighbours and lower-status men could travel and use physical force, and men with higher status or with access to some resource – money, connections and/or knowledge – could use these to get the *loco* out of trouble. Pedro Alonso, the *labrador* who discovers the battered Quixote after his encounter with the merchants, is typical of the first group and its role in the care of a *loco*. Alonso recognises his neighbour when he lifts up his visor, and his conduct thereafter is determined by this recognition of someone 'from his village . . . a neighbor of his' (I, v, 42). Whereas strangers were wary of engaging a delirious *loco*, Alonso interrupts his own errand to check Quixote for injuries, gives him his own horse and leads him back home. He is at first 'astounded' at the 'absurdities' that Quixote proffers, but as his neighbour continues to exclaim about the Marquis of Mantua – despite Alonso's repeated attempts to rationally find out 'how he felt and what was wrong' – Alonso becomes annoyed and 'he despaired at hearing such an enormous amount of foolishness; in this way he realised that his neighbour was mad' (42–3). While family members almost never expressed anger, the neighbours, one step farther removed from the *loco*, were not immune to frustration. Alonso's reaction to this 'impatience Don Quixote provoked in him' is common among neighbours; still, he does not abandon or abuse Quixote, but rather attempts to set him straight with reason ('Look, your grace . . . I'm not Don Rodrigo de Narváez or the Marquis of Mantua, but Pedro Alonso, your neighbor, and your grace isn't Valdevinos or Abindarráez, but an honorable gentleman, Señor Quijana' [43]). When Alonso over-hears the priest and barber explaining Quixote's disease, his newfound knowledge has the same effect that it had on the innkeeper pages before. He gains the confidence to joke about his neighbour's neurosis a bit, announcing their return not as Alonso and Quijana, but as Valdovinos and the Marquis of Mantua (44). Until he 'underst[ood] finally what his neighbor's sickness was' (Ibid.) he identified himself to Quixote stressing their relation as neighbours and Quixote's social superiority. Once he has confirmed his superior knowledge and capacity, he is able to make a joke about Quixote which involves the suppression of their neighbourly relations. But again, the joke is not at Don Quixote's expense, and Pedro Alonso only indulges in it for a moment before delivering Quixote to housekeeper and niece for medical and spiritual attention.

When Catalina Martínez first invoked the help of family, friends and local clergy, they too relied on reason and, when that failed, tried to eliminate the source of Sánchez's distress. Bartolomé de Mora, Sánchez's cousin, spent three nights with him, throughout which, he said, 'parece que [a Sánchez] se le querría salir el corazón y que no podía callar' ('it seemed that Sánchez's heart wanted to jump out of him and he could not keep quiet'). Seeing this, he decided to accompany Sánchez to a priest in Monteagudo, a town nearly fifteen miles away, to see if he could diagnose and remedy Sánchez's distress.[19] The visit did not help; after bringing Sánchez home, Mora and his friends asked him 'cómo había estado así y que respondió que se habían visto unos hombres de unas calzas amarillas, que aquellos lo venían a matar' ('why had he been that way and he responded that some men with yellow hose had been seen who were coming to kill him').[20] No one else had seen anyone, so they returned home, increasingly worried that Sánchez 'no estaba en su juicio y seso natural' ('was not in his right mind'). When Sánchez went off alone to Monteagudo again, Mora was sure that he 'había hecho algún desatino' ('had done something senseless') and he made the trip again to make sure he was safe.[21] Mora's dedication and concern is characteristic of a family member. His fear for his cousin led him at one point to tie Sánchez with rope, but when Sánchez protested and did not calm down, Mora and the two friends he had enlisted untied him and took him to the parish church. The physical restriction was clearly not a punishment; Mora thought that if Sánchez could be made physically still, spiritual and mental tranquillity might follow suit. When this failed, Mora turned to another, less confrontational remedy for spiritual anguish.

Sánchez's discussions with religious authorities only increased his obsession. Unbeknownst to his family, he had had a vision which he later saw reproduced in a Book of Hours, and he was driven to discuss it with priests and learned men near and far. Reasoned discussion about his ideas with local clergy had the same effect on Sánchez that the priest's admonishments about the proper way of reading books of chivalry had upon Don Quixote, inciting rather than appeasing. Sánchez did not make it to the monastery because, the night before his planned pilgrimage, his excitement overwhelmed him and 'cayó en el suelo de una silla en que estaba asentado, dando voces y diciendo, "vete maldito lucifer, no te dio *agra* que entres acá"' ('he fell on the floor from the chair in which he was seated, yelling and saying "Get out cursed Lucifer, I didn't give you permission to enter here"').[22] This was beyond what his wife and young sons were equipped to deal with, and they 'salieron a los vecinos dando voces como agollantados . . . y así se llegaron muchos vecinos, hombres y mujeres, y un clérigo' ('went screaming their heads off to the neighbours . . . and so lots of neighbours came, men and women, and a cleric').[23] The assembled community, from neighbours to clergy, restored him to his chair. When Sánchez was finally calm, a weaver named Garci Pérez said he wanted to stay with him through the night, 'para que a él le dijese lo que había; y así se quedó' ('so he could tell him what had happened; and thus he stayed'). Sánchez confessed his plan to visit the monastery, and Garci Pérez stalled him, telling him to wait until he (Garci Pérez) could consult with the local priest. Garci Pérez, like Pedro Alonso, felt out of his league and, having done what he could to ease Sánchez's immediate distress, he planned to bring the matter to the attention of a local authority. The fact that he sought Sánchez's cure and relief, and at no point expressed anger or a desire to humiliate his neighbour, did not prevent him from supplementing his strategy of nurturing and reason with a more preventive detention. When, the next morning, Garci Pérez went to see if the priest had awakened, he 'cerró el palacio por de fuera porque no se pudiese ir' ('shut the door from the outside so [Sánchez] couldn't leave').[24] Sánchez, like Quixote in his second and third sallies, had little trouble overcoming such precautionary measures; he merely waited a few minutes and had his son let him out. When Garci Pérez returned to find Sánchez gone, he chased after the escapee (quite possibly at the request of Catalina, who could not herself leave the house any more than the niece and housekeeper could take to the road after Quixote). Sánchez recalled that when Garci Pérez caught up with him, 'no le dejó ir e hizo tornar hasta que hablase con el cura, y le llevó a su casa y trujo el cura allí' ('he wouldn't let him go and made him go back until he talked with the priest, and he took him home and brought the priest there').[25] Like Pedro Alonso, who offers his mount to Don Quixote and endures being called a Moor, Garci Pérez went out of his way to bring his neighbour to mental, physical, spiritual and social safety. Home was the anchor of all of these. Only at home, fulfilling his societal role, could an early modern Spaniard be imagined as physically and mentally at peace.

As we see in Sánchez's case, when a neighbour's best efforts were insufficient, he and the family usually solicited help from someone with authority. The involvement of higher levels of authority often coincided with a more restrictive intervention, including tying someone up or sending him to a hospital. The decision to invoke restrictive measures did not necessarily come from the authority figures, but they alone could enforce it. Still, the authority figure *was* often more apt to invoke restrictive measures than family or friends, because as the level of familiarity between *loco* and *cuerdo* diminished so did the primary commitment to the *loco*'s well-being. This is not to say that priests, law officials and medical professionals were not interested in the health of the mad, but only that they were more likely to balance this concern with their duties to their offices or institutions, their identification with their own social group, their instinct for self-protection and their personal inclinations.

Like the priest in *Quixote*, the local priest who Garci Pérez brought acted more as a friend than as a standard bearer for institutional orthodoxy. The first priest Sánchez had consulted, a visiting preacher who did not know Sánchez's history, told him the vision had been the devil and refused to absolve him, instead ordering him to make a journey to a convent some twelve miles away and warning him that 'poco sería [su] vida' ('his life would be worthless') if he did not comply.[26] The local priest, in constrast, invited Sánchez out to talk on a hillside and asked him 'qué era que lo que había y a dónde iba' ('what was happening and where he was going'). Sánchez explained his journey to the convent and the local priest told him 'que no tuviese pena, que él le absolvía de todo aquello' ('he shouldn't worry, that he would absolve him of everything') and told him go to back home, work and tend to his family.[27] The visiting priest, acting purely as a representative of the Church, responded to Sánchez's heretical vision with doctrinal censure, just as the priest in the duke's palace summarily rebuffed Don Quixote for 'wandering the world and wasting your time and being a laughingstock to all who know you and all who do not' (II, xxxi, 665). Like Pero Pérez, the local priest took into account Sánchez's history, his family and his irrationality. His prescription showed that he had the same goals for Sánchez as did the wool carder's family and neighbours, but he had the status and knowledge to convince Sánchez (at least temporarily) where friends and neighbours had failed.

The priest's charitable, reasoned approach did not proscribe his taking practical measures to ensure that Sánchez did not provoke another crisis. Like the housekeeper in *Quixote*, the priest came to Sánchez's house and confiscated the offending Book of Hours. His position of authority enabled him to carry out the desires of family and neighbours, such as the one who, having heard Sánchez defend his heretical scriptural interpretations, had exclaimed, 'pluviera dios que nunca vos supiérades leer para que no deprendiérades esas herejías' ('I wish to God that you never learned how to read so you wouldn't learn these heresies').[28] The seizure of the book, however, was too little too late. Sánchez, like Quixote, had already internalised his obsession, and taking the text only fed into the irrational narrative he had created for himself, provoking him to more extreme measures. Sánchez became more insistent in his heretical views, promising 'que otras cosas más hondas había' ('there were other things deeper than this') and that he would say them in front of anyone who would listen.[29] Only the local priest had the authority to take action to solve what had become an unignorable problem. After nearly a year of frustrated local interventions, Bachiller Barca, the village priest,[30] finally sent a denunciation to the Inquisition and began to take depositions. Sánchez was imprisoned in the local jail during this process, but he escaped and Nalle notes that 'apparently no one was too concerned . . . it elicited no official reaction, and Sánchez did not go far'.[31]

Intermediate Authorities: Priests and Barbers

The local priest and village council's inaction here is indicative of their intermediary position in an institutional hierarchy. They were preparing a case for the Inquisition, and when Inquisitor Cortes sent for Sánchez seven months later, the local authorities found him and sent him to the secret prisons. But they did not seem to have acted out of malice or cruelty, allowing Sánchez to go free and at least provide for his family until the Inquisitors replied. Unlike Sánchez's wife and children, the officials did not have the family's well-being as their primary goal, but they did weigh it among their other concerns as civic and ecclesiastic authorities. As María Sacristán observes, 'the denouncers played a role between that of an authority and that of a relative/friend'.[32]

In the archival cases, this intermediary role was frequently played by local clergy or, less often, medical professionals. If we do not realise the role these figures played in real cases, Cervantes's selection of a priest and a barber might seem arbitrary, as the barber never performs the functions of his office and the priest's only clerical activity comes in the last scene. Indeed, critics reading on a strictly symbolic level seem not to know what to do with the priest and barber. Félix Martínez Bonati writes that the pair are 'inverisimilar', as at times they are 'affectionate and well-intentioned friends of Don Quixote' and at other times they are 'mockers, at times insensitive and even cruel'. He concludes that:

> This inverisimilar discrepancy truthfully allegorises human imperfection. If we tried to interpret these characters' conduct as realistic and consistent, we would have to conclude that they are unfeeling, idle hypocrites, and somewhat perverse. But that would go against the strong impression of good sense and bonhomie that at least the Priest makes in so many passages, and against his global function in the economy of the story.[33]

The archival material shows that inconsistent and seemingly contradictory (at least to a contemporary reader) ethical stances are not 'inverisimilar' – that, in fact, they were common, and particularly so among those figures who mediated between groups with different, and often conflicting, relations to the *loco*. Far from suggesting an allegorical reading, the map of mockery and compassion, protection and restriction that Cervantes charts is realistic, a sign that he is exploring the human comedy and not simply allegorising. The 'global function' of the priest and barber in 'the economy of the story' is as transitional figures between the world of home and the world of law and order, a prominent role for doctors and medics in almost every recorded case of madness I consulted.

The priest and barber's map of charity and cruelty corresponds fairly closely to their map of La Mancha. While they are at home with Quixote and his primary caretakers, they act more as family, carrying out the housekeeper and niece's requests. When they are still at home but the housekeeper and niece are not present, as we find them at the opening of Part II, they begin to act more as educated, professional, sociable men with goals that include, but are not limited to, preserving Don Quixote's health and social conformity. We see a clear example of the way they balance familiarity and authority in the scene of the destruction of the library. While the niece and housekeeper had both expressed their hatred for the books of chivalry, they would not dream of destroying their master's property. It is the priest who has the knowledge of literature to plan the careful examination of the library and the social authority to incinerate it.[34] He first consults 'at great length' with Pedro Alonso about the state in which the farmer had found Don Quixote (I, v, 45). Thus the level of intervention passes from a lower-status community member to an educated professional, and, at the same time, the restrictiveness of the intervention increases. But the priest is by no means going beyond the caretakers' wishes; niece and housekeeper gladly hand over the keys to the library and give orders not to 'pardon' any of the offending tomes.

When the niece and housekeeper are not present, the priest and barber give more free rein to their desire for entertainment, which, as Martínez Bonati noted, sometimes borders on cruelty. In general, the priest and barber only laugh *at* Don Quixote in such a way that he does not perceive it or suffer from it, and rarely does their laughter obstruct their main goal of reuniting Quixote and his wits. The barber's anecdote of the madman of Seville is one of the few instances where they miscalculate. When Quixote declares that he shall 'die a knight errant', shattering the pretence of sanity that the housekeeper had so delicately tried to protect, the barber indulges his desire for social cohesion and superiority by immediately recalling a story 'very much to the point here'. He expects that the joke's ironic humour will impress and amuse the priest, while the point (and Quixote's role as its butt) will go over the knight's addled head. He achieves his first goal, but the Bergsonian laughter of the group is quickly cut short by Quixote's own, even wittier and more 'to the point' reply, which revealed that he had not only understood the story perfectly but also the less-than-friendly motives of the barber in telling it. The barber, humbled and now unsure of the dynamic of the relationship, retreats quickly to his 'friend' role, apologising and assuring him that 'my intentions were good, and your grace should not be offended' (II, i, 466). By incorporating a conventional representation of madness and inscribing it into something new – a social world, where madmen are *men*, with feelings and relationships – Cervantes is marking off the distance between traditional literary madmen and his own approach.

The warmth of Don Quixote's relationship with the priest and barber is affirmed in the novel's final pages. As his end approaches, Don Quixote asks his niece and housekeeper to call for 'my good friends . . . the priest, the bachelor Sansón Carrasco, and the barber Master Nicolás' (II, lxxiv, 935). The priest pronounces Quixote sane and takes his final confession, once again acting as a representative of the Church, but one whose relation with his congregant is based on the same goals and shared past as that of a close friend or family member. (No Inquisitional theologian would spend two minutes with an accused and pronounce him to have 'truly recovered his reason' [936].) After this final rite, barber, priest and *bachiller* leave behind their affiliations with any external social or professional circle and join Quixote's closest kin and closest friend.

The archival perspective challenges many critical readings of the priest and barber in the *Quixote*, and an attention to the ways in which hierarchies of authority engaged with the mad can challenge interpretations of the work as a whole. Where Martínez Bonati sees the priest and barber as non-verisimilar 'allegories of imperfection', the Romantic and the Foucauldian schools of criticism have seen them as near-villains: to the former, Quixote becomes a tragic figure, felled in the pursuit of his noble ideal by the repressive state or the conformist bourgeoisie,[35] while to the latter, the priest and barber and *bachiller* return a nomadic, socially destabilising Don Quixote to his 'proper' place in the social hierarchy, back to where he can be observed and regulated by institutions. There is, of course, some truth in all this. The purge of the library does attempt to destroy the source for Quixote's imagination and individuality, and they do at one point place Don Quixote in a cage. The priest is undoubtedly affiliated with an often repressive institution. James Iffland, applying the critical categories of Deleuze and Guattari, sees Don Quixote in the role of nomadic warrior usurping the role of the State and the role of prophet usurping the role of the Church. We see the threats he poses, Iffland argues, in the repressive response his actions provoke. Quixote is brought home, or 'reterritorialised', through the cooperative efforts of a priest and the 'agents of Royal authority, members of the Santa Hermandad. That is to say, the two sides of political sovereignty.' The 'warrior' is 'effectively defined as mad, deformed, a usurper (wielding an authority that does not correspond to him)'.[36]

Such a reading assumes that persons affiliated with Church or State become its functionaries. The archival accounts problematise this metonymic equating of members of an institutional body with the institution itself. In many of the cases, we see different members of the same institution respond to the same irrational subject in markedly different ways. In almost all of these instances, the officials who had known the subjects for a longer period, who knew their family and history, were more likely to reason and console than to punish. Bartolomé Sánchez's experience with the local and visiting priests, and then his ordeals at the hands of the Inquisitors, give one compelling example. The cases like Sánchez's, which involved or brought into dialogue officials at varying levels of authority within the same institution, highlight the heterogeneity of these organs of power and the extent to which degrees of proximity of power (both geographically and hierarchically) affected attitude and behaviour.

The Inquisition certainly intended its *familiares* to be undercover spies devoted to the eradication of heresy, but in practice the *familiares* often acted more as community members than agents of the Holy Office.

In the case of Antonia Núñez,[37] a *familiar* got into an argument with a townsperson over how much attention should be paid to the blasphemous Antonia, with Andres Gonzalez, the *familiar*, insisting 'que la dicha Antonia era loca' ('that the said Antonia was mad') and thus should not be disciplined, and the townsperson retorting 'que harto más loco era él, dando a entender que la dicha Antonia estaba en su juicio' ('if she was crazy, then he was even crazier, by which he meant to convey that the aforementioned Antonia was in her right mind'). A resident of the inn where Antonia was staying recalled that when he chastised her for some heretical statement, she retorted that she had spent three years in an inn run by Andrés González and, in all that time, 'no la había reñido otro tanto como la habían reñido este declarante y los demás desta posada' ('he hadn't scolded her as much as this witness and the other guests at the inn had'). The resident replied that this must have been because she had not said such heresies then, and Antonia retorted that 'las decía y muchas más y callaba el dicho Andrés Gonzalez porque veía que decía verdad' ('she said them and many more and the aforementioned Andrés González didn't say anything because he saw she was telling the truth'). Gonzalez explained that he kept quiet because he thought she was insane and thus deserving of pity, not punishment. He said he had known Núñez for ten years:

> y los cuatro dellos la conoció con juicio natural y los seis restantes la conoció loca sin juicio porque andaba por las calles de noche y de día tirando piedras a los muchachos . . . que estando así decía muchos disparates y locuras como persona privada de juicio . . . y este testigo no hacía caso della porque la tenía por loca y que este testigo muchas veces la quería dar de palos porque callase y de lástima la dejaba.

> and for four of them he recognised her to be in her right mind and in the remaining six he recognised her as out of her mind because she would wander through the streets night and day, throwing stones at young boys . . . and in such a state she would say a lot of nonsense and crazy things like someone out of her mind . . . and this witness paid her no mind because he held her to be mad and that many times this witness wanted to beat her so she would be quiet and out of pity he let her be.

This attitude is in stark contrast to the position taken by the *comisario*, a stranger to the town and to Antonia, who took the initial depositions and sent the denunciation to Toledo. He was much more preoccupied with his Inquisitional duty to prevent the spread of heresy, and with possible legal skirmishes with the secular branch, than he was concerned for Antonia's plight. He wrote that:

aunque se da a entender del modo de la rea que puede proceder de falta de juicio, cuando sea así todavía por lo menos me parece que por orden de Vuestra Alteza se había de recoger por el escándalo que causa, sin esperar a que la justicia seglar lo haga, porque es conocido el descuido que en esto tiene, y de derecho le puede suplir el eclesiástico en algunos casos que [¿?] no son de su jurisdicción ... mucho mejor podría Vuestra Alteza en este caso remediar este inconveniente en que concurre la circunstancia del lugar, que es esta corte, y la de la materia, que es de fe, la cual de suyo es tan grave como se ve.

although from the behaviour of the accused one could understand her to be mad, even if this is so it seems to me that your Honour ought to at least order that she be taken in, due to the scandal she is causing, without waiting for the secular justice to do so, because their negligence in doing this is well known, and by law the ecclesiastical tribunals can step in in certain cases which are not under their jurisdiction ... in this instance your Honour is much more able to remedy the inconvenience caused by the coincidence of the place, which is this court, and the subject, which is faith, which in itself is so serious, as can be seen.

The *comisario* feels it important to insist that he was not being cruel or vindictive, adding that 'no digo esto para que se castigue si es loca sino para que se recoja ... en Toledo hay casa de locos donde se podía poner' ('I do not say this so that, if she is mad, she be punished, but so that she be taken in ... in Toledo there is an asylum where she could be placed'). He was acting to protect the interests of the Church and the Inquisition (in its ongoing rivalry with the secular arm). Yet the testimony from the *familiar* reveals that such institutional devotion was not uniform throughout the Office's hierarchy.

Another set of documents that challenge binary oppositions between power and the powerless are the records of applications for admission to the Hospital de los Inocentes in Seville. As discussed in Chapter 1, mental hospitals in early modern Spain were still run as medical and charitable facilities, and they were still refuges of last resort. The language of the applications supports these conclusions, but it also shows how even the poorest members of society could engage highly placed officials to act on their behalf. The family's applications almost always included a letter of recommendation from a local authority, typically a parish priest, but often letters from doctors and higher officials as well.[38] Pedro González's elderly widowed mother, for example, had written a plea to the Archbishop of Seville, begging him to use his authority to have her son admitted. The letter reveals her desperation: she writes that her son has been demented and violent for five years and that she fears death at his hands, 'que a no haberme liberado de ellas Dios milagrosamente en muchas ocasiones hubiera perecido' ('if God had not miraculously freed me from them on many occasions I would have died'). It is hard to imagine a more socially marginalised subject than this woman whose 'fuerzas no alcanzan a poderle ya buscar el pan' ('whose means are not enough to allow [her] to seek out bread'). Yet this poor widow had, in support of her case, gathered a doctor's medical certificate and a letter of reference from the local vicar, in which he affirmed that, were it not for his 'pobre y anciana' ('poor and ancient') mother, Pedro 'careciera del sustento ordinario y se dejara morir por ser sujeto incapaz siempre dementado' ('would be without basic sustenance and would be left to die, as he is an unfit, permanently demented individual'). The vicar knew how to use the language of the Church to make an argument with an archbishop, ending his letter by noting that the archbishop's assistance would be 'muy del agrado de Nuestro Señor' ('an act most pleasing to Our Father').[39] The town doctor, for his part, also combined the language of authority and affection in his supporting letter. He wrote that he had known Pedro for over two years, during which:

> le ha visto siempre con delirios ferinos cogitabundo, señales todas de una manía confirmada y por la experiencia le ha visto hacer siempre extremos de locura confirmada . . . y que será del agrado de Dios por la quietud de los vecinos de esta villa y por la necesidad que padece en ella, que su Ilustrísima se sirva mandar recogerle.

> he has always observed him meditating with wild deliria, all signs of a verifiable mania, and in his personal experience he has always seen him committing extreme acts of verifiable madness . . . and that God would be pleased if, for the sake of the peace of the residents of this village and the poverty which is suffered there, your Highness would take it upon himself to order him to be taken in.[40]

The doctor's appeal on the grounds of the public good shows that his motives were not limited to the relief of a crazy man or his suffering mother, but clearly the priest's and doctor's personal knowledge of the case was essential to their intercession and its success.[41]

Attention to the diversity of motives and allegiances among agents of the State is important in complicating the allegorical abstractions of theory. Returning to the 're-territorialisation' scene Iffland cites, we see that there is a vast difference between the behaviour of the agents of royal authority and Pero Pérez, supposed agent of ecclesiastical authority. The officers of the Holy Brotherhood are the last in a chain of visitors to arrive at the inn of Juan Palomeque, where they are informed of Quixote's insanity and soon have opportunity to observe it firsthand (I, xlv, 389-95). At first, despite having been attacked by Don Quixote, they are willing to forgo personal revenge (396). However, when one of them remembers that their arrest warrant is precisely for Don Quixote (for his liberation of the galley slaves), they recognise their duty as agents of the State. At this point, their language and behaviour change completely. One of the officers 'seized Don Quixote so tightly by the collar that he could not breathe' (despite having just seconds before resolved not to engage him further) and loudly declared his institutional authority to all assembled, both through words ('In the name of the Holy Brotherhood!') and symbols (producing the royal arrest warrant and challenging all to read 'this warrant ordering the arrest of this highway robber') (Ibid.). The scene devolves into a repeat of the earlier brawl, but this time the officers are fighting on behalf of institutions they are sworn to serve, and their personal judgements of sanity or futility can no longer determine their actions. They insist that Don Quixote be arrested 'and that the others assist in binding him and committing him to their authority, *as demanded by their duty to the king and the Holy Brotherhood*, which once again was asking for their help and assistance in the arrest' (italics mine, 396–7).

This appeal to the loyalty owed by all Spaniards to their governing institutions should, according to a Foucauldian model, find particular resonance with the priest, that 'other side of political sovereignty'. This is not what happens, however. The priest rushes to Don Quixote's defence, persuading the officers that 'Don Quixote was not in his right mind, as they could see by his actions and his words', and so an arrest was pointless, as he would have to be released as mentally incompetent (II, xlvi, 398). The officer gives in essence the same answer that the Inquisitor gave in his letter accompanying Antonia Núñez:

> it was not up to him to judge the madness of Don Quixote, but only to do what his commanding officer ordered him to do, and once Don Quixote had been arrested, it was all the same to him if they let him go three hundred times over. (Ibid.)

The officer's allegiance is to his superior and he has no personal motive or competing alliances which limit his compliance with orders from above. The priest is no more legally entitled to disobey a royal order than the officer, but he acts in a double capacity: member of the Church and friend of Don Quixote and his family, to whom he has promised to return their loved one safe and sound. His appeal to legal technicalities, then, can be seen not as evidence of a lack of compassion but as a compassionate use of his professional authority and rhetorical training to honour his commitment as a neighbour. It is precisely *because* he is a figure of authority and knows how to use its language that he is able to convince the officers to violate their own orders.

Barber Nicolás also draws on his professional background to resolve the other pending conflict at the inn, the theft of the other barber's basin. The priest 'without Don Quixote's knowing anything about it paid eight *reales* for the basin, and the [second] barber gave him a receipt promising not to sue for fraud then or forever after, amen' (Ibid.). The narrator's sudden incorporation of this hybrid liturgical-economic formula is comical, but it recalls the juxtaposition of various discourses of authority – religious, economic and medical – in the applications for admission to the Seville Hospital. In both cases, professional authority and official discourse are required to realise an ultimately personal, emotionally motivated end. A certain amount of deception is also required; the priest has to settle things with the aggrieved barber 'without Don Quixote's knowing anything about it', but it is a deception for the deceived's benefit.

This small deception is immediately followed by one that seems more ethically troubling: the caging of Don Quixote. In a typical Foucauldian reading, James Iffland describes the entrapment as 'an act of immobilization, of subjection, which is the first step in whatever operation the State takes against one who breaks its rules'[42] and highlights the similarity between Quixote's cage and 'the jails used by the State as part of its punitive machinery',[43] concluding that 'games and schemes notwithstanding, the image projected here must necessarily allude to the state system of control and punishment'.[44] Indeed, upon first encountering the procession and the caged Quixote, the residents of the canon's village make the same assumption, that Quixote 'must be some highway robber or another kind of criminal' (I, xlvii, 409). However, the rest of the scene makes it clear, both to the canon and to the reader, that not all prisons are alike. The moment the canon and his neighbours begin to ask questions, they discover that centrally imposed disciplinary repression is not the dominant narrative. The officers, asked who they are transporting, remit the question to the transported himself. Don Quixote, given a voice, calmly recites his own version of his enchantment. The canon risks his own honour and name by authorising Don Quixote's freedom, with only Quixote's 'word as a gentleman and knight' that he will not run off (I, xlix, 422). His lecture to Quixote on proper reading practices is what we might expect from a representative of the Church: more Scripture, less romance. Yet he speaks not to defend the Church from a heretic but 'moved by compassion' for Don Quixote and his 'profound madness' (423). Of course the proper indoctrination of Church dogma does also reinforce the Church's power, but Cervantes goes out of his way to detail the canon's compassionate motives here, and does not mention any other. For the canon, like the priest and the barber, individual well-being and socio-institutional order are not necessarily in opposition.

Cervantes is not giving us an idealised view of power, however; in the very next scene, Don Quixote gets into a fight with a goatherd and, despite the violence of the encounter, 'the canon and the priest doubled over with laughter' and 'the officers of the Brotherhood jumped up and down with glee'. Here the authority figures bond based on their shared sense of superiority, even provoking Quixote and the goatherd 'as if they were dogs involved in a fight' (I, lii, 439–40). The sudden animalisation of Quixote, the provocation of violence and the cruel 'diversion and amusement' at his expense are in direct contrast to the more generous interventions and gentle laughter of previous scenes. Yet cases such as Bartolomé Íñiguez's and the Seville patient Amaro's remind us that such ethical inconsistency was a real fact of social encounters with the mad. The jailers who made a spectacle of Íñiguez and allowed children to throw stones at him also untied him when he seemed ready to harm himself with the rope. The bishop who allowed Amaro to take to the streets each day for public ridicule and attack also gave him safe haven and a sense of purpose.

In fact, compared with the violence that repeatedly breaks out between Don Quixote and strangers in his way, the violence in the caging scene *brilla por su ausencia* ('is notable for its absence'). Priest and barber manage to tie Quixote up while he is asleep, and deliberately construct a narrative for Quixote which will make his entrapment acceptable to him. The scene is a paradigmatic example of Cervantes's integration of literary and historical referents. The prophecy concocted by the priest is both an allusion to and a parody of literary (and historical) prophecies. Yet the fact that the barber delivers the prophecy at all shows that his purpose is not to facilitate repression but to alleviate it: a 'true' jailer would not worry about how the already-imprisoned victim had interpreted his experience, to make sure that he was 'consoled by the prophecy he had heard' (I, xlvi, 404). Like Bartolomé Íñiguez who, after being removed from the roof, talked his way out of being taken to jail and was instead put to bed in his wife's inn, Don Quixote is able to negotiate the terms of his imprisonment, and his imprisoners never cease to regard him as a fellow man with feelings and opinions.

The most important distinction between the priest and barber's intervention and the repressive model is its end result. Priest and barber are taking him *home*, in order to care for him and return to him his physical and mental freedom. Upper-level officials might discipline and punish but friends and neighbours were more likely to protect and restrain. In drastic cases and for the right reasons, restraint could be much more compassionate than liberty, as we see in Part II, when Don Antonio Moreno and then the viceroy protest Sansón Carrasco's scheme to bring Quixote home, complaining that 'the benefit caused by the sanity of Don Quixote cannot be as great as the pleasure produced by his madness' (II, lxv, 889). There is a large ethical difference between their deliberate resistance to a plan to restore Quixote to home and health, and the priest and barber's ruses in the service of such a return.

The conversion of a human being into an unfeeling object of pleasure depended on an a priori dehumanisation of that person. In the archives and in the novel, such an attitude was only sustainable in two environments: among the most miserable and wretched (drunks, beggar children, criminals) and in the Court. The vast majority of real *locos* never entered the latter, while their lives were filled with low-level officials who act as do the priest and barber. These local authorities, in *Don Quixote* as in the archives, had to find ways to reconcile the demands of personal affection, doctrinal teaching, hierarchical obedience and civic responsibility. They were also humans, eager for status and pleasure. Their actions were necessarily morally complex, and it is this very human, very real complexity which Cervantes explores in the characters and actions of the priest and barber.

Friends and Neighbours in Avellaneda's *Quixote*

The absence of priests, barbers and neighbours in Avellaneda's 'false' *Quixote*[45] is a key to a fundamental difference between the two authors. Once Avellaneda's Don Quixote sets out on the third sally (at the end of the third chapter), he never again crosses paths with neighbours or family. Avellaneda's Quixote leaves the world of provincial authorities behind, heading first for the jousting tournament in Zaragoza and then for the Court at Madrid. The courtly entertainments in Avellaneda resemble the Hapsburg spectacles discussed in Chapter 1. Fernando Bouza Álvarez considers the phenomenon of the court *loco* as intrinsically connected to the rigorous proscriptions of etiquette for the 'good courtesan'.[46] Baltasar Gracián, whose *El discreto* defined proper courtly behaviour, wrote that the good courtesan had to possess 'proper decorum in laughter', which consisted of knowing how to 'discern the occasion and the person with whom one may laugh, both in moderation and in hilarity'.[47] According to Gracián, there was only one situation in which the good courtier could relax and let such obsessive self-discipline behind, in which 'he is allowed to enjoy himself at another's expense'. This form of 'cruel humour . . . was permitted if the object of the joke was none other than a jester or buffoon'.[48] It was the buffoon (*hombre de placer*)'s job to be the butt of jokes. And in the majority of cases, it was a job, and the 'employee' a savvy and entirely sane man who, like other would-be courtiers, came from outside the capital to present himself for the position.[49] The royals who laughed at his folly knew nothing of his past, his needs or his motivations; it was imperative not to know or wonder about these things in order to be able to laugh at him. Furthermore, he was already marked as 'mad' and the proper reactions to his 'madness' prescribed. Outside the Court, no such neat categorisation or prescribed behavioural dynamic existed. For the stranger, the only way to discern whether the irrational man was a threat, a drunk, a joker, a prophet or a faker was to investigate further. The framework of the Court made such ambiguity and tentative interaction unnecessary.

For those who had known a madman prior to his madness or in his lucid periods, the possibilities of *placer* could never fully displace the relation between *hombres*. The priest and the barber at times get pleasure from Don Quixote's antics, but their games never subvert their main goal of returning him home. The nobles and aristocrats in Avellaneda, in contrast, have no goal but their own entertainment. Since they do not know or have any feeling for the source of their diversion, their pleasure is in no way tempered by his suffering. While the priest and barber take care that when they do laugh at Don Quixote he is unaware of the insult, the assembled aristocrats in Zaragoza deliberately provoke and get enjoyment from Don Quixote's anger, frustration and humiliation. This is Bergsonian laughter par excellence, 'incompatible with emotion',[50] demanding 'anesthesia of the heart'.[51] When Quixote ceases to provide them with entertainment, Don Álvaro Tarfe and Don Carlos deceive him in order to bring him, not to home and freedom, but to the Toledo madhouse where 'one tied him by his sword, and another by his arms . . . he offered all the resistance he could; but it did him little good'. He is quickly 'very well-tied up' and locked in a cell (xxxvi, 354). This is not a means to an end; it is, figuratively and literally, the end.

Avellaneda's decision to bring Cervantes's *man* of La Mancha out of La Mancha and into the Court, where he is assimilated into the role of a *man-of-pleasure*, is much more than a simple change of scenario. If we examine the characterisation of Don Quixote and Sancho even before they arrive at the Court, we see that Avellaneda's narrator shares the aristocratic attitude towards his protagonists. Avellaneda's Don Quixote is irrevocably, indisputably mad. He inspires no diagnostic doubt, he sustains no ambiguous or complex relationships, and his mad discourse never touches on truth. Avellaneda explores neither the other characters' interpretations of Don Quixote nor Quixote's interpretation of reality. His Quixote is a *personaje de placer* (a character of pleasure), a conjunction of symptoms and obsessions designed to inspire laughter and a sense of superiority in the reader. Avellaneda may pick up *where* Cervantes had left off, but his Don Quixote and Sancho are not Cervantes's. Indeed, even before they get to the Court, Avellaneda's Quixote and Sancho already conform to the stereotypical and well-defined roles of court spectacle: the madman and the simpleton. Their actual journey to the Court and assumption of these roles is predetermined, redundant. They cannot be accompanied by friends, family and neighbours because friends, family and neighbours are undeniable evidence of a past, a psyche, a human being. The disappearance of housekeeper, niece, priest, barber and the like, and the caricatural nature of Avellaneda's characters are really one and the same. Real madmen, as the archives show, were constantly being protected, diagnosed, explained and controlled by a hierarchy of social actors. A writer who eliminated these could not have – and probably did not wish to – explore real madness.

It is impossible to say what Cervantes might have had in mind for Quixote had Avellaneda never appropriated his destiny. As it was, Cervantes's Part II is shaped by his desire to engage Avellaneda just enough to reject him. His Quixote would now have to have his own 'authentic' experience in the Court – a fictional duchy rather than that of Zaragoza or Madrid – and, to some extent, this shift entails a reduction of social verisimilitude and a shift toward a more theatrical mode of madness. Yet Cervantes, unlike Avellaneda, does not fully assume the attitude of the court spectator. In Avellaneda, the narrator is as uncurious and as willing to accept a flat, inhuman Don Quixote as is the noble audience. Cervantes, having moved his protagonists away from friends and family and into the hostile pageantry of the duke's palace, no longer can explore social relationships to the extent he did in Part I, but instead of returning to a stock portrayal of madness, he shifts the verisimilitude of his portrayal elsewhere. In fact, the deprivation of a full field of social and interpersonal relationships which the move to the palace entails gives Cervantes room to explore in more depth the relationship between his two central characters and the subjective experience of his hero. In what Edwin Williamson identifies as a 'critical shift of narrative interest from action to character', the novel truly breaks free from its epic, picaresque and satiric forebears.[52]

Don Quixote and Sancho

The development of the relation between Don Quixote and Sancho Panza is fundamental in this transition. In Avellaneda, both Quixote and Sancho are stock types, and where there is no individual depth or complexity, there can be no deep or complex relationships. However, a writer's development of an individual character does not necessarily entail a development of that character's relationships. In *Lazarillo* or *Guzmán de Alfarache*, for example, the episodic structure and overpowering narrative voice preclude an extended exploration of a dynamic between two people, with two points of view evolving in response to one another. Edwin Williamson, building on Ramon Menéndez Pidal's theory of the evolution of *Don Quixote*, characterises the decision to present a mad protagonist, and then to give him a sidekick, as 'fortuitous', because it provided 'a creative space beyond verisimilitude' in which Cervantes could 'assert the freedom of his imagination'.[53] The archival material makes one question just how 'fortuitous' this 'invention' of Sancho was, as well as the opposition that Williamson creates between Cervantes's imagination and the constraints of verisimilitude. The relationship between Sancho and Don Quixote may begin as a simple game between mad and sane, and it does undergo a series of ingenious permutations as the identities of mad and sane switch and blur, but the idea of the reversibility of sanity and madness had been expressed before, perhaps most notably in Erasmus's *The Praise of Folly*. Don Quixote and Sancho have become an archetypal pair in large part because Cervantes went beyond Erasmian paradox to explore the way that these men experience the constantly shifting ground that is their understanding of the other. As Sancho comes to suspect his master's sanity, he is forced to question their relationship and the ethics of his actions. The confusingly partial madness of Don Quixote, combined with Sancho's doubts about his own powers of analysis, place the squire in an uncomfortably ambiguous position. While no Inquisition file aspires to novelistic detail, the glimpses that the archives give us into family, friend and neighbour's confused responses to the mad suggest that this was a not an atypical response. The paired figures of Quixote and Sancho have become archetypes because their relationship is not an allegory.

It is Sancho's progressively more complex response to Quixote's madness that drives the increasing complexity of their relationship as a whole. He first enters the novel in I, vii, when Don Quixote seeks him out to serve as his squire. This Sancho, a farmer on Quixote's lands, is 'a good man . . . but without much in the way of brains' (I, vii, 55). His lack of education and critical faculties keeps him from grasping the irrational premises behind Quixote's fantasies. When he does notice discrepancies between Don Quixote's view of the world and his own, he is easily convinced that Quixote, his superior in education, social standing and worldly experience, is in the right. Sancho is doubly unable to doubt or challenge Don Quixote – he is his social inferior (and at this early stage of the narrative, their relationship is still defined primarily as one of *hidalgo* and *campesino*) and his character is defined as being incapable of critical thought. When he cannot follow Quixote's interpretations and explanations, rather than doubt them, he shrugs his shoulders and assumes that his own limited understanding is at fault. Throughout Part I, Cervantes emphasises Sancho's preoccupation with physical comfort and obedience rather than his mental or emotional experience. His character poses interesting questions for other characters in the novel (and for the reader) regarding the relation between insanity, simplicity and conformity,[54] but Sancho himself does not pose questions or ponder character.

In Part I, the relationship between squire and knight does not fundamentally change. Don Quixote must invent increasingly complex and farfetched explanations to reconcile the growing discrepancy between his reality and everyone else's (a task the other characters assist him with), but Sancho only quibbles at details and inconsistencies; throughout Part I, his steady faith in Don Quixote is the constant that unites all the new encounters with the characters of the Castilian countryside. Sancho knows that 'there [isn't] any reason to pay attention to the words of a madman', as he says in dismissing Cardenio (I, xxv, 191), but the diagnosis of madness must be done for him.

In the metafictional space between the two volumes, this is precisely what happens. The fame of Don Quixote's first and second sallies reaches the public and becomes a topic of gossip, debate and critique. The metafictional Sancho cannot but hear these reports and all the charges of madness and misreading from which the priest and barber had protected him. When, at the beginning of Part II, Quixote asks Sancho what people are saying about him in his village, the farmer reports frankly that 'the common people think your grace is a great madman'. There are many varying opinions, he goes on, of Don Quixote: 'Some say, "Crazy, but amusing"; others "Brave, but unfortunate"; and others, "Courteous, but insolent"' (II, ii, 471–2). While Don Quixote explains this away as the natural jealousy of inferiors, and Sancho seems convinced for the moment, the scene marks an important change in Sancho's character. Not only has he been made aware of Don Quixote's possible madness but also he recognises and can recount competing interpretations of events, showing a critical acuity absent in Part I.

Many critics, including several within the narrative itself, comment on Sancho's sudden IQ-lift. However, it is important to distinguish between a simple reversal of types – from country bumpkin to country sage – and a genuine deepening of character.[55] Cervantes undeniably plays with the former. Sancho's sudden insight into governmental policy and human nature draws on a long literary tradition of wise fools, and can also be read as social criticism or as a metatextual rejection of Avellaneda's brutish Sancho. However, Sancho's increasingly complex relationship with Don Quixote is not a necessary consequence of his sudden *agudeza*. A fool who unwittingly speaks truth should be no more capable of weighing ethical choices or social obligations than a fool who unwittingly speaks folly. Sancho's new attitude towards Don Quixote is, however, if not a necessary then at least a very natural result of his realisation *entre tomos* that his master might be mad. We can examine two nearly parallel scenes in Parts I and II to see the effect that the suspicion of Quixote's madness has upon Sancho's character.

In both volumes, Sancho tells a lie to Don Quixote about an encounter with 'Dulcinea'. In the first, Sancho is merely following the orders of the priest and barber, who emphasised that the deception was necessary to set Quixote 'on the road to becoming an emperor or a monarch' (I, xxvii, 214). We are told nothing of Sancho's reaction to this, other than that he listened carefully and 'thanked them profusely for their intention to advise his master to be an emperor and not an archbishop' (Ibid.). Because he is incapable of questioning the motives or sanity of his social superiors, he cannot question his obligation to obey their orders. He deceives Don Quixote just as he might unload his horse: unquestioningly fulfilling the commands of a superior.

Once Don Quixote has relayed to Sancho his mission and sent him off, the narrator abandons the squire and does not pick him up again until he arrives at Juan Palomeque's inn and is greeted by the priest and barber. Sancho alone in the forest does not make a noise; incapable of thought, he cannot sustain a narrative. In II, x, Don Quixote sends Sancho on a very similar mission. Now, however, when Sancho departs from Don Quixote, the narrator accompanies him. Once Sancho is alone, he 'turned his head, and seeing that Don Quixote was nowhere in sight, he dismounted his donkey, sat at the foot of a tree, and began to talk to himself, saying: "Now, Sancho, my brother"' (II, x, 514). This new Sancho is capable of reflection, of internal monologue and, furthermore, of weighing practical and ethical choices within that monologue. It is no coincidence that these practical and ethical choices all stem from Sancho's newfound recognition of Quixote's possible madness. He does not simply sit down and ponder the best way to get a good meal, he mentally replays a dialogue between what can be seen as the 'new' Sancho and the 'old' Sancho. The 'old' Sancho passively repeats his mission as it has been relayed to him by Quixote: 'I'm going to look for a princess . . . who is the sun of beauty and the rest of heaven, too' (515). The 'new' Sancho is aware of the illogic of his mission, telling himself, after reviewing his mission: 'All that's very fine. Do you know where her house is, Sancho? . . . Have you, by chance, ever seen her?' (Ibid.) Based on this imbalance between what his master has told him and what reason tells him, Sancho arrives at the only logical conclusion: 'I've seen a thousand signs in this master of mine that he's crazy enough to be tied up' (Ibid.).

This recognition immediately, *necessarily*, opens the way to a plethora of doubts and dilemmas that stem from the nature of madness. The newly reasoning Sancho must now question the conflict between his duty as a servant/squire, his duty to himself and his duty as a moral being; his decisions threaten his understanding not only of his own character but also of his own sanity. If, as he recognises, 'I follow and serve [Don Quixote]' despite these 'thousand signs' of madness, then 'I'm not far behind, I'm as much a fool as he is' (Ibid.). However, the ambiguity of Don Quixote's madness, Sancho's duty as a servant and his own desire for reward prevent him from refusing his mission. He decides to deceive Don Quixote by making him believe that the first peasant girl he runs into is Dulcinea. Having invented a deception, rather than blindly carrying out another's script, Sancho must now consider the ethical dimensions of his act. At first, 'his spirit was calm, and he considered his business successfully concluded', anticipating that Don Quixote's own madness would protect him and cause him to assume that an enchanter had turned Dulcinea from beauty to beast (516). This is, in fact, exactly the assumption the Quixote makes, and Sancho, after so many days of being pummelled, laughed at and otherwise inconvenienced by Don Quixote, has a very human reaction to this newfound recognition of his superiority and power. After his ruse works even better than he expected, 'it was all the scoundrel Sancho could do to hide his laughter . . . when he heard the foolish things said by his master, who had been so exquisitely deceived' (520). Despite the obvious fictional nature of the deception, the dynamic Cervantes reveals here – madness's destabilisation of social hierarchies – is entirely real, as is the social inferior's instinct to find someone more powerless than he upon whom to repeat his own humiliations and misfortunes. Sancho, who has been laughed at and 'exquisitely deceived' by just about everyone in Part I, suddenly realises his own power to deceive, to provoke someone else to be ridiculous and to ridicule him.

In Part I and the archives, past familiarity with a *loco* was a key factor in determining the ethics of a person's engagement. In Part II, we see that continuous or future familiarity has a similar effect: an innkeeper can be a *socarrón* to Don Quixote because the object of his laughter will soon be out of sight and he will not be forced to think about his actions or to witness their consequences. When Sancho first planned his way out of the Dulcinea errand in Part II, his only considerations were his own self-preservation and pleasure. As long as he avoided Don Quixote's wrath, his master's reaction was relatively unimportant. 'Maybe I'll be so stubborn he won't send me out again carrying his messages . . . or maybe he'll believe . . . that one of those evil enchanters' is responsible (II, x, 516). As the scene plays out, the latter prediction is fulfilled, more perfectly than Sancho could have dreamed. Unlike the innkeeper, however, Sancho stays on with Don Quixote and sees that his master's complete belief in this new, insidious intervention of the evil wizard has cast the normally swaggering Quixote into a depression. Sancho knows that he is responsible for this melancholy, and takes it upon himself to redress it, encouraging Quixote to cheer up 'and come back to yourself . . . the well-being of a single knight errant is worth more than all the enchantments and transformations on earth' (II, xi, 521). Sancho now tells essentially the same lie he told just one scene before, but this time out of compassion, seeking precisely to undo the effects of the previous lie and perhaps expiate his own guilt in telling it. His position is not simple nor are his motives unequivocal. Later on, when he explains the episode to the duchess, he reflects on these motives and laments their consequences. 'I made it up to avoid a scolding from my master, Don Quixote, not to offend him,' he protests, but he also recognises that 'it's turned out wrong' and asks God to understand and forgive him (II, xxxiii, 681). Beneath the comic surface, Cervantes is now in the territory of complex human relations, fleshing out the ethical effects of sudden shifts of power on friendship and duty.

From this point in Part II, Sancho ponders the proper diagnosis of his master in much the same way as the characters in Part I. However, these characters, having made, or chosen not to make, their judgements, promptly left the narrative. Cervantes's intensified focus on Sancho and Don Quixote in Part II means that Sancho makes judgements, acts upon them, and then sees and feels the results, which often leads him to adjust his opinions. After Sancho sees the results of his first deception, he becomes noticeably more charitable and even protective towards Quixote. When Don Quixote threatens to chase down the company of actors who have made off with Sancho's mule, Sancho, recognising that Don Quixote is a danger to himself and others, convinces his master not to pursue the company further (II, xii). The sudden wisdom in his argument, which combines the knight's own theories of the proper engagements of *caballeros andantes* with scriptural exegesis, does not go unnoticed – either by Don Quixote ('every day Sancho . . . you are becoming less simple and more intelligent' [II, xii, 527]) or by critics.[56] But what has gone largely unnoticed is that Sancho's new powers of reason, which first appear in the moment when he realised that his master – the one to whom he is obliged to *ceder la razón* – was without reason, are consistently used to protect Don Quixote from himself, to take the place of the reason which his master lacks.

Sancho's recognition of his master's madness places him in a position with no clear social guidelines. How can he serve someone who cannot serve himself? At the same time, how can he abandon someone whom he knows, as he tells Tomé Cecial, is 'as innocent as a baby; he doesn't know how to harm anybody, he can only do good to everybody, and there's no malice in him: a child could convince him it's night in the middle of the day' (II, xiii, 536). Sancho describes Quixote as a child, echoing both popular comments and legal definitions for the mad.[57] He resolves to stand by his master, he explains to Cecial, both despite and because of this: 'Because he's simple I love him with all my heart and couldn't leave him no matter how many crazy things he does' (Ibid.). He resolves his social and personal dilemma by redefining his role as servant, tending not to Quixote's physical needs but to his emotional and analytical ones. In this single scene, Cervantes touches on how madness both puts established social relations into crisis and how it forces difficult and paradoxical ethical responses. We need not believe that our author set out with such a lofty thematic goal in mind, only that by creating a character 'truly' suffering from madness (true to the experience of madness in his day), he ended up confronting the social and emotional puzzles that madness creates. Neither the romance nor the satire nor the exemplary story had room for such complexity and ambiguity.

From this point on, Sancho is constantly pushing and retreating from the boundaries of insubordination and offence. When Quixote recounts his visions in the Cave of Montesinos, Sancho boldly asserts, 'may God take me . . . if I believe a single one of all the things you've said here' (II, xxiii, 600–1). When the *licenciado*'s cousin, also present, pushes this to its logical conclusion – that Sancho must be accusing *sir* Don Quixote of lying – Sancho retreats, defending himself not by attesting to his master's madness (which surely would have angered or further depressed Don Quixote) but by again exploiting Don Quixote's paranoia about invisible and omnipresent enchanters. Indeed, Don Quixote incorporates the narrative of Sancho's first deception into his new fantasy, a logical fallacy which Sancho quickly detects and recognises as invalidating the entirety of Don Quixote's professed experience in the Cave. Sancho recognises that since he had been Dulcinea's enchanter, this proved 'beyond the shadow of a doubt that his master was out of his mind and completely mad' (611).

Like his initial diagnosis of his master's madness (II, x), this inversion of the 'natural' social hierarchy produces a range of conflicting emotions and reactions in Sancho, making him doubt whether to 'lose his mind or die laughing' (611). On the one hand, he has come to such a shocking conclusion that he is more inclined to doubt his own unlettered, oft-insulted mind than accept that the reason of an educated aristocrat might be faulty. On the other hand, he is tempted to accept his observation and use it to assert his superiority over his supposed superior. He dares to tell Don Quixote directly that he is 'saying the most foolish things that anybody could imagine' and when Quixote replies that he will not pay attention to Sancho's words, the newly empowered Sancho shoots back:

> And I won't pay attention to your grace's . . . not even if you wound me, not even if you kill me on account of the ones I've said to you, or the ones I plan to say if you don't change and correct yours. (612)

His recognition of his mental leverage has also given him physical courage. Where earlier he cowered from Quixote's threats of violence, here he practically dares the knight to punish him for his insolence.

Sancho's reproof, both calling for a return to order ('change and correct') and seizing the opportunity that this order's collapse offers, combines two of the most frequent reactions to madness in a social superior that we see in the archives. In numerous Inquisition cases, parishioners pleaded that a blasphemer 'callase y no hablase aquellas herejías' ('be quiet and not speak those heresies') or demanded, '¿Cómo dice esos disparates? Tenga mas fundamento y mire lo que dice' ('How can you say that nonsense? Have more sense and watch what you say').[58] At the same time, some marginalised figures jumped at the opportunity to turn the tables, as we saw in the reactions of the students, street merchants and vagrants to Don Amaro (once a distinguished lawyer), and of the 'muchachos' to Juan de Santaren (a defrocked and clearly insane priest), who would swarm around him 'haciéndole cantar y decir coplas y versos con disparates de loco' ('making him sing and recite couplets and verses full of a madman's nonsense').[59] Sancho's response at the Cave of Montesinos contains, in just a few lines, all these competing impulses.

Sancho's confidence in his position is further tested by Quixote's moments of great wisdom and eloquence. After hearing Don Quixote proffer erudite monologues on the ideal wife or the relative merits of arms and letters, Sancho remarks to himself ('entre sí') upon the discrepancy between 'the impossible foolishness that he says he saw in the Cave of Montesinos' (II, xxiv, 619) and the latest display of wisdom. The poetry and acuity of Quixote's thoughts exceeds what we might expect to have been said by most early modern madmen when they suddenly spoke well; Cervantes is clearly engaging in multitextual allusions here and perhaps also voicing his own thoughts. However, the general dynamic – the destabilisation of previous diagnoses caused by a sudden and inexplicable return to reason, or by unreason's blurry borders with reason – is entirely verisimilar.

Increasingly, Sancho treats Quixote as a wise and good man who is occasionally possessed by a madness which he cannot control and for which he bears no responsibility. As he assures Maese Pedro, just after Don Quixote had destroyed all of his figurines in an attack of mad fury and confusion, 'my master, Don Quixote, is so Catholic and scrupulous a Christian that if he realises he's done you any harm, he'll tell you so and want to pay and satisfy with you, with interest' (II, xxvi, 634). This is notably different from Sancho's role in the destruction of the wine casks, a similarly delirium-induced property destruction in Part I. That Sancho, still essentially a stock simpleton, is tangential to the scene, providing only comic touches as he unquestioningly accepts Quixote's version of reality. In Part II, we see that Sancho is capable of making decisions and is aware of the possibilities for taking advantage of Quixote, but that he chooses to use his new power to protect and assist him. We sense Sancho's humility, compassion and virtue as a character, not because an omniscient narrator tells us that he is simple and good but because he tells the duchess that 'it's clear to me that [Quixote] is a fool' and that 'if I were a clever man, I would have left my master days ago', and yet he resolves to continue on because 'we're from the same village, I've eaten his bread, I love him dearly, he's a grateful man, he gave me his donkeys, and more than anything else, I'm faithful' (II, xxxiii, 678). The fact that at other moments his inclinations are less generous – in fact, just before running into the duchess he resolved to abandon Quixote on the road 'without engaging . . . in explanations or leavetakings' (II, xxx, 653) – does not diminish this declaration. On the contrary, it makes it *more* believable and honourable, because the character who utters it reveals himself as subject to the complex motives that drive actual people and from which actual friendships emerge.

Quixote's inconsistent behaviour makes Sancho not only doubt his master's sanity but also his own. He concedes the duchess's point that,

since he knows his master to be mad and yet still follows him, 'there can
be no doubt that he is more of a madman and a dimwit than his master'
(II, xxxiii, 678). He finds himself in the same position as Don Quixote
– unable to sort out his perceptions from reality – but unlike Quixote,
painfully aware of the discrepancy, of the unreliability of his 'poor
wits' (Ibid.). Where Quixote can chalk everything up to evil enchanters,
Sancho is left turning logical circles as he tries to figure out why everything seems to have 'turned out wrong' (II, xxxiii, 681). Without the
logical sophistication to argue his way out, he can only fall back on his
good intentions, pleading that the duchess not judge 'a dolt like me' as
malevolent for having 'enchanted' Dulcinea (Ibid.). He cannot explain
his own experience or actions to the duchess, particularly when she is
doing her best to confuse him further for her own entertainment, but
his utmost concern is that he defend his moral conduct. If anything, his
weakness and sense of inferiority in the duke and duchess's Court makes
him more sensitive to the power he holds over Don Quixote, and more
resolved not to abuse it. Sancho's reaction to Don Quixote's madness
shows his loyalty and generosity. He overcomes his social subjugation
precisely because he does not take advantage of the opportunity he has
to overcome his social subjugation. By shifting the stock joke in Part I –
that Sancho must be as mad as Don Quixote since he is following him
– from a third-person accusation to a first-person declaration, and by
making this declaration an affirmation of solidarity within a context of
abuse of power, Cervantes completely changes the meaning and impact
of the statement. Instead of a flippant accusation ('you must be crazy'),
we get a moment of self-doubt ('I must be crazy') and an affirmation of
the ways in which madness can transform relationships and character ('I
may be crazy, but I would rather be loyal and honourable than deceitful
and sane').

Quixote, when he is in his more rational and pensive states, notes and
appreciates this, and his appreciation leads him to give Sancho greater
liberty and more affection than are found in a typical 'master-servant'
relation, to the point that when Sancho leaves Quixote to govern his
island the knight immediately laments his absence. Yet Quixote has
many non-rational, non-contemplative moments; his madness is not
(like so many other literary madnesses) limited to amusing but inof-
fensive delusions, nor is it a saintly nonconformity which only threatens
the evil and the corrupt. Quixote loses control of his mind and his body,
and he lashes out, not only at hypocrites and aggressors but also at his
best friend.

There are various episodes in Part I in which Sancho expresses doubts
about the rationality of Quixote's quest, and Quixote responds with

violence. Both when Sancho laughs at the non-adventure of the *batanes* (I, xx) and when he unfavourably compares Dulcinea to princess Micomicona (I, xxx), Quixote explodes, grabbing his lance and giving his squire two thwacks. This may be comic violence, but the circumstances which set it off and the characters' reactions to it reveal that the comedy obeys real social dynamics. In both cases, after the physical attack, Don Quixote asserts his social superiority (reminding Sancho that a nobleman like himself has never seen a *batán* before, unlike the 'lowborn peasant that you are' [I, xx, 150] and, in the second case, recalling for Panza that it is thanks to him he has been 'raised from the dust of the earth' [I, xxx, 255]). Each time, the physical disciplining and social reprimand crush any nascent criticism on Sancho's part, who responds by exaggerating his own humility and inferiority. The two then proceed as if nothing had happened. Despite Quixote's *ex post facto* acknowledgment in both scenes that he was unable to control his anger, Sancho seems to accept that physical abuse is a fitting response to his social disobedience.

This continues all the way through Part I. Near the end of the volume, as the guests are preparing to leave Juan Palomeque's inn, Sancho complains and Don Quixote responds with fury, lashing out with a string of insults and 'signs of the great anger raging in his heart'. Sancho thinks only of his own safety – 'he did not know what to do except to turn and leave the enraged presence of his master' (I, xlvi, 401–2). Cervantes here gives us a window into Sancho's thoughts and feelings, and all there is to see is an instinctive desire for self-preservation. There is no register of any puzzlement as to the suddenness or excess of this uncontrolled, animalistic violence. Dorotea is able to placate Quixote's fury, Sancho is called back, and upon returning 'very humbly, fell to his knees, and begged his master for his hand; Don Quixote gave it to him [and] allowed him to kiss it' (402). Sancho does not reflect on the bizarre change of treatment, nor does he question the explanation which Quixote gives him for his own behaviour. Sancho in Part I is characterised chiefly by his attention to his physical needs and his social role, and this scene emphasises both: the fleeing Sancho thought only of his physical safety and the returned Sancho unquestioningly acts out the role of an inferior who has transgressed against an authority. At no point does Sancho question the validity of that authority, nor does Cervantes give us a glimpse of private discontent or suspicion. This Sancho is not yet capable of thinking or speaking privately, to himself ('entre sí').

When Don Quixote sets upon Sancho in Chapter lx of Part II, the squire's reaction is very different. By this point, the pair are only nominally master and squire; not only have they been through danger together and at various times expressed their affection or dependence on the other but also Sancho has come off a successful stint as the governor of an island. After six days on the road, the pair settle down under some trees and Sancho drifts off to sleep. Suddenly and without any logical cause beyond his own infirmity, Quixote is beset by 'imaginations' and obsessive thoughts, a mix of voices and visions regarding Sancho's 3,000 lashes. Unable to silence the voices, he grabs Rocinante's reins, sneaks up on the sleeping Sancho and tries to untie his breeches in order to administer the beating. At this point, Sancho awakens and asks what exactly Quixote thinks he is doing. Whereas his response to Quixote's violence in Part I was physical, here it is cerebral. He takes hold of the logical fallacy in Quixote's plan, astutely reminds him of the stipulation that his lashing be voluntary, and, confident in his logic and right to protest, he orders that Quixote back off. A madman obsessed by a desire for violence cannot, however, be dissuaded by reason. Quixote continues to grapple with Sancho's breeches, 'seeing which, Sancho Panza got to his feet, rushed at his master in a fury, and tripped him so that he fell to the ground and lay there face up'. Sancho pins Quixote down with his knee on his chest, 'not allowing him to move and barely permitting him to breathe' (II, lx, 850). This is neither peasant revolt nor slapstick. Rather, the scene evokes archival accounts of friends and family physically restraining violent madmen: Bartolomé Sánchez's neighbours,[60] Juan de Larrea's mother and stepfather,[61] Alonso Hernández's wife and neighbours,[62] to recall just a few discussed in this chapter. Knowing that the attack is unjustified but that the attacker is incapable of malicious intent, the victims resist but do not take the violence personally. They are not afraid to use force, but their goal is only to restrain the other, to 'hold down his hands' until the threat of attack is over (851).

Just as the scene in Part I was marked by Sancho's physical cowardice and social submission, this scene moves from his physical dominance to his social self-assertion. Physically disarmed by Sancho, Don Quixote attempts to reimpose the social hierarchy between the two, reminding him he has raised his hand against his 'natural lord and master'. Sancho rejects this outright, declaring that 'I depose no king, I impose no king . . . but I'll help myself, for I'm my own lord' (Ibid.). Despite the modified adage's allusions to royal betrayal and murder,[63] Sancho does not behave as an offended rival or subordinate seeking power. He is not interested in revenge or victory; having neutralised Quixote's immediate threat, he makes him promise 'that you'll stay where you are, and won't try to whip me now' and in exchange 'I'll let you go and set you free'. Quixote, the fury having passed, promises 'to leave the administering of the lashes entirely to his free will and desire' (851). Madness has, as it very often did in real cases, inverted the social hierarchy; the master is physically dominated by his servant, and then reduced to apologising and promising to respect that very servant's 'free will and desire'.

When he realised Quixote's madness, Sancho, after suffering the guilt caused by his initial deception, made the decision not to take advantage of his infirmity. In this scene, his charity extends further; he does not simply abstain from actively harming Don Quixote, he pardons the harm that Don Quixote, completely unjustifiably, attempts to do him. Neither Sancho nor Cervantes insists on the inversion of power implicit in both Sancho's resistance and his 'pardon'. Sancho resumes his role as the subordinate, literally sealing off the scene of Quixote's humiliation ('Sancho got up and moved a good distance away' [Ibid.]) and Cervantes shifts the narrative to Roque Guinart and a picaresque interlude. Yet we recognise the effect that Sancho's charity has had on the relationship when, in Chapter lxxi, Don Quixote again tries to get Sancho to whip Dulcinea (via his own buttocks) into shape.

This time there is no need for an ambush. The main spur to Sancho's sudden acquiescence is Quixote's offer of money, but since Don Quixote has always had money and presumably Sancho could have stipulated a pay-per-lash deal earlier (as he negotiated his salary), it seems that Sancho is also moved by his master's increasing melancholy.[64] In any event, even before Sancho begins his penitence, Don Quixote begins to back peddle in his demands, calling after his squire, 'Be careful, my friend, not to tear yourself to pieces' (921). Sancho, after a sincere effort at actual self-flagellation proves more painful than he can withstand, arrives at another deception: the enthusiastic whipping of a nearby tree. Unlike the duke and duchesses's elaborate ruses, this is a deception conceived without pleasure in deceiving. Sancho seeks to give Quixote some mental relief and to protect the stability of their relation. Don Quixote, who is no longer in a furious state, can rationally appreciate the extent of Sancho's sacrifice. When Sancho's performance of self-flagellation sounds too convincing, Quixote runs to interrupt him, pleading that he stop, or at least postpone this self-injury which is so painful for him to hear. Quixote still believes in the enchantment of Dulcinea but, when not in the most intense throes of delusion, he shows that he values Sancho's health even above Dulcinea's fate and his own happiness. In one of the most touching moments of the book, Quixote removes his own cape and 'in his shirtsleeves, he covered Sancho, who slept until he was awakened by the sun' (922). This time the inversion of roles – the master asking the servant to stop the discipline that he himself had ordered, and then covering the servant with his own cloak – is initiated by Don Quixote. Both characters, by this point, have come to place the physical and mental well-being of the other above their own desires and above society's dictates. They have become friends.[65]

This friendship is confirmed in Don Quixote's final days, with the theme of madness (in this case, its sudden disappearance) again driving the interaction. Don Quixote, on his deathbed, renounces his past *locuras* and begs Sancho's forgiveness for 'the opportunity I gave you to seem as mad as I, making you fall into the error into which I fell' (II, lxxiv, 937). The words make explicit the role of madness in his dereliction of his social duty, but the speech act itself – a *hidalgo* humbly asking for forgiveness from a *labrador rústico* – proves the extent of the social disruption. Don Quixote's madness has not just led Sancho into error, it has provoked the awakening of Sancho's consciousness, it has tested the character of each, and from these tests a simple, clearly defined hierarchical relationship has become a complex friendship.

Madness is certainly not the only means by which a figure of authority is rendered vulnerable; a physical infirmity, a loss of fortune or any number of other external calamities could give a servant the opportunity to take liberties. However, external calamities and physical infirmities tend to be one-time events, with fairly well-defined implications for those affected. Madness is particularly rich as a source of narrative because it is by nature unstable and unpredictable; it forces a constant revision of relationships, as adjustments to a madman's behaviour one day often prove untenable the next. As we have seen, much of Part II of the *Quixote* consists of Sancho's adjustments to some new behaviour of Don Quixote's and then Quixote's reaction to this new adjustment on Sancho's part. Quixote's madness means that his reactions always involve considerable misinterpretation and unpredictability, guaranteeing that Sancho will always have some catching up to do and that the relationship will never find a status quo (lovely in real life but death to narrative). In addition, in the process of detailing Sancho's responses to each new episode with Don Quixote, Cervantes gives us a progressively deepening insight into a progressively more complex character. The inherent instability of madness, particularly when it is outside institutions of diagnosis of control, sparks a sort of positive feedback cycle, with narrative creating character creating narrative, and so forth.

The final spin in this narrative-character cycle comes when Quixote lies on his deathbed. Sancho, faced with the prospect of his friend's death, forgets past inconveniences and indignities. His concern for his master's spirit leads him to propose something which does *not* have any parallel in the archival materials. As I have shown, the concept of a healthy or ultimately beneficial insanity did not exist (outside satire) in Cervantes's time. A man without will or reason could not fully enjoy

God's grace. But Sancho proposes to Quixote that he renounce his newly found sanity, that he get up from bed and that together they 'go to the countryside dressed as shepherds, just like we arranged' (Ibid.). This is not the equivalent of the students or courtesans playing at shepherds – staple of the pastoral and previous chapters in the *Quixote* – because the proposal is made as a negotiation in a relationship. Sancho's development in Part II has been his discovery that Dulcinea is Aldonza Lorenzo, that the books of chivalry are just fictions, and that he can use this information for his own benefit. His suggestion to Quixote that they might find Dorotea 'disenchanted . . . behind some bush' and his consolation that 'your grace must have seen in your books of chivalry that it's a very common thing for one knight to topple another, and for the one who's vanquished today to be the victor tomorrow' is the final inversion of that earlier 'enchantment' of Aldonza Lorenzo; he re-enchants Dulcinea here, not for self-preservation but for Quixote's preservation. And the Sancho who had for so long complained of being blamed for things he could not help or punished for things that were not his fault, pleads that 'if you're dying of sorrow over being defeated, blame me for that and say you were toppled because I didn't tighten Rocinante's cinches' (Ibid.).

Aristotle, in the *Nichomachean Ethics*, differentiates between three types of friendships.[66] Imperfect friendships may be based on utility or pleasure; the perfect friendship is of those who are equals, both good in themselves and both 'desiring the good of their friends for the friends' sake' and not their own. There are plenty of historical and literary examples of this purest friendship – Damon and Pythias, David and Jonathan, Achilles and Patroclus. In each story, the friendship is the constant; it is the dedication of the two to each other, against the sacrifices and hardships imposed by the outside world, which creates a narrative. Cervantes gives us something different and new: he shows a friendship forming, moving from one of utility and social prescription *towards* a more perfect form. Rather than an idealised portrayal of altruism, Cervantes shows us how selflessness emerges from a relationship born out of the fracture of the self. The movement is neither uninterrupted nor is it the sole focus of the narrative; however, I would argue that Cervantes can surprise the reader with episodes that return to pre-novelistic patterns and archetypes precisely because he has been leading the reader to assume verisimilitude. In Part II, even these decidedly non-realistic moments are increasingly folded back into a narrative of the central relationship of Don Quixote and Sancho (i.e., Sancho evokes his success in the hardly verisimilar interlude of Barataria in order to challenge Quixote's natural right to dominance. The re-calibrated power dynamic changes the parameters of their relationship). The shift from Part I to

Part II is Sancho's transformation from a character defined solely by his pragmatism and self-interest to one represented as capable of making ethical, and unethical, decisions. It is typical of Cervantine irony that the culmination of this increasingly verisimilar relationship is Sancho's offer to sacrifice reality. Madness is both the vehicle that enables the two to transcend their initial utilitarian relationship (making friendship possible), offers the temptations to pervert that friendship (making that friendship novel and real) and finally offers an escape from the limitations of that reality.

Notes

1. 'El pueblo' is 'the people', but in the sense of 'the popular' (what United States politicians mean when they refer to 'Main Street' as opposed to 'Wall Street') (Morón Arroyo: 315).
2. Sacristán is writing about New Spain, but all the documentation I have seen from the peninsula confirms her observations.
3. See Iffland: Chapter 5.
4. Sacristán: 76, 79.
5. Ibid.: p. 28.
6. Nalle: 136.
7. Ibid.: 20.
8. For an introduction to the various readings of housekeeper and niece see Monedero.
9. Obviously the immediate speaker here is not Cervantes himself but Cide Hamete. Still, while there are certainly moments when Cervantes plays with the complex relation between author and narrator(s), this is not one of them.
10. See Close, *Romantic Approach*.
11. The best-known song from the 1965 musical *Man of la Mancha*, an extreme Romantic adaptation of Cervantes's work.
12. It jumps from 3.5 per cent in the seventeenth century to 42 per cent in the nineteenth and twentieth (López Alonso: 65).
13. López Alonso: 52.
14. Joseph Valles, AHN Inq. Lib. 944, Fol. 266.
15. Sadly, there is no indication in the file of what those *instrumentos* might have been.
16. Pedro Rodríguez Herrero, AHN Inq. Leg. 101, Exp. 9.
17. Andrés Hernández Tejero, AHN Inq. Leg. 38, Exp. 6.
18. See Chapter 3.
19. Nalle: 15–16.
20. Ibid.
21. Ibid.
22. Ibid.: 20.
23. Ibid.
24. Ibid.

25. Ibid.
26. Ibid.: 19.
27. Ibid.: 20–1.
28. Ibid.: 24.
29. Ibid.: 23.
30. It is not clear from the *proceso* whether this was the same local priest who had absolved Sánchez and taken the Book of Hours.
31. Nalle: 25.
32. Sacristán: 29.
33. Martínez Bonati: 87.
34. Cervantes refers him to as 'el licenciado' in this section (and almost no other), emphasising the intellectual authority which enables him to think of and effect this plan.
35. See Close, *Romantic Approach*, Ch. 2
36. Iffland: 204.
37. Antonia Núñez, AHN Inq. Leg. 2106, Exp. 24 (*sumario*), Leg. 206, Exp. 43 (*proceso*).
38. López Alonso: 65.
39. Ibid.
40. Ibid.: 266.
41. Although relatively few complete admission files from the seventeenth century remain in the Seville archives, López Alonso asserts that the case 'serves as an illustration of what probably was a good deal more common than what is attested to by the remaining documentation' (López Alonso: 65).
42. Iffland: 221.
43. Ibid.
44. Ibid.
45. The 'false' sequel to Cervantes's Part I, published in 1614. Fernández de Avellaneda. All translations are mine. For comparative readings of Cervantes and Avellaneda, see Gilman; Riquer; and Iffland.
46. Bouza Álvarez: 93.
47. Qtd in Bouza Álvarez: 94.
48. Bouza Álvarez: 96.
49. Bouza Álvarez, citing research by Moreno Villa: 120–7.
50. Bergson: 180.
51. Ibid.: 62.
52. Williamson: 174.
53. Ibid.: 90–1. Menéndez Pidal.
54. The fundamental difference between Cervantes's and Avellaneda's Sanchos: Cervantes's Sancho is less stupid than truly *simple* – he avoids complexity, and thus conflict, hardship, and nonconformity; Avellaneda's Sancho does little more than eat and spout irrelevant refrains – not only does he not think but also does not provoke thought.
55. Eduardo Urbina argues that Sancho's alternance between literary archetypes is the source of comedy and creativity, and it is a Romantic projection to try to connect these 'types' into any sort of 'coherent' character. While I agree that these literary types and models do inform Sancho's character, I clearly disagree that they *are* Sancho's character, or that it is a projection to speak of Sancho as a character.

56. Salvador de Madariaga coined the term 'Quixotification of Sancho' for this phenomenon.
57. Madmen were often compared to children, both in informal descriptions and by medical and legal experts. H. C. Erik Midelfort cites a Bruges jurist who wrote in 1555 that 'we excuse the *furiosi et phrenetici* . . . just as we do children and infants, for they all lack true consent of will and of mind' (196).
58. The quotes come from, respectively: AHN Inq. Leg. 213, Exp. 5 (Juan Arias), AHN Inq. Leg. 103, Exp. 1 (Juan Calvo). While it might be argued that the reproof of heresy is not comparable to a reaction to secular 'disparates', in all of these cases, the speaker was suspected to be mad before the encounters described in the depositions. Also we should keep in mind that Don Quixote's fantasies do have threatening religious and social implications.
59. Juan de Santaren, ADC Leg. 708, No. 636.
60. Bartolomé Sánchez, ADC Leg. 196, No. 2216.
61. Juan de Larrea, AHN Inq. Leg. 2106, Exp. 28 (*sumario*); 225, Exp. 21 (*proceso*).
62. Qtd in Sacristán: 39–40.
63. From Francisco Rico's footnote: 'Sancho modifies a saying which originated in the war between Pedro the Cruel and his brother Enrique of Trastámara' (*Don Quixote* II, lx, 850).
64. Even the demand for money does not, if we refrain from reading through a Romantic filter, make Sancho a greedy, materialist foil to Don Quixote's pure idealist. As we have seen earlier in the chapter in the cases of Pedro Rodriguez, Bartolomé Íñiguez and Bartolomé Sánchez's wives, financial self-protection was not seen as incompatible with love and compassion for a *loco*. Sancho frames his material interests in exactly these terms – he is not looking to defraud Don Quixote, it is only 'the love I have for my children and my wife makes me seem greedy' (II, lxxi, 920).
65. In *Cervantes and the Material World*, Carroll Johnson traces the changing relationship between Sancho and Don Quixote according to their economic relation, arguing that the narrative is fuelled by the conflict between a feudal relation (master and loyal squire, payment in *mercedes*) and a capitalistic one (employer and employee, payment in salary). Johnson notes the conflicting terms with which Sancho and Quixote try to define their relation, but does not offer a rationale as to why their demands change, why Sancho would feel able to demand a salary at one point and settle for patronage at another. Sancho's recognition and understanding of his master's insanity – which renders him fundamentally unable to serve as patron or reliable employer – generates these changes and enables/forces the relation to go beyond a purely economic one (since Quixote, as a *loco*, no longer has a clear place in the socioeconomic hierarchy).
66. Aristotle.

Chapter 5

Madness, the Mind and the Novel

Most attempts to define the novel make United States Supreme Court Justice Potter Stewart's definition of pornography[1] seem scientific.[2] Yet while the land of the novel is impossible to map with precision, we can make some general observations about the territory. The novel is 'a prose fiction in which the characters, plot and/or themes develop through the work'[3] and through each other.[4] Acknowledging that any more precise definition inevitably opens itself to counterexamples and exceptions, we can state that *as a rule* the novel separates itself from its literary forebears (the epic, the romance, the satire) by its realism, complexity of characters and formal experimentation.[5] The ambiguity of the novel is an element and a result of all of these: complex characters interacting in a complex social world and represented by unstable narrators all contribute to the novel's resistance to univocal interpretation. The novel evokes the real world, but it destabilises the concept of a single, representable reality, both from within (ambiguous characters) and without (ambiguous narrators). In *Don Quixote*, both of these stem not only from Cervantes's choice of a mad protagonist but also from Cervantes's choice of a protagonist whose madness is that of Cervantes's own time and place.

Madness From Without: What Is He Thinking?

Put yourself in the place of Anamaría Ballesteros, a woman living in a boarding house in Toledo. At seven o'clock in the evening, she hears strange shouting and pounding noises coming from the floor below, and peeks through a hole into the room. There she sees the following scene: by candlelight, the tenant, completely alone and in his nightclothes, is screaming:

Puto jodido dios maldito quien te hizo quien te creó, si te cogiera con cuatro garfios . . . maldito sea el espíritu santo . . . maldito sea el verbo y tus hígados y huesos y tripas y ojos y cuánto tienes y quien te parió, maldito tu culo y tu cuerpo, malditos tus cielos que te sustentan y el sol, luna y estrellas que te dan luz, maldito el criador que te crió, perro hereje yo te haré polvos.

Fucking goddamn whore god who made you, who created you, if I could get at you with four hooks . . . goddamn the holy spirit . . . goddamn the word and your liver and bones and guts and eyes and everything you have and whoever gave birth to you, goddamn your ass and your body, goddamn your heavens who support you and the sun, moon, and stars that give you light, goddamn the creator who created you, heretic dog I'll beat you to a pulp.[6]

At the same time, he is gazing about wildly, spitting on the ground and pounding the walls. She sees him tearing and burning pieces of paper, throwing stones and bricks he runs and gathers from outside, and wildly waving a pair of scissors 'como si viera con quien hablaba' ('as if he could see who he was talking to'). Intermittently he runs to open and close the door, 'y algunas veces se sentaba a comer nueces y a beber . . . y en haciendo esto se levantaba como toro rabioso y tornaba a la calle a hacer lo mismo' ('and sometimes he sat down to eat nuts and to drink . . . and then upon doing this he would get up like a rabid bull and return to the street to do more of the same'). Finally, after three hours, 'comenzó a hacer su cama diciendo las mismas palabras referidas y dejaba la cama e iba corriendo a la calle . . . hasta que la acabó de hacer y luego se le murió el candil y a oscuras estaba diciendo las mismas palabras' ('he began to make his bed while saying the same words already recounted and he left his bed and went running into the street . . . until he stopped doing this and then the candle went out and he was in the dark saying the same words'). Yet the next day this fellow leaves his apartment as if nothing had happened and chats normally with his co-workers.

You could not help but ask: *what is he thinking?* The answer held vital consequences; the distinction between rogue, heretic, madman and demoniac, to name just a few of the options, could mean the difference between life and death, and these distinctions all depended on an understanding of internal processes. How was this determination made? The typical markers by which men judge the thought and character of others assume a unity between external signs and internal states. In most daily interactions, we note physical appearance, actions, speech and biographical information, and, using past experience and reason, fit them into patterns that we know and recognise. Based on these assumptions we anticipate future actions and we make moral judgements and, based on these, we shape our own actions.

These external signposts should lead us to a sense of the other's invisible, intangible 'self'. In the *loco*, they lead to nowhere, they contradict each other. The inconsistency of these – with each other, with their context, over time – makes it impossible for others to react accordingly and sustain relationships based on inferences from their own experiences. They must find some other narrative to explain the behaviour – to decode these signposts so that they realign into a meaningful map. We have seen in Chapters 3 and 4 that the common Spaniard usually tried to avoid prolonged encounters or get second opinions. The artist, however, is not at the risk of being swindled or attacked by his own characters; he or she can sit, 'with the paper in front, pen behind the ear, elbow propped on the writing table' (I, 4) and instead of merely describing the behaviour of a mad character, think about what it means to think 'madly'.

As we have seen, the early modern experience of madness in Spain was defined precisely by its incomprehensibility: the contradiction between external and internal signs and the absence of any 'master narrative' to explain the contradiction. The uncertainty and ambiguity presented by the madman in the street is in stark opposition to the symbolic clarity of sixteenth-century literary *locos*; the traditional literary *loco* had little relation to the everyday experience of *locura* and *locos*. A writer who set out to portray the existence of a mad individual in early modern Spanish society had two options: either to choose one of the available narratives of disordered interiority – one which neatly defined and united cause, symptoms and implications – or to rethink concepts of consciousness, language, the self and truth. Cervantes, as we will see, chooses the latter, but in order to understand the novelty of his choice it is worthwhile to consider what the available narratives of madness looked like, the genres not taken.

Madmen before the Novel: Epic and Satire

There is no shortage of madmen in the dominant premodern literary forms against/from which *Don Quixote* emerges: the romance epic and the satire. As Northrop Frye writes in *Anatomy of Criticism*, the romance epic is 'an intermediate between the novel, which deals with men, and the myth, which deals with gods'.[7] Myth is inherently allegorical; the gods are gods *of* some other attribute and the stories explain some universal human experience. The heroes of the romance epic are human, but they inherit much from their godly forebears. Their 'self' is constituted by their acts. External forces will oppose them in their goals, creating narrative, but as Georg Lukács writes:

There is not yet any interiority, because there is not yet any exterior, any 'otherness' for the soul. The soul goes out to seek adventure; it lives through adventures, but it does not know the real torment of seeking and the real danger of finding; such a soul never stakes itself; it does not yet know that it can lose itself, it never thinks of having to look for itself.[8]

Because the epic character is what he does, only his situation changes, never his nature. Only supernatural intervention can keep Odysseus from being sly or Orlando from being brave, and, in each case, eventually the supernatural spell is lifted and the character returns, instantaneously, to who he truly *is*. A 'mad' epic character is defined only by his 'madness' and will always act 'madly'; Orlando 'furioso' will rage across the countryside uninterrupted until Astolpho finally brings him (via a magic potion) back to his senses and he is no longer Orlando 'furioso'. Madness here is no more interior or subjective than deafness or a plague of locusts.

It seems fairly obvious that a character who does not yet experience a tension between inner and outer, *fuera* and *sí*, cannot be *fuera de sí*.[9] There are 'mad' characters in epic and romance, but their madness, like all of the character traits in these premodern forms, has a clear cause and meaning: it 'illustrate[s] an abstract hypothesis about the moral essence of the world'.[10] Typically madness is a punishment for a transgression against the gods or, later, God: Oedipus' madness is penance for ignoring the gods and sleeping with his mother, Orlando's madness is punishment for abandoning a Holy War and lusting after a woman. The causes and meaning of the madness are clear, both to the reader and to the characters. It is precisely the non-allegorical madness, a madness which *may mean nothing*, which appears in the Renaissance and cannot exist in the epic forms.

The comic tone may make satire seem a closer relation to a work like *Don Quixote*, but if we look closely at madness in the satire most often seen as a direct influence on *Don Quixote*, *The Praise of Folly*, we see that the same allegorical certainty holds. In Erasmus's work, Dame Folly looks down from on high and informs her audience of the nature of each breed of folly she sees on Earth, and, at the end, she ties these together in a moral lesson. The characters she summons are not characters, they are human embodiments of diverse follies who could no more exist in the text if they ceased to be foolish than could Dame Folly herself. They do not have names, families or life stories, much less thoughts and doubts. Many of the characters of the *comedia* are similarly 'flat', to use the formulation of E. M. Forster: they do not suffer internal struggles, and thus they do not change, and their relationships do not grow.[11] They too satisfy Erasmus's literary precepts, according to which 'character is the name given to the depiction of a lover, rake, miser, glutton, drunkard, sluggard [etc.]' and the author's role is to 'show the wealthy man as haughty, the poor man as humble and diffident' and so forth.[12]

The realistic setting of the picaresque moves it closer to the novel, insofar as one of the novel's defining features is the shifting of the action from an ideal past to the flawed present, and the characters from the mythic to the mundane. Yet the realistic setting does not necessarily lead to a greater complexity, interiority or individuation of character. In the picaresque, the idyllic world of the epic is inverted: its characters represent anti-ideal types, 'just as idealized as the exemplary heroes of the Greek, medieval, or pastoral novels, in the sense that their qualities are reduced to salient traits that coincide with the unifying theme of the novel'.[13] Recent criticism has argued against the reading of certain picaresque works as episodic, inverted epics,[14] but it is generally true that even the most ambiguous and sophisticated of picaresques, *Lazarillo de Tormes*, has only *one* complex and continuing character (the first-person narrator),[15] and its overarching purpose is to 'denounc[e] society for its faults' rather than explore social dynamics.[16] Characters and relationships are still circumscribed to the illustration of 'an abstract hypothesis about the moral essence of the world'.[17]

With *Don Quixote*, Cervantes did not immediately shatter past types and give his audience a radically new madman. In fact, the Don Quixote we meet at the beginning of Part I, and several of those described at some point as *locos* in the intercalated stories, do not seem all that different from the *locos* of Cervantes's literary predecessors and contemporaries. In order to highlight the differences between Don Quixote's madness, as it develops, and the literary *locuras* from which it separates itself, it will be useful to look briefly at one of Cervantes's other *locos*, the *licenciado* Vidriera.

El licenciado Vidriera and Don Quixote

Tomás Rodaja is the eponymous protagonist of Cervantes's short story 'El licenciado Vidriera'.[18] His madness begins in a manner fairly similar to Quijano's, with an omniscient narrator unequivocally stating a cause (in the *licenciado*'s case, mis-eating rather than misreading). Rodaja, 'although he was restored to physical health . . . was afflicted with the strangest form of madness ever witnessed' (113).[19] Vidriera's 'strangest madness' is to believe he is made of glass. The narrator tells the reader, and Rueda tells all who approach him, that 'he really and truly was unlike other men, because he was made of glass from head to foot'

(Ibid.). An uncontested pronouncement gives both characters and reader immediate access to the faulty logic which connects Rodaja's acts and thought, a diagnosis that fits with and explains all of Vidriera's behaviour. The *licenciado*'s madness is not entirely divorced from everyday reality; there are documented cases of similar delusions,[20] and the variety of reactions to the *loco* among the cast of characters, ranging from protection to cruelty to 'amazement' (114), is not unlike what we find in *Don Quixote*. Had 'El licenciado' continued in this vein and had Quixote's journey ended with his first sally, the treatment of *locura* in the two works could hardly be said to differ.

Yet at this point, *Quixote* and 'El licenciado' part ways. After a page or so of discussing the effects that Vidriera's *locura* has on his perceptions and on the way he is treated, the narrator introduces a new twist. Vidriera, it is soon discovered, is not just a man who thinks he is made of glass, he is suddenly willing and able to 'reply to any question correctly and intelligently' (Ibid.). He switches from being principally a character with a never-before-seen *locura* to a very-often-seen literary type: the wise fool.[21] The narrator's focus shifts from exploring Vidriera's relationships and the underlying dynamics of his 'fragile' condition to quoting his witticisms on a wide variety of topics, his satirical take on all the familiar types of Spanish society. Two years and twenty-four pages pass without any discussion of Vidriera's life, feelings, changes or relationships. He is not a 'rounded' character but a wise talking head, a rhetorical trope through which Cervantes can – depending on whose interpretation of the story you prefer – express his own criticisms of society or parody his literary contemporaries.[22] Finally, a compassionate priest 'cures and heals' Rodaja and, again, the omniscient narrator assures us of the complete and immediate return to health (129). The joke is that while he is still as witty and satirical as ever, now no one will listen to him, but because we have no sense of Rodaja (now Rueda) as an individual, this can be nothing more than a punch line. It is the perfect zinger of an ending, but it does not push any boundaries or create any new genre.

The similarity between 'Vidriera' and the first chapters of the *Quixote* fits with what we know of Cervantes's process of creation of the latter.[23] In all likelihood, the *Quixote* began as a *novela ejemplar* which would satirise the tales of chivalry, with Don Quixote's madness providing a vehicle through which Cervantes could parody a genre. The recurring pattern of the early encounters is: Quixote has a mundane experience, the narrator informs us of the knight's misinterpretation of the scene, and then the reader, aware of the irony, can appreciate the humour of the encounter. Yet there are already differences with 'Vidriera'. In the *Quixote*, the majority of the figures who become the protagonist's audience and victims are unaware of his condition, creating a multiplicity of perspectives and sympathies already richer than anything we see in 'Vidriera'. Yet while the relationship between characters is already more complex, the narrator's control of characterisation still follows the mould of the exemplary novel.

Let us look at one of the early encounters as an example. Quixote sees a company of merchants on their way to Murcia to buy silk. The omniscient narrator immediately steps in to explain to the reader the workings of Quixote's mind and how they elicit his apparently irrational actions:

> No sooner had Don Quixote seen them than he imagined this to be a new adventure; and in order to imitate in every way possible the deeds he had read in his books, this seemed the perfect opportunity for him to perform one that he had in mind. And so . . . he waited until those knights errant, for that is what he deemed and considered them to be, had reached him. (I, iv, 39)

A few pages later, with Quixote stuck under his horse, the narrator again enters Quixote's mind to explain that 'seeing, then, that in fact he could not move, he took refuge in his usual remedy, which was to think about some situation from his books, and his madness made him recall that of Valdovinos and the Marquis de Mantua . . . ' (I, v, 41). The narrator performs this function throughout the exchange that follows between Pedro Alonso and Quixote. Each ridiculous speech of Quixote's is accompanied by the narrator's account of the knight's new literary exegesis. The logic – such as it is – is completely spelled out; there is a seamless movement from motivation (Quixote was thinking of Book X and thus interpreted Situation Y a certain way) to action (leading him to say or do Z). This is not a verisimilar psychology; it is literary parody.

How do we know that this is not a verisimilar psychology? Let us look at some of the attempts of *locos* to account for their own irrational behaviours when pressed by the Inquisition. Because the line between heresy and mad speech depends on the will and thoughts of the speaker, the Inquisitors wanted nothing more than an omniscient narrator to reveal what an accused had *really* been thinking. While it was certainly not their only method of investigation, they always began by asking the prisoner to account for his own actions and recording the response. When the accused wished to argue that apparently heretical actions had not been the result of heretical thoughts, he had to try to explain his own psychological processes. It would seem that there could be no one more authorised to act as omniscient narrator than oneself, yet, as we will see in these testimonials, when reason attempts to recover unreason, something is always unknowable or inexpressible. The omniscient narrator who can perfectly convey the inner states that give rise to specific outer actions is a literary fiction. When the madman must convey his experience via language to others who have not lived it, fractures appear.[24]

The Madman's Self-Examination: What Was I Thinking?

The Inquisitors always opened questioning by asking the accused if he knew why he had been brought before the Inquisition. Among the defendants pleading insanity, there were many who proclaimed they had no idea but, rather than insist that they had committed no offence, they explained that they might have done something, anything, because they periodically suffered attacks of unreason. Joseph Valles, for example, explained that he did not know why he had been arrested but, he explained:

> habría como nueve u once años que padece un achaque que le saca de sí y le priva de juicio, y algunas veces está con alguna advertencia y percibe algunas de las cosas disparatadas que dice, pero otras se enagena totalmente y no le queda memoria de lo que ha hecho o dicho mientras ha estado así; y que esto le sucede regularmente desde después de comer . . . y esto aunque bebe medianamente vino, y nunca ha conocido se haga daño . . . y si en las ocaciones que estaba fuera de sí . . . entre los disparates que hablaba, ha dicho algunos tocantes a Nuestra Santa Fe Católica, habrá sido por estar enagenado, pero no por tener voluntad de decirlos . . .

for nine or eleven years he has suffered attacks which take him out of his senses and deprive him of his wits, and sometimes he has a certain awareness and he perceives some of the nonsense he says, but other times he is out of his mind entirely and is left without any memory of what he has said or done while he was in that state; and this regularly occurs to him after eating . . . although he drinks wine in moderation, and as far as he knows he has never done any harm . . . and if on the occasions he was out of his mind . . . among the nonsense that he said, he said things touching on Our Holy Catholic Faith, it would have been due to being out of his mind, but not because he wanted to say them.

Andrés Martínez, when asked to explain his bizarre behaviour, told the Inquisitors that that he did not know why he had been arrested, but:

> sospecha podría ser que por respecto de una pedrada muy grande que le dieron en la cabeza unos ladrones habrá más de catorce años, de que quedó falto de juicio, de suerte que muchas noches se iba de su casa dando voces, diciendo mal de sus padres y maldiciéndolos, sería posible que a vueltas de decir males dellos, haya dicho alguna palabra contra Nuestra Santa Fe, estando fuera de sí, y que no sabe que por otra razón haya podido ser preso.

he suspects it could be for something related to a big blow to the head that some robbers gave him more than fourteen years ago with a rock, which left him out of his mind, in such a way that many nights he would go out from his house yelling, speaking badly about his parents and cursing them, and it is possible that, having been speaking badly of them, he might have said something against Our Holy Faith, being out of his mind, and he doesn't know any other reason he could have been arrested.

This is more or less what Cardenio suffers in *Don Quixote*; his attempt to account for his own behaviours may very well constitute the first literary entry into the inner consciousness of a *loco* that reveals the ruptures between perception and reality from the inside out, instead of relying on the report of an infallible narrator. Cardenio's madness is, at least externally, not unlike that of Orlando in Ariosto's epic: both are spurned by a lover and go raving into the forest. However, Orlando's epic madness is announced by the poet and Cardenio's is not announced by anyone; it must be surmised by the goatherds (the ones who, in Ariosto, would have been killed ten at a time)[25] who, like so many early modern Spaniards, could only observe an irrational man and speculate as to the causes of his unreason. Sancho first hears of Cardenio's strange behaviours from the goatherd, who recounts with perplexity the acts of the intermittently courteous and violent stranger. The goatherd's tale is an attempt to understand the ragged gentleman from the outside in – he has no privileged access to Cardenio's thoughts, but knows what he sees with his own eyes and hears from his fellow goatherds. He recounts his successive impressions and confusions as Cardenio's behaviour changes. When the young man first appears asking for directions to the most inhospitable part of the forest, the shepherds are all 'pleased by his good looks and surprised at his question and at how fast we saw him riding back' (I, xxiii, 180). They do not see him until several days later, when he intercepts a shepherd in the road and, with no apparent motive or explanation, attacks him, strips his donkey of all its provisions and disappears again into the woods. The shepherds get together to find this strange fellow and try to make sense of him. We have seen this in several of the archival cases cited so far: the monks who gather to assess Juan Egujo, the townspeople who come to check out Bartolomé Iñiguez, or Anamaria Ballesteros's invitation to various neighbours to spy on her downstairs neighbour. Cervantes keeps reader, goatherds and protagonists equally in the dark about Cardenio's true state of mind. Like Spanish villagers in the presence of a *loco*, they can do nothing but observe external speech and actions, swap notes and try to resolve inconsistencies.

Meeting Cardenio himself comes far from resolving matters. Cervantes gives us a *loco* who is as confused and alienated at the spectacle of his own inconsistency as those who observe him from without. In a sane moment, Cardenio recognises that his actions seem mad. 'Perhaps you consider me a man whose power of reasoning is weak and, even worse, one who is completely mad,' he admits to Quixote and Sancho, 'and it would not be surprising if that were the case' (I, xxvii, 217). Like Valles or Martínez in the tribunal, he has an idea of the source of his condition – in his case 'the power of [his] afflictions' upon his imagination – but this in no way helps him control or understand it. 'I am powerless to prevent it and I become like a stone, bereft of all sense and awareness.' It is through the reports of others that he becomes conscious of his own actions. He is in the terrifying position of having to rely on external signs – what 'people tell me and show me [of] the evidence of the things I have done while that terrible attack has control over me' – to understand himself (Ibid.). Cervantes emphasises this self-alienation by making Cardenio not only psychologically but 'grammatically' *fuera de sí*, relegating his own existence to the margins of dependent clauses and direct objects. Cardenio explains:

> *The drovers and goatherds* who wander these mountains, moved by charity, *sustain me, placing food for me* along the paths and around the rocky crags where *they know* I may pass by and find it; and so, although I may be out of my mind at the time, *the demands of nature allow me* to recognize sustenance and *awaken in me* the desire to want it and the will to take it. When *they find me* in my wits, *they tell me* that at other times I go out onto the paths and take food by force, though they willingly give it to me, from the shepherds . . . (italics mine, 225–6)[26]

The shepherds provide his basic sustenance, and they are able to do so because they, not he, know where he might wander. Only his natural instincts enable him to take advantage of this generosity, and he only knows about all of this because they tell him. His acts of forceful self-assertion – what he takes 'by force' – are sadly embedded in the narrative of what 'they tell me'. It is no wonder that he characterises his life as 'extreme' (226).[27] It has passed to the extreme of not being his.

Martínez, Valles and others similarly afflicted also must accept outside accounts of their behaviour. Juan de Trillo, arrested for shouting in a church, protested that all he remembered was that 'un día, no se acuerda que tanto ha, le prendieron y azotaron unos frailes del lugar, y no sabe por qué' ('one day, he doesn't remember how long ago, some friars from the area arrested him and whipped him, and he doesn't know why').[28] Valles also seems to have given up resisting or trying to assert a self that is his. He repeatedly calls his own *audiencias* to plead with the Inquisitors that 'en las ocasiones que estaba fuera de sí no sabe lo que pudo decir o hacía' ('on the occasions that he was out of his mind, he doesn't know what he could have said or what he did'), but, while in his 'juicio y acuerdo natural' ('right mind and natural state'), he had never done or said anything heretical. It is clear that the constant fear of his own actions has filled his life with terror and shame. He told the Inquisitors that 'por conocer, que con los accidentes referidos podría decirlas [algunas cosas] y dar ocasión a que se burlase de él, ha más de seis años que huía los concursos y festejos publicos y de muchas conversaciones' ('knowing that during one of the aforementioned attacks he might say [certain things] and give people occasion to make fun of him, for over six years he has avoided gatherings and public celebrations and many conversations'). While Cardenio's initial retreat into the mountains might have been for the literary motive of lamenting a lost love, the shame he expresses at his violence towards the shepherds and his resigned acceptance of his 'miserable and intemperate life' spent in hiding in a tree 'to shelter this miserable body' (I, xxvii, 225–6) suggest that, as for Valles, shame and fear are equally powerful in keeping him from public interaction.

Cardenio's experiences are perhaps all the more terrifying for his partial consciousness of them as they occur. Once the shepherds told him of his behaviour *sin juicio*, he admits:

> I have felt that I am not always in my right mind, and my reason is so damaged and weak that I do a thousand mad acts, tearing my clothes, shouting in these desolate places, cursing my fate, and repeating in vain the beloved name of my enemy, having no other purpose or intention than to shout my life to an end; when I come back to myself I am so tired and bruised I can barely move. (225)

He is not completely without reason, but rather he holds on to its most tenuous 'damaged and weak' threads, just enough to register his actions and 'intention' but without the power to control them. Other *locos* spoke of a similarly alienated, but not entirely severed, relation to their own minds and bodies. Andrés Martínez tried to explain his bouts of fury to the Inquisitors:

> Ha estado enfermo de la cabeza y que éste muy de ordinario ha traído un terror y una carga consigo que le parecía que era espíritu, y que veía su rostro como de hombre, y que estaba esta figura renegando y otras veces llorando y mofando, y que algunas veces que lo veía en la pared encendía papeles para quemarlo y con un carreón de llevar las sillas daba golpes por las paredes, y salía otras veces a la calle y tiraba piedras por los tejados porque le parecía venir de los nubes un bulto como colorado ... y así decía algunas palabras maldiciéndole y que podrá ser que haya dicho la palabra que el testigo dice ... mas que su intento no era hablar contra Dios Nuestro Señor sino con aquel terror y espíritu que tiene dicho, que es lo que le obligaba a decir los

disparates que decía . . . con aquella rabia que siente muchas veces maldice la luna y las estrellas y dice mal de los nublados entendiendo que de allí le viene el daño . . . que lo que le parece ha dicho [es] que si cogiera unos garfios y la enfermedad que ha dicho tiene se subiera a los cielos la alcanzara y arañara con ellos si pudiera . . . y dijo que se acuerda que estando una vez con el dicho mal sin saber cómo se cortó un dedo de la mano de que está manco y se dio de porrazos y calabazadas por los paredes sin ser poderoso para resistir al ímpetu que le viene, y que como ha hecho estas cosas podía ser haber hecho otras muchísimas de hombre fuera de juicio . . . de que no se acuerda.

He has been sick in the head and this has regularly brought a terror and a weight upon him that seemed to him like a spirit, and he saw its face which was like a man, and that this figure was cursing and at other times crying and making fun, and that sometimes he saw him on the wall and he set paper on fire in order to burn him and with a [carreón?] for carrying chairs he pounded on the walls, and at other times he went out in the street and threw stones at the rooftops because a reddish mass seemed to him to come from the clouds . . . and in such a state he said certain words cursing it and it might be that he said the word that the witness says he did . . . but that his intention was not to speak against God Our Father but rather with that terror and spirit that he has described, which is what forced him to say the nonsense that he said . . . and with the rage that he frequently feels he often curses the moon and the stars and speaks ill of the clouds, understanding that the harm comes from there . . . that what it seems to him he said is that if he could grab some hooks and the sickness he has told them he has he would rise up to the skies he would reach and claw at it if he could . . . and he said that he remembers that one time while he was suffering with the said illness without knowing how he cut off one of his fingers, which is still damaged, and he beat with his fists and his head against the wall without the strength to resist the urge that comes over him, and as he has done these things he might have done many other things typical of a man out of his mind . . . which he does not remember.

This is a fascinating glimpse, not just into one man's attempt to understand his own physical violence to himself but also into his attempt to work through his own processes of unreason. In the moment of Martínez's testimony, when he is not suffering one of his attacks, the world of these attacks is almost, but not entirely, closed to him. He can recall certain delusions and unreasonable actions, but he is left to deduce, using reason, how he might have ended up at the unreason he could no longer remember. If ascending to the heavens with a pair of hooks to attack his illness seemed like a logical proposition, he reasons, he *might* have unwittingly confused secular and divine agents.

The reader should recognise here a paradox at the heart of much of *Don Quixote*: how reason produces unreason and vice versa. Cervantes is not the first to take up this paradox, at least in superficial form. When it is isolated from any larger story or character interaction, the surprising jumps from unreason to reason and back form the basis of many jokes and fables, such as in the joke about the *loco de Sevilla* at the beginning of Part II. These are intellectual barbs, appealing to the wit and not the heart. (Who feels bad for the *licenciado* tossed back into prison?) What makes the testimony of men such as Martínez different is the insight into the effect that the instability between sanity and insanity has on his emotions and sense of self. The psychological depth which Cervantes gives Cardenio, allowing us to see him not just as the shepherds do but to hear his confused and sad reflections on his state, makes him different from the *loco* of Seville and so many other literary *locos*.

Cardenio does not remain at the forefront of the narrative for long. Immediately after this scene, Cervantes reinscribes him into a traditional romance narrative. His *locura* disappears, as (not coincidentally) does any representation of his interiority. Yet his *mise-en-scène* foreshadows a shift in Cervantes's treatment of Don Quixote's madness. It is as if Cervantes saw the possibilities that an exploration of the psychological effects of inner crisis could offer and recognised that such an inquiry could not be contained within a secondary character. In fact, it is in the scenes which bookend the encounters with Cardenio that Don Quixote's madness takes on an ambiguity and complexity unseen in previous literary representations of madness.

Two Kinds of Madness: Black Holes and Grey Areas

The archival *locos* are about evenly split between those who, like Andrés Martínez and Joseph Valles, assert their own insanity and those who, like Juan Egujo or Giraldo París, resist such a diagnosis but find it asserted for them. Cardenio falls into the first category, Don Quixote into the second. To understand the two categories, it is useful to consider the division made at the time between melancholy and fury. Attacks of fury tended to be sudden and absolute – one either lacked reason or one had it. The melancholic, in contrast, was never completely alienated from his senses; he experienced subtle degrees of obsession and delusion that he could more easily rationalise and integrate into his self-narrative. Paradoxically, then, the more 'real' the delusions of the melancholic seemed to him the more evidence he would find for his narrative, and thus the less likely he would be to accept a diagnosis of madness. This is certainly Quixote's situation in Part I. His security in his own sanity manifests itself in his confident opposition to all those who disagree with him. Many of the *locos* in the archives at times shared such confidence; had they always realised the falsity of their perceptions, they would not have acted upon them and thus ended up before the Inquisition. In their moments of greatest madness, they were the most convinced that they were rational and the least willing to allow others to cast doubt on their rationality. Juan García, the day labourer with dreams of grand knowledge and wealth, dismissed all those who sought to correct him as being themselves madmen and rogues. When a co-worker mentioned that his claims would get him in trouble with the Inquisition, García invited him to make a denunciation, boasting that:

> no se pondría[n] con él letrados ni licenciados ni frailes ni abades a disputar con él en caso de aquellos sueños que él soñaba, que a todos los metería en un zapato . . . diciéndole este testigo y sus compañeros que era loco o hereje pues decía aquello el dicho Juan García les decía que más herejes y bellacos eran ellos, que sus sueños eran muy buenos y verdaderos.

> neither lawyers, university graduates, friars nor abbots would get into it with him nor dispute him in the matter of those dreams that he dreamed, that he would stuff all of them in a shoe . . . when this witness and his comrades told [García] he was mad or a heretic since he said that, the aforementioned Juan García told them that they [the witness and his friends] were the real heretics and rogues, that his dreams were very good and true.

Quixote is often equally confident in his own misreadings, telling the canon, for example, that 'it is my opinion that the one who is deranged and enchanted is your grace, for you have uttered so many blasphemies against something so widely accepted in the world' (I, xlix, 425).

Yet the melancholic did not dwell securely or exclusively within his delusional world. Although at times fully convinced of his perceptions, he was not always unaware of their incongruence with others' perceptions, or their failure to produce the expected results. Madmen such as Cardenio, whose fits brought them completely out of their senses, could not make sense of the experience later, and were at a loss to represent or explain their *locura*. In their lives, the line between reason and unreason was clear and impermeable. 'Padece un achaque, que le saca de sí' ('He suffers an attack, which takes him out of his senses') was about as much as could be explained. Whatever happened during that attack was lost to memory, words and logic. Cardenio, even had he never discovered Dorotea and magically recovered his reason, could not have sustained a novel, because every period of lost reason would have been the same, producing an identical black hole in the text. An omniscient narrator could attempt to recreate that experience within total madness, but it would be akin to imagining the internal life of a wild animal. There could be no psychological verisimilitude because verisimilitude depends on the reader's recognition of the experience. By definition, the madness whose experience is utterly lost to consciousness, memory and hence language will never be recognisable.

It was for those who, like Quixote, lived in the ever-shifting borderlands of unreason that representation and rationalisation was possible. The *procesos* show the different narrative potential of a Cardenio and a Quixote. Juan de Larrea's *audiencias* were interrupted by Cardenio-like descents into incoherence. He called one *audiencia* to declare that 'ha estado loco', and in that state he might have said some 'bad things'. The Inquisitors asked him to specify, in response to which:

> se quedó por un rato suspenso y sin hablar ni decir cosa alguna, y dijo después que pedía perdón y misericordia, y diciéndole que de qué la pedía, se volvió a quedar suspenso sin hablar, aunque se le hicieron muchas instancias para que dijera en razón de qué pedía la misericordia, no respondió palabra alguna más que mirar a una y otra parte sin decir cosa alguna, y diciéndole si tenía más que decir, dijo 'no señor.' Preguntado si hoy siente que está sano de la locura que dice tuvo, de que le curaron, dijo sonriéndose y mirando otra vez hacia una y otra parte y encogiendo los brazos, 'no señor.' Preguntado si se acuerda de haber hecho o dicho en el tiempo que dice estuvo loco alguna cosa contra Dios Nuestro Señor . . . les dijo, como suspenso y despacio, 'sí señor, bien me acuerdo de eso,' y advirtiéndole que fuese diciendo qué era lo de que se acordaba, quedó otra vez suspenso sin decir ni responder cosa alguna, y volviéndole a hacer instancia si tenía qué responder, dijo 'no señor' . . . visto que no decía cosa alguna, los dichos señores inquisidores le mandaron volver a su cárcel.

> he remained still a moment and without talking or saying anything at all, and then he said that he begged for pardon and mercy, and asking him what he begged it for, he went still again, without speaking, and although they urged him many times that he say why he begged for mercy, he did not say a word more other than to look one place and then another without saying anything, and asking him if he had anything more to say, he said 'no sir'. Asked if today he feels that he is cured from the madness that he said he had, of which they cured him, he said, smiling and looking again from one spot to another and clutching his arms, 'no sir'. Asked if he remembered having, in the time he said he was mad, done or said anything against God Our Father . . . he said, slowly and as if he were in a trance, 'yes sir I remember that well', and advising him that he say what it was that he remembered, he went still again without saying or responding at all, and once again urging him on if he had something to reply, he said 'no sir' . . . and seeing that he wasn't saying anything, the said Inquisitors ordered him back to his cell.[29]

Each time this occurred, the Inquisitors had to end the *audiencia* and the transcription: narrator and narrative go blank. In order to find out about a rupture of the self, the Inquisitors depended on a continuity, however tenuous, between reason and unreason. When the self in the present could not access the ruptured self of the past or could not express in language that past self, they stopped taking notes; as far as they were concerned, narrative stopped.

Precisely because, in moments of sanity, they recognise the black holes in their self-narratives, men like Cardenio and Larrea were generally forced to admit that they suffered from insanity. However, Quixote and others whose self-narrative moved in a twilight zone were less likely to accept that their reason was faulty. For all of the reasons outlined in Chapter 1, to accept one's own *locura*, particularly if one had any sort of social status, was an almost unthinkable renunciation of one's own subjectivity – both in the social sense (one's rights as a subject of the King) and the epistemological one (the implicit inverse of the Cartesian formula: I cannot think, therefore I cannot be). In order to sustain their very selves, these madmen had to subject to reason those behaviours and thoughts which escaped rationality. Because reason and unreason were so close, so fragile and so intertwined in these men, the process of understanding and representing the irrational could easily become tinged with the same delusional elements that it was trying to explain. It is impossible to disentangle truth from error in these narratives; they reveal that, rather than representing two sides of a coin, reason and unreason are more like two sides of a Mobius strip.

Self-Narrative and Self-Esteem

Navigating this Mobius strip in life is never a purely intellectual exercise. To spend one's life chasing after an elusive narrative of self, constantly having to revise one's own account of the mind and the world in order to retain the right to that mind and that world, has profound emotional effects. This is the driving force behind much of *Don Quixote*: Don Quixote has a theory about himself and the world; the world responds in a way which would seem to negate this theory; and Quixote adjusts his hypothesis in order to explain the new situation without having to call into question his theory of self. However, as each hypothesis fails, the work of revision becomes more difficult, the gap between self and world becomes harder to deny, and Don Quixote's spirits fall lower.

The *locos* in the archive recounted similar struggles to explain behaviour with seemingly no rational basis without acknowledging that they were mad. Juan Egujo had initially denied one of the charges against him by claiming he did not remember having said what he was accused of saying, but, if he did say it, 'no ha sido de su voluntad sino estando fuera de juicio' ('it was not willingly, but rather when he was out of his mind'), and indeed his erratic behaviours make this seem probable.[30] Yet by the next *audiencia,* his sense of dignity had gained the upper hand, and when the Inquisitors asked him about his previous statement, essentially extending an olive branch by means of which he could climb out of prison, he denied everything (adding perjury to heresy). He insisted on affirming all of the heresies he was charged with.[31] When the Inquisitors read back to him his claim of ignorance and insanity, he said that 'no le está bien para su honra y reputación confesarse por ignorante, por eso ha dicho ahora que no procede[n] de ignorancia sus proposiciones' ('it isn't good for his honour and reputation to confess to be ignorant, and that is why he has now said that his propositions do not stem from ignorance') and that 'no es reputación suya volver atrás de lo que ha dicho' ('it is not his reputation to go back on something he has said'). He was willing to burn at the stake rather than admit that he was not a man of 'honour and reputation'.[32]

If a wandering beggar was resistant to call himself mad, we can imagine what such a charge would have meant to a *hidalgo* like Don Quixote. Quixote's main strategy for explaining the failure of the world to match his idea of it is to postulate interventions by evil enchanters. The first time Quixote evokes the enchanters to explain away a tangible difference between his perceptions and those of others comes when he gets the barber's basin that he believes to be Mambrino's helmet.[33] Sancho knows a basin when he sees one, and his shock at his master's inability to recognise a quotidian object threatens to topple his faith in his master entirely:

> I even imagine that everything you tell me about chivalry, and winning kingdoms and empires, and giving me ínsulas and granting me other favors and honors, as is the custom of knights errant, must be nothing but empty talk and lies . . . Because if anyone heard your grace calling a barber's basin the helmet of Mambrino without realizing the error after more than four days, what could he think but that whoever says and claims such a thing must be out of his mind? (I, xxv, 194–5)

So Quixote is defending not only the status of a single object but also the future of his quest, the basis for that quest, and his own sanity. The rhetoric of enchantment saves him and convinces Sancho. As he explains it, the ever present enchanters 'alter and change everything and turn things into whatever they please, and so, what seems to you a barber's basin seems to me the helmet of Mambrino, and will seem another thing to someone else' (195). Not only does this explanation stave off any possible recognition of a failure of reason but also it affirms his decisions and perceptions. The 'wise man who favors him' must have made the helmet seem like a basin to everyone else because otherwise everyone would try to steal it from him (Ibid.). For the moment, his irrational rationalisation enhances his spirits and his faith in his delusions.

However, this does not last. A man who was completely and inescapably mad – Avellaneda's Quixote, perhaps – could have used the enchantment rationale *ad infinitum*. There is nothing inherent in the belief in an uncontrollable, unappeasable magical force with the power to affect all aspects of life that would fail to explain any particular conflict. But Don Quixote, like most real *locos,* did not suffer from this acute, solipsistic unreason; he is at least a part-time resident of the rational world. Insomuch as he is a man motivated to anger, affection and fear by the same things which motivate others to anger, affection and fear, and insofar as he is aware of the way others see the world and see him, he senses the insufficiency – others do not come to share his view – and inaccuracy – he becomes progressively less sure himself – of his narrative for himself and the world.

As Quixote is increasingly unable to explain away encounters which challenge his reality, he takes a larger view, still affirming the overall narrative but no longer claiming to understand all of the details. He shifts from being the author of his own adventures to a character carrying out a destiny that is already determined, or that is being forged on a higher plane by enchanters and magicians. As a point of reference, let us recall one of his first seeming triumphs, the liberation of Andrés from Juan Haldudo's lashes (I, iv). Quixote emphasises his own agency in enforcing what he is certain is an act of knightly justice, boasting to Haldudo that 'I am the valiant Don Quixote of La Mancha, the righter of wrongs and injustices' and threatening that, if the stingy employer does not live up to his word, 'by that same vow I vow that I shall return to find and punish you, and find you I shall' (37–8). As he rides off, Cervantes tells us that Don Quixote was 'exceedingly pleased with what had occurred, for it seemed to him that he had given a happy and noble beginning to his chivalric adventures' (38). When the first adventures go awry, Quixote knows exactly why – his horse has failed him (40), a specific knight has attacked him (I, vii, 54), a specific magician has it in for him (I, viii, 59). He is convinced of these rationales, and thus his spirits remain high: even as he is gathering his wits after being nearly decapitated by farm implements, he is sure that in the end, 'evil arts will not prevail against the power of my virtuous sword' (Ibid.).

But the sheer number of these failed encounters begins to take its toll. When Quixote proposes to free the galley slaves, Sancho warns him against it. There follows a typical exchange of narratives. Quixote gives his, which involves 'my profession: to right wrongs and come to the aid and assistance of the wretched', and Sancho responds with his, which happens to be the one shared by society, that the galley slaves are being justly punished for their crimes (I, xxii, 163). The same type of exchange occurred before the windmill/giant episode, but this time, after the adventure fails, Don Quixote remembers Sancho's warning and we see the first signs that reality's insistence on favouring Sancho's narrative is beginning to weigh on him. 'If I had believed what you told me, I should have avoided this grief,' he begins, teetering on the edge of rejecting his entire world-view. But this is untenable, just as it was for Egujo and Alarcón.[34] Quixote's best defence is stoic dismissal: 'what is done is done, and so patience, and let it be a lesson for the future' (I, xxiii, 172).

The humiliations that Don Quixote suffers during his second stay at Juan Palomeque's inn further challenge the validity of his knightly narrative. Don Quixote cannot deny the reality that a wench has tricked him into dangling by his arm just inches from the ground for two hours (I, xliii) and that a group of police officers and hotel guests – whose opinions carry much more weight and authority than do Sancho's – all contradict his readings of the helmet and caparison. Don Quixote concedes that he cannot explain any of this, and in fact relinquishes his authority of interpretation not just of past events but of anything that may occur at the inn in the future. 'So many strange things have happened to me in this castle on the two occasions I have stayed here, that if you were to ask me a question about anything in it, I would not dare give a definitive answer,' he tells the assembled guests (I, xlv, 392). For the first time, he doubts not just his perception of a particular object, but his power of perception itself. Again, he teeters on the edge of despairing of his own sanity, admitting that any opinion he offered at this point would be 'a rash judgment' (Ibid.).[35] The only explanation that fits within his larger narrative is the assignation of blame to evil enchanters. Still, while his self-diagnosis of enchantment does not carry the long-term stigma of an admission of insanity, it has the same short-term effect: he is lost in the world. Just as Cardenio had to rely on the reports of others for his own conduct, Quixote will have to 'leave . . . to the judgment of your graces' the realities of the world around him (Ibid.). His situation is perhaps even more difficult because Cardenio had no competing reality to offer for his own past; the accounts of others filled a black hole. Quixote, in contrast, sees what to him is unquestionably an enchanted helmet, and yet must cede to the opinions of those who tell him that what he sees is not what is there. He must accept that the others see things 'as they really and truly are' and the way 'they seem to [him]' is an illusion (Ibid.).

Seeing Things That Can't Be There: Don Quixote and Torquato Tasso

The experience of the Cave of Montesinos marks a turning point in the conflict between Don Quixote's rational and irrational selves – or more precisely, a turning point in Cervantes's characterisation of this inner state.[36] The vision in the cave may not represent a new level of hallucination – Cervantes implies that Quixote was envisioning an entire fantastic narrative when Pedro Alonso found him trapped under his horse – but Quixote's doubts about this vision, and the degree to which Cervantes describes his protagonist's mental processes and their effects on his emotional state, is entirely new.

Quixote's relation of his experience in the cave is a watershed moment in his characterisation (similar to the appearance of Sancho's interiority discussed in the previous chapter). The knight does not just describe a delusional experience he believes he has had, nor does an omniscient narrator tells us what Don Quixote thought. From the moment Sancho and the *licienciado*'s cousin slap him awake, Don Quixote tells us of his own doubt as to whether he actually had the experience that he proceeds to relate. Once in the cave, he begins, he found a rock, and he 'sat on it, becoming very thoughtful as I considered how I would reach the bottom' (II, xxiii, 605). Here we have one level of thought, seemingly a conscious and rational one, but already marked by confusion. Then:

> when I was deep in this thought and confusion, suddenly, and without my wishing it, I was overcome by a profound sleep; and when I least expected it, not knowing how or why, I awoke and found myself in the midst of the most beautiful, pleasant, and charming meadow that nature could create or the most discerning human mind imagine. (Ibid.)

The rational side of Quixote is suspicious; rational human experience does not provide for sudden transport from caves to Edenic landscapes. This is, he recognises, dream logic, and yet he feels he has just *awakened* from a dream. The rational Quixote insists on some external confirmation of this irrational experience. While the mind is capable of flights of unstable fancy, the body is subject to reasonable laws, and so Quixote seeks to back up his mind's claims with his body's evidence.

> I opened my eyes wide, rubbed them, and saw that I was not sleeping but really was awake; even so, I felt my head and chest to verify whether it was I myself or some false and counterfeit phantom sitting there, but my sense of touch, my feelings, the reasoned discourse I held with myself, verified for me that, there and then, I was the same person I am here and now. (Ibid.)

After Quixote finishes recounting the episode, Sancho expresses his doubts, and Quixote again acknowledges that the improbable story does sound more like an enchantment than a real experience, but he cites as proof of its reality the corporeality of his perception. 'It is not [an enchantment],' he counters, 'because what I have recounted I saw with my own eyes and touched with my own hands' (611). The circularity of these statements reveals the lie behind Quixote's certainty and, implicitly, behind all attempts at self-knowledge. Whether or not one is conscious, just like whether or not one is sane, can only be determined from an external, objective state of 'awakeness' or 'reason'. The dreamer who dreams he is awake cannot confirm his own conscious state with his own eyes *because* they are his own eyes. There is always the possibility that his process of diagnosis, however rational and scientific it may seem to him, may be part of the dream. The madman who thinks he is sane can never be sure that his own seemingly 'reasoned discourse' is not also inscribed within his illogic. Quixote's certification that he 'was the same person I am here and now' is both true (he is mad when he says this and was mad when he was hallucinating) and completely false (insofar as it leads him to confirm the reality of a hallucinated experience).

Quixote, when his reason has the upper hand, recognises the paradox of his logical process, or at least that it has provided him with an illogical result. The ontological status of his Montesinos experience continues to bother him in a way that similar hallucinatory experiences in the first part never did. Thus when he has the opportunity to ask the fortune-telling monkey any question, he asks if 'what happened . . . in the Cave of Montesinos is true' (II, xxv, 627).[37] Later, when a company of actors (following the duchess's script) claim to be sent on an errand from Montesinos, Don Quixote is confused, 'because he could not be certain if what had happened to him in the Cave of Montesinos was true or not' (II, xxxiv, 688). Near the very end of the novel, Quixote asks the enchanted head the same question. This lingering doubt and confusion was completely absent after the wine-cask debacle. Then, after Quixote was put to bed, the narrative shifted back to *El curioso impertinente;* Quixote never tried to understand or justify his experience, to himself or to others. Because he was immediately able to incorporate the vision into his narrative of enchanters, the experience provoked no emotional crisis or response. Or, what is one and the same, Cervantes was not at that point interested in exploring the emotional crisis provoked by a mind caught between sanity and insanity.

The private letters of Torquato Tasso are full of this emotional crisis, all the more striking because of the contrast with the visions and apparitions in Tasso's literary works. In Tasso's poetry, the visions are always explained by an omniscient narrator who reveals their divine source and fixes their message and meanings. While the poet was in the asylum of Santa Ana, he wrote a series of moral dialogues, some of which are between himself and a fantastic spirit. In the beginning of one of the dialogues, the poet expresses doubt that the spirit is real, but the apparition, using typical Scholastic arguments, soon convinces him and proceeds to offer theological and moral lessons.[38] These are clearly the point of the literary exercise, and if we knew nothing about Tasso's madness there would be little reason to find anything remarkable about his visionary interlocutors. As Allen Thiher notes, despite the fact that Cervantes and Tasso were near contemporaries, the differences between the representations of non-rational experience in their fictions are so 'extraordinary' that they 'tempt the historian to speak of a rupture'.[39] Yet there is evidence suggesting that the rupture occurred not in the understanding of madness but in the understanding of literature. Tasso's correspondence with his friend and patron Giovanni Batista Manso reveals that his visions were far more problematic and contested than his literary rendering of them would suggest. On the one hand, as Tasso told his friend, his visions could be a source of great inspiration and beauty. Quixote too complains when he is awakened after emerging from the Cave that his friends 'have taken me away from the sweetest life and most pleasant sights that any human being has ever seen or experienced' (II, xxii, 604). Unreason, in its purest form and isolated from the nagging doubts of reason, is a transcendental and revelatory experience. On the other hand, when reason encroached upon this certainty, the visions become the source of a wide range of emotions, including embarrassment, self-mockery, terror and despair. 'Sono infermo, e l'infermità non è da giuoco, nè senza periocolo' ('I am sick, and the illness is not a game, nor is it without danger'), Tasso wrote. In some letters, he insisted his maladies were caused by humoral imbalances, while in others he ascribed his sufferings to demonic possession or magical enchantment. And when his visions did provide him with solace – in particular an apparition of the Virgin Mary which came to him in the midst of an attack of terrifying and non-transcendent hallucinations (mice, frightening whistles, the sensation of being trampled by a horse) – he was so unsure of his mental state that he doubted even these. After the apparition of the Virgin, he lamented that 'potesse facilmente essere una fantasia, perch'io sono frenetico, e quasi sempre perturbato da varii fantasmi, e pieno di malinconia infinita' ('it could easily be a fantasy, given that I am frenetic, and almost always bothered by different phantoms, and full of infinite melancholy').[40] He described his vision in a sonnet but, notably, not the fear and doubt of the visionary,[41] his fear that the 'flusso e il riflusso de miei pensiere' ('ebb and flow of my thoughts'), far from providing his spiritual or literary salvation, would be 'la rovina di tutte le mie azioni' ('the ruin of all my actions').[42]

Tasso's letters are relevant for a reading of *Don Quixote* even beyond the evidence they provide for the verisimilitude of Quixote's symptoms and hence a non-symbolic reading of madness in the *Quixote*. They also highlight two fundamental aspects of madness in *Don Quixote:* the way that madness and reason can coexist in a single mind, and the effects that madness has on human emotions and relationships. Like Quixote, Tasso suffers attacks of rage which overpower all his faculties of reason and judgement, but, once they pass, he can return to a state in which his general delusion persists, but from which he can reflect and, within that delusion, be very reasonable. Manso recounts a conversation in which Tasso attempted to convince him of the reality of one of his visions. Manso, like Sancho after Quixote recounted his vision in the cave, attempted to convince Tasso with 'i più severi ragionamenti' ('the most serious arguments') that his visions 'non possono essere vere' ('cannot be real').[43] Tasso met reason with reason (and contemporary theory on the discernment of visions), arguing that the duration of the visions, the unchanging forms of the envisioned spirits, and their revelation to him of things he could not otherwise have known, all proved that the visions were not delusions.[44] After going back and forth about the reality of the images, like Quixote and the barber about the identity of the *baciyelmo*, Tasso shifted tactics. Seeing that reason could not prove itself, Tasso, like Quixote, recurred to the evidence of his own eyes: 'E farò che voi con gli occhi stessi veggiate quello spirito, di cui prestar fede non volete alle mie parole' ('I will make you see that spirit with your own eyes, since you do not want to trust my words about it').[45] Of course when Tasso looked out of the window and declared, 'Ecco . . . l'amico spirito . . . miratelo; e vedrete la verità delle mie parole' ('There's the friendly spirit . . . look at him; and see the truth of my words'), his friend saw nothing. Both left the scene confused and frustrated.

The discursive pattern at the heart of this dispute – the inscription of logical argument into a greater illogic – is the same that we find in Quixote's refutation of Sancho. Every appeal to an external point of truth ('the sense of touch, my feelings, the reasoned discourse I held with myself' [II, xxiii, 605]) is, in the end, the product of the very mind whose judgement and perception is in doubt. Michel Foucault identifies this 'pure reason . . . located in the paradoxical truth of madness . . . [as] madness's organizing form, the determining principle of all of its manifestations, whether of the body or of the soul'.[46] Yet the descriptions of Quixote's contemporaries suggest a different understanding of reason and unreason. These men were understood as men who suffered unreason, and were mad insofar as they did so, but they were *not* madmen a priori, whose every word and movement was mad. In Tasso's case, like so many others, delusional logic is not the 'paradoxical truth' of madness, but rather the result of a reasoning man's attempt to explain his unreasonable perceptions or beliefs without renouncing his claim to rationality and validity as a rational being.

Mad Confidence and Rational Despair

The Inquisition narratives are filled with stories in which a defendant's partial recovery of sanity is linked to an increasing despair, as it impelled him to question his previous self-narrative without providing a completely convincing alternative. Because Bartolomé Sánchez was allowed to speak so freely during his two trials and because the file is complete, his is a particularly useful example. In Sánchez's first trial, he dominated his interactions with the Inquisitors, lecturing the Tribunal on his ideas and requesting and ending *audiencias* at his will. This all fit with his declared belief that he was the new Elijah-Messiah, and that God would come that All Souls Day, rescue Sánchez and punish the Inquisitors if *they* did not repent. Sánchez's sufferings in prison and the Inquisitors' arguments and threats did not bother him because they fit into his narrative identity; Jesus too was persecuted and suffered. When 1 November passed without any climactic event, Sánchez still did not despair, because he was able to adapt the narrative: he believed 'God was testing him to see if he would be a worthy bearer of his Word'.[47] Even when the Inquisitor, *licenciado* Cortes, threatened him with death if he did not revoke his heresies, he challenged the Inquisitors to throw him in the fire and add 'cuanta leña quisiesen . . . que él tenía por cierto que Dios le libraría y no se quemaría' ('as much wood as they wanted . . . he was certain that God would rescue him and he wouldn't be burned').[48] But at the moment of truth, as Sánchez was to ascend the scaffold, his narrative failed him. He saw that God was not going to rescue him and he not only confessed but also broke down entirely.[49] He referred to his past heresies and delusion of grandeur as 'boberías y locuras' ('nonsense and craziness') which he claimed 'la imaginación y locura que él tenía se lo hizo decir' ('his imagination and insanity had made him say').[50] Although the Inquisitors had suspected Sánchez's mental health for some time, this was the first time that Sánchez accepted the narrative of his own insanity. Before, like Quixote in his moments of confidence, he was sure that the madmen were those who doubted him. Now he was forced to face the fact that the Inquisitors' reality had prevailed over his own and that he could not trust his own mind. Where he had previously threatened and lectured the Inquisitors, Sánchez now did nothing but cry in the *audiencias*, pleading to Inquisitor Cortes to 'sacarle de la soledad y oscuridad y prisiones en que está o si no lo merece, que le maten o hagan dél lo que más mandaren' ('remove him from the solitude, darkness and captivity in which he is held or, if he is not worthy of that, that they kill him or do to him what they most want').[51] These are completely reasonable responses to prolonged Inquisitional confinement, but he had shown no such desperation during his longer period of incarceration prior to the *auto de fe*; in fact, he seemed to relish the opportunity to speak truth to power. He had not become a sane man after his brush with execution (his declarations continued to be disordered and he began to confess to bizarre and delusional things of which he had never been accused), but he had lost the narrative which, in his mind, had made these delusions and obsessions make sense.

It is, thus, no coincidence that the point where Quixote begins to doubt his delusions and obsessions is also the point that marks his emotional decline. His disillusionment in Part II is not tied to any change in his objective fortunes; he is, if anything, more successful in Part II than in Part I. The arrival at the ducal palace should restore all of his confidence, as he finally sees his self-narrative confirmed by others. However, after a brief interlude of restored spirits, his doubts return. Unlike I, i, when the narrator declared that Quixote had lost his mind, there is no narrative pronouncement here that Quixote's delusion is fading. Instead, Cervantes presents actions, speech and occasional windows into his thoughts, and the reader must piece together clues and imagine the 'self' that is struggling to find coherence. In a series of successive defeats, Cervantes not only shows us a progressive decline in Quixote's spirits but also, crucially, he connects that decline, manifested in external actions (staying in bed, refusing adventures), with thoughts. After his defeat by a bag of cats, for example, Don Quixote stays in bed for six days, 'dejected and melancholy . . . sleepless and awake, *thinking about his misfortunes*' (italics mine) (II, xlviii, 765). Melancholy here is not a symptom of madness, it is the result of madness's dissipation, its inability to describe reality. In the description of Don Quixote's encounter with Doña Rodríguez, Cervantes opens up another level of interior space: now Don Quixote is thinking about thoughts. Like Tasso, suffering the 'flusso e il riflusso de miei pensieri' ('ebb and flow of my thoughts'),[52] Quixote thinks to himself 'I cannot be in my right mind, saying and thinking such nonsense' (II, xlvii, 1110). After being trampled by a herd of cattle (II, lviii), Quixote offers his most disillusioned monologue yet: 'Let me die *at the hands of my thoughts* and by means of my misfortunes,' he implores Sancho (italics mine) (II, lix, 842). And in the scene immediately prior to his defeat by Sansón Carrasco, Don Quixote, 'tall, scrawny, lean, sallow, wearing tight-fitting clothes, awkward, and not at all graceful' (II, lxii, 868), exhausted 'not only in body but in spirit', cries out, 'Leave me in peace, *unwelcome thoughts.*' In this one scene, Cervantes performs a narrative zoom, describing the body, speech, spirit and thought, and showing the continuity between each level. We have seen earlier that madness was marked by a disjunction between body, speech and thought. Quixote now looks, speaks and thinks with melancholy, not because he is mad but because he is becoming sane. He is not yet confident enough to reject his entire past but, as he confesses to Sancho after his defeat at the hands (sword) of Sansón Carrasco in the next scene, 'my mind is shaken and confused' (II, lxvi, 895).[53] As we saw with Tasso and Bartolomé Sánchez, the psychological anguish of madness comes not from the unreasonable delusion itself but from the anxiety of being literally *of two minds*, of simultaneously believing the irrational and knowing it not to be so.

Tomás Rodaja was sane. El *licenciado* Vidriera was mad. Tomás Rueda was sane again. There were mad selves and sane selves, and never the two could meet. Cervantes has transcended the pre-novelistic character because he has created *one* character that can be of two minds, a self that is somehow both the sum of its thoughts and acts and yet is greater than any thought or act.

Notes

1. 'I shall not today attempt further to define the kinds of material I understand to be embraced within that shorthand description ["hardcore pornography"]; and perhaps I could never succeed in intelligibly doing so. But I know it when I see it' (Concurring opinion in *Jacobellis v. Ohio*).
2. For example, the entry on the 'novel' begins by asserting that the 'only common attribute is that they [novels] are extended pieces of prose fiction' and then backtracks by noting that the word 'extended . . . begs a number of questions' (Cuddon and Preston: 561).
3. Auger: 203.
4. 'The representation of character occurs . . . in the process of development as the result of events or actions' (Harmon: 354).
5. The various 'schools' of the novel have emphasised each of these elements at the expense of others; we might say that the eighteenth-century novel focused on realism, the nineteenth on character and the twentieth on formal experimentation. This has prompted Francisco Ayala to note that

'everything is in the Quijote' (qtd in Juliá: 17). See my Epilogue, however, for a questioning of any facile genealogical narrative.

6. Andrés Martínez, AHN, Inq. Leg. 40. Exp. 27. I have mixed accounts from three witnesses who observed the scene on various occasions (Ballesteros invited the other two, a notary and a *familiar*, to witness the scene and advise her on what to do).

7. Frye: 7.

8. Lukács: 30.

9. To be 'fuera de sí' is literally to be 'outside one's self' and is a common expression for what would translate most closely in English to being out of one's mind.

10. Pavel: 11.

11. See Forster.

12. Erasmus: 583.

13. Pavel: 11.

14. For a summary of arguments about the integration of the various episodes of *Lazarillo de Tormes*, see Deyermond: 33–43, 71. For an argument for a more 'novelistic' reading of *Lazarillo*, see Cruz, 'Don Quixote', and Friedman.

15. Even Deyermond, arguing for a more 'novelistic' reading of *Lazarillo*, notes that 'The book is Lázaro-centred to an extraordinary degree; after the first few paragraphs, which name his parents and stepfather, no character apart from Lazarillo himself has a name' (Deyermond: 97).

16. Cruz, 'Don Quixote': 24.

17. Pavel: 12.

18. Various critics have compared the two characters and works, in general stressing their similarities. Luís Rosales, for example, calls Vidriera 'a little Don Quixote' (Rosales: 84).

19. English translations and page numbers are from Cervantes Saavedra, *Exemplary Stories*.

20. For discussion of historical cases of glass delusions, see Sevilla Arroyo and Rey Hazas: xl–xli; Speak. Casalduero, *Sentido y forma de las Novelas ejemplares*, vol. 1; El Saffar, *Novel to Romance*; Bunn; and others have done psychoanalytical readings of the tale which find a coherent psychological interiority to the character. I do not dispute the possibility of such coherence, but the language in which these critics express this interiority – 'neurosis', 'shadow projection', 'the ego ideal' – are obviously foreign to the seventeenth century. My argument is to show the way that *Vidriera* and *Quixote* dialogue with conceptions of madness in their own time.

21. For an Erasmian reading of the story, see Sampayo Rodríguez.

22. The most intriguing reading in this vein is offered by Schindler and Jiménez Martín. Building on Martín de Riquer's 'unmasking' of the pseudonymous Avellaneda as Jerónimo de Pasamonte in *Cervantes, Passamonte y Avellaneda*, they make a compelling argument that the Vidriera episode is a response to an episode in Pasamonte's autobiography. This reading confirms our sense that 'Vidriera' is an intertextual game, a satire and *not* an exploration of the experience and effect of madness. See Pasamonte.

23. See Menéndez Pidal.

24. The same argument could be made for those who experienced other

types of nonrational visions for which they were called to account by the Inquisition (or other authorities). As mentioned earlier, the very same behaviours which in men would arouse suspicions of madness were almost always, in women, interpreted as either mystic or demonic visions. In the trials of *beatas* and supposed witches, we see the same demand to account for nonrational experiences. Cañizares's story in 'El coloquio de los perros' shows that the crisis of narrating other types of nonrational experience had similar possibilities for literary innovation; indeed, many consider 'El coloquio' to be more akin to *Don Quixote* in its novelistic approach than to the other *novelas ejemplares* in the collection (Cervantes Saavedra, 'El casamiento engañoso'). See Rey Hazas: 203; El Saffar, 'Montesinos' Cave', for a discussion of the novelistic aspects of 'El casamiento'.

25. Orlando 'Seizes a shepherd, and plucks off his head' (24, v) and 'Twice he ten peasants slaughtered in his mood' (Ariosto 24, x).

26. I have modified Grossman's translation somewhat to restore the indirect objects, which sound somewhat awkward in English but show the degree to which Cardenio has been made an indirect object of his own life.

27. Grossman translates 'extrema' as 'intemperate'.

28. Juan de Trillo, AHN Inq. Leg. 47, Exp. 60.

29. The trial ended soon afterwards and Larrea was set free. The trials of those who suffered from spells of total incoherence or unconsciousness tended to be much shorter than those of the defendants for whom unreason and discourse were not incompatible, but rather inseparable (Juan de Larrea, AHN Leg. 2106, Exp. 28, #28 [*sumario*], Leg. 225, Exp. 21 [*proceso*]).

30. See Chapter 2.

31. A motley assortment of propositions, which he made much worse by insisting whenever corrected that he believed everything he was being told 'si era verdad' ('if it was true').

32. He was indeed, after a four-year trial, sentenced to death and transferred to civil authorities for execution, but one of the jailers in the secular prisons came before the Inquisition to testify that Egujo seemed thoroughly insane, and in the end he was freed.

33. The idea has been suggested to him by others (In I, vii the priest and barber conspire to explain the 'disappearance' of the Don's library by means of this convenient magical scapegoat), but this is the first time Quixote himself offers the explanation to explain a new situation.

34. Alonso de Alarcón. AHN Inq. Leg. 11, Exp. 11. Alarcon claimed that 'si dijo alguna de las díchas blasfemias seria estando loco, más que los que están en la casa del Nuncio' ('if he said any of the aforementioned blasphemies it would have been when he was mad, even more so than the people in the Toledo madhouse') but also that 'siempre ha tenido buen entendimiento y nunca ha hecho ni dicho cosa que parezca de hombre falto de juicio, ni nadie le ha dicho a éste otra cosa ni lo podrá decir' ('he has always had a sound mind and has never done or said anything typical of an insane person, nor has anyone told him otherwise, nor could they').

35. 'Juicio temerario' is literally 'rash judgment' but echoes 'faltar el juicio', 'no tener juicio' et al. (all ways of saying 'mad', damaged powers of judgement, madness).

36. Various critics have seen this episode as a turning point, although they

differ on what is being turned from and to. For Helena Percas de Ponseti, it is Quixote's movement from deluded idealist to impotent realist. For Henry Sullivan, the scene initiates the movement from madness to sanity, but in terms of a metaphoric journey into and out of Purgatory.

37. The question is suggested by Sancho, but Quixote agrees, as he 'still ha[s] certain scruples in that regard' (II, xxv, 922).
38. Tasso, 'Dialogo'.
39. Thiher: 92.
40. Roncoroni: 51–2. I thank Gian Maria Annovi for his assistance with the Italian translations.
41. Tasso (Giovanni Gaetano Bottari and Giovanni Battista Manso).
42. Roncoroni: 165.
43. Ibid.
44. Ibid.: 49.
45. Ibid.
46. Foucault, *Madness and Civilization*: 97.
47. Nalle: 74–5.
48. Ibid.: 95.
49. In fact, the Inquisitors, not wanting to burn Sánchez because of their lingering suspicion that he was mad, had decided beforehand *not* to burn him, but instead to lead him to the stake with the hopes that he would recant. It is not entirely clear whether Sánchez acceded to this plan beforehand. If he did not, then his irrational prophecy of last-minute salvation ironically was fulfilled, in the same way that Quixote's fantasies of giving Sancho an island are fulfilled. If he did, as Nalle suspects, this is evidence of the degree to which the Inquisitors accepted the co-existence of reason and unreason in a subject: they were willing to enter into a rational agreement with him, the necessity for which came from their belief in his unreason (Nalle: 102).
50. Nalle: 106.
51. Ibid.: 107–8.
52. Roncoroni: 165.
53. I have again modified Grossman's translation of 'juicio'.

Chapter 6

Madness, Authority and the Novel

And what to make of the final complete return to sanity? Don Quixote himself presents it as a radical about-face, but the text, as we have seen in the preceding chapter, suggests otherwise; Quixote had been losing faith in his chivalric identity ever since the Cave of Montesinos. There is a sudden reversal here, but it is at the level of form rather than character.[1] Throughout Part II the reader has had to proceed like José Ortega y Gasset's prototypical reader of the novel, 'by trial and error . . . work[ing] out as best he can the actual character' of the figures that the author 'refuses clearly to define'. We have had to 'shape and assemble' Don Quixote 'step by step';[2] now, a (seemingly) omniscient narrative voice re-emerges and gives us a preassembled, predefined protagonist. Not since Cervantes's opening declaration that Don Quixote 'came to lose his mind' (I, i, 21) has Quixote's mental state been so unequivocally announced.[3] From that point on, certainty regarding Don Quixote's condition has steadily eroded. The text's increasing ambiguity occurs on two levels: the characters' growing confusions about Don Quixote's state and the loss of an omniscient narrator guiding the reader to a 'correct' interpretation. And then suddenly, at the end, both ambiguities disappear. Don Quixote declares definitively that 'I was mad, and now I am sane; I was Don Quixote of La Mancha, and now I am, as I have said, Alonso Quixano the Good' (II, lxxiv, 937). His certainty in his own beliefs is nothing new, but for the first time it coincides with the prescribed social narrative. His friends, after an initial suspicion that the conversion might be a 'new madness', agree with the priest that 'Alonso Quixano the Good . . . has truly recovered his reason' (II, lxxiv, 936). And after Quixote's death, Cide Hamete Berengeli makes a definitive declaration of authorial purpose. His 'only desire' in chronicling Quixote's exploits was to 'have people reject and despise the false and nonsensical histories of the books of chivalry' (940). If the books of chivalry are 'false and nonsensical', then Don Quixote, when he believed them, must have been equally senseless; in death, having renounced them, he has finally arrived at the proper perspective. Cide Hamete leaves the reader not just with the proper interpretation of Don Quixote's mind but with a prohibition of alternate readings. Don Quixote was born for him, and any other reading which strays from his own is illegitimate. An astute reader, of course, will note that this strident authorial certainty does not come from the voice of the prologue. Still, the other, original narrator does not contradict or relativise Cide Hamete here, as he has done in the past, and Cide Hamete's repeated reference to the physical act of writing and ceasing to write, and the coincidence of this cessation with the end of the text, makes it natural to conflate the two narrators.

Perhaps it is this final re-emergence of the certainty that was a constant in pre-novel forms, but which Cervantes had so thoroughly eroded, that makes the ending so difficult to swallow for modern (and postmodern) readers. Ambiguity, indeterminacy and the possibility of multiple interpretations are defining attributes of the novel, and the explicit announcement of our main character's mental state and the moral we should take from this raises the suspicion that the work should not be read as a novel but rather as a satire, and Don Quixote's madness as fundamentally similar to that of *el licenciado* Vidriera.

Narrative Experiments

Up to this point, Cervantes has been experimenting with form and narrative voice, emphasising the polyphony of experience and the subjectivity of interpretation. Moreover, this experimentation is consistently tied to the representation of Quixote's madness. Shoshana Felman is, to my knowledge, the only critic to make the connection between the radical formal experimentation of *Don Quixote* and its dominant theme: her intuition may have been correct, but her reading (which, after the initial observation about *Don Quixote*, shifts to Balzac and then Henry James) is anti-historicist and uses modern definitions of madness.[4] Cervantine criticism has instead assumed that *Quixote* drew on earlier literary treatments of madness, an assumption which impeded a connection of the treatment of madness to generic innovation. Yet, the archival accounts of madness regularly betray an indeterminacy regarding the accused's mental state. The resulting undermining of narrative omniscience and authority, although foreign to most premodern literary genres, makes its way into Cervantes's fiction and into the novel.

Indeterminacy of character is directly related to the undermining of authorial authority because one of the main effects of an all-seeing narrator is to dispel interpretive ambiguities. It is the omniscient narrator's opening declaration that Don Quixote had lost his mind which fixes the reader's interpretive starting point. As detailed in the previous chapter, however, somewhere along the line Quixote, like most madmen, begins to show that he has not jumped off a cliff of unreason but is on a road that straddles – and often unexpectedly criss-crosses – the border between sense and madness. It becomes increasingly difficult for outsiders either to pinpoint his location at any given time or to reconcile his varied behaviours with a univocal diagnosis of mad or sane. Not only do the opinions of the characters contradict each other, but also many of the characters who interact with Don Quixote are unable themselves to come to a conclusion. The priest, the canon, Cardenio, Don Diego and his son, Sancho and various minor characters express bewilderment about the would-be knight's mental state. The confusions are twofold: those who suffer Quixote's violence wonder if he is a rogue or out of his mind, while those who witness his saner moments are confused as to whether he is 'mad' or 'wise'.[5]

Doubts voiced in the same terms recur frequently in the testimonies of friends and family called upon by the Inquisition to give their accounts of a questionably sane prisoner. I will cite only a representative few. A neighbour of Juan Antonio Lázaro,[6] when asked to judge the defrocked priest, said:

> que [a él] muchas veces le ha parecido que era loco este reo según las acciones y casos intempestivos y descompuestos que obraba, otras veces se pone a dudar si era verdadera locura o no, con que está confusísimo en hacer juicio si es loco o no lo es, aunque le parece se resolviera más hacia la parte de locura, que de malicia, aunque de cierto no se atreve a confirmar sea verdadera locura, ni tampoco a que sea verdadera malicia, siempre se queda en mucha confusión, y no quisiera hacerle agravio ni faltar a la verdad . . .

> that many times it has seemed to him that the accused was mad, according to his actions and the inopportune and disordered things he did, other times he would start to doubt whether his madness was real or not, and so he is very confused as far as judging whether he is mad or not, although he leans toward saying it is madness rather than malice, although he does not dare to confirm for certain that it is true madness, nor that it is true malice, he has always remained very confused, and he doesn't want to offend him but nor does he want to be untruthful . . .

A co-worker of Juan García, the visionary day labourer discussed in Chapter 2, judged that, based on García's claims of omniscience and other strange statements, he was an 'hombre que hablaba mal' ('a man who spoke badly'), but said that 'fuera de aquello que le tenía por hombre concertado y de buen juicio' ('outside of that he held him to be an organised and reasonable man'). A priest in Almadén said of the defrocked priest Juan Calvo:

> En conclusión no hace juicio fijo del estado de dicho presbítero porque en medio de experimentarle con buen juicio le ha oído algunas veces hablar entre sí, y en preguntándole algunas cosas divinas da buena razón . . . mas en reprehendiéndole de todo lo referido se altera y dice que no lo entienden y si responde algo es de modo que no se puede hacer juicio de lo que dice por no entenderlo; y estando solo habla entre sí preguntándose y respondiéndose y algunas veces ríe muy recio y habla y luego que entra alguna persona se quieta y cesa en todo y habla en forma . . .

> In conclusion, he can't make a fixed judgement as to the said presbyter's state because in the midst of finding him to be in his right mind he has sometimes heard him talking to himself and on asking him about sacred things, he [Calvo] gives well-reasoned answers . . . but upon reprimanding him for everything to which he [the witness] has testified, he [Calvo] becomes upset and says that they don't understand him and if he responds at all it's in such a way that one can't make a judgement about what he says because it can't be understood; and when he is alone he talks to himself, asking himself questions and responding and sometimes he laughs very loudly and speaks and then when someone enters he quiets down and stops altogether and speaks properly . . .

In many cases, the local (lack of) consensus about an individual could be summed up with what one man said of Alonso de Alarcón:[7] 'unos decían que era locura y otros que no lo podía ser' ('some said it was madness and others that it couldn't be').

Yet these witnesses, like the various characters in *Don Quixote* who express confusion or who contradict each other in their diagnoses, are inscribed within a larger narrative, and this larger narrative seemingly has the power to comment on and select among the various opinions expressed, thereby reinscribing heteroglossia within monologic order. The Tribunal could ask further questions of the witnesses, interview the accused and call in doctors to make 'expert' diagnoses, so that the final verdict would provide the 'correct' reading which could account for and thus erase the internal ambiguities. This is more or less what happens in *The Praise of Folly*, *Orlando Furioso* and other precursors of *Don Quixote*: an authoritative voice emerges to provide the proper interpretation.[8] In *La ambigüedad en el Quixote*, Manuel Durán says of Ariosto that, in order to maintain the overall harmony (of language and meaning) of his work, the poet exercises:

> a constant intervention in order to gently modify the march of events, to straighten out those fragile figures and situate them at the necessary distance, each from the other, and all of them before the poet, who continuously con-

trols them and whose power is recognized by all – characters, readers, the poet himself – as the essential element of the work . . . Ariosto intervenes, again and again, in the story.[9]

The same could be said of Erasmus in *The Praise of Folly* or Lope's *Los locos de Valencia*; either before or after the presentation of apparent discord and contradiction, a character or narrator with an unproblematic claim to authority steps in and gives the true explanation.

There is every indication that Cervantes had similar intentions when he began *Don Quixote*. In the prologue, the author seems to declare a simple, didactic intent to ridicule and thus delegitimise books of chivalry. In retrospect, we can find abundant clues that this narrator is not so unproblematically authoritative as his literary predecessors, but the reader, accustomed to confiding in the prologuist's voice, is initially inclined to chalk such disavowals of authority up to modesty. The narrator of the first chapters seems to be an extension of the Prologue's authorial voice, equally omniscient, equally committed to parodying the books of chivalry and those who read them uncritically.

How does this break down? How does Cervantes proceed from this fairly conventional, if delightful, didactic parody to something that resembles a novel precisely because, as Durán affirms, 'the didactic-satiric message *is not clear*',[10] a work so ambiguous and complex that 'the word "perhaps" should never be very far from the critic's lips or pen?'[11]

The Inquisition archives give us a clue as to what produces this onrush of uncertainty. For if we view the Inquisition *proceso* as a text, we see in the more complex insanity defences a similar undoing of authority. The Inquisitors also began each trial with a declaration of authority and intent. Everything in the Inquisition 'genre' was designed to endow the Inquisitors with absolute authority, in matters of heaven and earth, body and soul. When a case did not immediately fall into a known pattern, the Inquisitors, like Ariosto, would begin 'a constant intervention' to 'modify the march of events', to 'straighten out' the defendants and witnesses and 'situate them at the necessary distance, each from the other'. Just as Ariosto introduces John as an apostle *ex machina* to reveal the hidden truth of Orlando's madness, the Inquisitors invoked outside experts – doctors and clergy – to uncover the hidden truths of those who seemed mad or claimed madness.

Yet the *procesos* show that these experts were decidedly less successful than Ariosto's John. Juan Antonio Lázaro's case is typical. In the preliminary testimony gathered by local authorities, a doctor testified that, after consultations, 'concluye en decir, que bien por cierto, que padece un delirio mixto de manía y melancolía, aunque no continuo, por lo cual no se atreve a asegurar si estaba en el delirio actual cuando profirió estas proposiciones' ('he concludes by saying that it is certainly true that he suffers from a delirium that is a mixture of mania and melancholy, although not continuous, due to which he does not dare to say for certain if he was in his current state of delirium when he proffered these propositions').

Of course the last was the key point which would determine whether Lázaro should be punished or pitied, so the local bishop re-examined this doctor and called upon other authorities. Instead of clarifying the matter, however, they only confirmed the inadequacy of contemporary discourses of medicine and religion to understand someone who seemed neither completely rational nor completely mad. On a re-examination, the doctor was asked his opinion of Lázaro's 'accidentes y achaques' ('accidents and attacks'). He responded that after consulations with all of the physicians in town, 'confiriendo la materia y proponiendo todos las especies de delirio individuándoles a este sujeto, no halló ninguno que adecuadamente le conviniera' ('conferring on the matter and proposing each of the types of deliria and fitting them to this subject, they could find none that adequately suited him'). This doctor thus asked another doctor for his opinion, and the second physician responded that 'era materia muy dificultosa, y que necesitaba de tiempo para verla' ('it was a very difficult matter, that he needed time to consider it'), but that he was leaning toward a diagnosis of mixed mania and melancholy. Based on this, the first doctor said that his judgement was that Lázaro 'tiene el celebro muy débil y flaco' ('he has a very weak and flaccid brain'). Still, in order to be sure he went to see him several times to ask questions. Lázaro seemed to respond 'muy en su ser' ('very much in his wits'). Stuck, the doctor:

> encargó a algunos religiosos atendieran a sus acciones y le hicieran algunas preguntas; y que después les preguntó qué juicio habían hecho, [y] respondieron . . . habían observado en él muy buena inteligencia, y que discurría muy bien, y le parece debe ser así.

> ordered some religious men to attend to his actions and ask him some questions; and afterwards he asked them what judgement they had made, and they replied . . . they had observed him to have very good intelligence, that he held forth well, and it seems to him this must be the case.

Having heard these conflicting diagnoses, the local authorities voted to refer Lázaro, along with the records of these various opinions and doubts, to the Inquisition – essentially passing on the problem. The Inquisition, unhappy with the less-than-authoritative 'must be the case' of the local experts, assumed the task of constructing a convincing narrative, ordering that 'se tengan con este reo diferentes audiencias extraordinarias para reconocer por ellas su capacidad, tratando en ellas diferentes materias' ('they hold various extraordinary *audiencias* with the accused in order to recognise his capacity, touching on different subjects in each one'). But after three such meetings, the only thing they could definitively state was that 'no se puede formar entero juicio de la capacidad o incapacidad total de este reo' ('they cannot form a definitive judgement of the accused's capacity or total incapacity' and thus they suggested continuing and then, after the accusation and his responses, 'se vuelva a ver y votar' ('they return to consider and vote').

By proceeding, they maintained the semblance of the traditional Inquisitional narrative, but the fact that they could not, despite ample testimonies and interviews, determine Lázaro's inner state undermined their role as omniscient narrators, for the Inquisition's jurisdiction *was* this very inner state, the human soul. Their inability to synthesise the voices of the various characters in 'their' text, and their call to re-examine all of the witnesses interviewed in the preliminary investigations as well as all other 'religiosos principales' ('prominent religious men') who had come in contact with Lázaro, 'informándose del modo con que se portó . . . y qué juicio hicieron de él' ('informing them of his manner of conducting himself . . . and what judgement they made of him') revealed the failure of their own omniscient authority. Six more months of *audiencias*, medical examinations and depositions followed.[12]

Juan Calvo's case followed a similar trajectory. The first doctor to examine him noted the inconsistencies cited above and gave the exceedingly unhelpful final verdict that 'se halla neutral en el sentir y conocimiento del estado y dolencia que haya padecido o padece dicho presbítero, y en singular por ser punto que toca su conocimiento más a los físicos que a los cirujanos' ('he finds himself neutral in his feeling and knowledge of the condition and ailment that said presbyter has suffered or suffers, and in particular because it is a matter that corresponds more to the knowledge of a physician than a surgeon'). The Tribunal, without a definite lead to follow, called upon a full team of 'médicos y cirujanos, y exorcistas inteligentes, personas que convengan' ('physicians and surgeons, and intelligent exorcists, and all other suitable people') and also asked functionaries to write to the other Tribunals to check their archives for any trace of previous offences. The net result of the consultations was a variety of conflicting opinions, as we see in the Inquisitors' summary:[13]

Juan Calvo estuvo tenido por loco o espiritado . . . dicen los testigos últimamente examinados y el primer médico que le tienen por de sano juicio y no espiritado. El cirujano no se atreve a dar censura. El segundo médico, motivado con fundamentos físicos, se inclina a que está leso de la cabeza.

Juan Calvo was held to be mad or possessed . . . the most recently examined witnesses and the first doctor say they hold him to be of sane mind and not possessed. The surgeon does not dare to make a judgement. The second doctor, based on medical principles, leans toward declaring him mentally damaged.

A letter from the *familiar* who had gathered the testimonies was more blunt: 'en vista de la ultima declaración . . . quedo más confuso que estaba y suspendo mi dictamen' ('in view of the ultimate declaration . . . I am left more confused than I had been and I suspend my judgement'). The very *proceso* ends ambiguously. In the last recorded meeting, the Inquisitors seemed inclined to keep digging, voting to continue the case. Yet there is no record of further proceedings, and on the cover of the *proceso* we read 'soltado por loco' ('released as mad'). How the case passed from imprisonment and confiscation to 'released as mad' is a mystery, as abrupt and frustrating to this reader as the break in *Quixote* I, viii is to the 'the second author of this work' (64).[14]

Blocked in their claim to omniscience, the Inquisitors sought out other archives, other opinions, other recorders of human actions and minds. In the search for anyone who might bridge sudden ruptures in knowledge and speech, they ended up authorising (both giving authority to and making into authors) new voices and typically marginalised or invisible figures, just as the abrupt end of the first *Quixote* manuscript gave authority to an Arab historian and a *morisco* translator. If we look at the *procesos* where such shifting of narrators occurs, we see an operation that is at the heart of the narrative structure of *Quixote* and much subsequent fiction: a rivalry between narrators' competing claims to truth.

Bartolomé Sánchez's case shows clearly how the inability to represent and comprehend unreason created multiple narrative authorities but also destabilised them. In his first trial, Sánchez's delusional self-confidence and penchant for sharing his thoughts made him an atypical defendant. Nalle notes that Pedro Cortes, the judge in his first trial, 'did not conduct a normal trial with the wool carder'.[15] While the judge-accused relationship was typically adversarial:

because Cortes was convinced that Sánchez was not mentally competent to stand trial, his primary concern was to save his prisoner's life – he did not want a judicial murder on his conscience. To this end, he spent many hours in conversation with Sánchez before the formal indictment of the prisoner, all in an attempt to persuade the wool carder to recant. The result is a document that records a lively debate between two individuals, each equally committed to the justice of his position.[16]

Of course these same discussions provided the *source* of Cortes's suspicion that Sánchez was not sane, but the more articulately Sánchez presented his thoughts the less inclined the Tribunal was to accept a plea of insanity. The discussions became the means through which Cortes, who logically did not believe in the prisoner's capacity to repent (as this would require that he had knowingly sinned, something the madman cannot do) would try to exhort him, via reason, to do exactly that. In analysing the motives for Cortes's unusual willingness to listen to and engage the accused, we cannot discount the fact that Sánchez was, like Don Quixote, 'a natural-born storyteller, a good debater, and at times a convincing liar'.[17] Nalle finds it unusual for the accused to be allowed to speak without interruption as much as Sánchez did, but, in fact, we frequently see this same freedom to narrate granted: as, for example, to Alonso Mendoza, Juan Egujo and Alonso Hernández Tejero.[18] The nature of these men's mental state – reasonable enough to represent themselves coherently but not enough not to recognise the inappropriateness (if not folly) of doing so – made them seductive and complicated narrators. The Inquisitors had to listen to them because within their discourse lay the key to a judgement and verdict, and they very well may have *wanted* to listen to them, as drawn to colourful stories and entertaining logic as is every reader and listener in *Don Quixote*. At the same time, the contradiction between the defendant's linguistic competence and logical incompetence made the Inquisitors' judgement and verdict – that pretext for allowing the speech to begin with – more difficult. To resolve this difficulty, the Inquisitors called in additional experts and witnesses. But the intractable paradoxes of madness, in an age without a language to speak of them, tended to confound the experts as much as the Inquisitors, and, rather than offering a narrative which could restore the hierarchical model of authority, the proliferation of expert opinions quite often destabilised the proceedings even further. New narrative voices emerge from 'above' and 'below'; in several cases, not only do the experts and witnesses, whose contributions should theoretically be subordinate to the judge's narrative frame (i.e., the Inquisitor functions as the omniscient author who allows, within his text, these voices to speak, but has the final word), resist incorporation into a clear narrative, but other equally authoritative voices – the *Suprema*, the prosecutor – began to intervene and protest. As a student of narratology, aware that 'authorial distance is the prerequisite of control',[19] would expect, these more distant authorities were less sympathetic to the contradictions and circular discourses which the judges and the accused were constructing. In one trial for blasphemy,[20] we find a letter from the *Suprema* chastising the Tribunal for stretching the proceedings out for five years as they attempted to 'sentar el juicio' ('establish the mental state') of the accused. The Suprema pointed out the inconsistency of simultaneously proceeding with the prosecution and the investigation of an insanity defence – 'si tuvisteis duda del juicio, ¿para qué fueron las sesiones de los calificadores?' ('if you had doubts about his mental state, what was the purpose of the sessions with the *calificadores?*'). The Suprema was obviously unconvinced by the insanity defence, concluding from the transcripts of the sessions that 'se conoce su ficción y malicia' ('his fiction and malice are manifest'), but they reserved their harshest judgement for the local Tribunal itself, almost mockingly recounting all the years of sessions and inaction and chiding them for 'hacer esta causa inmortal' ('making this case go on forever'). The letter ends with the order that, 'sin perder hora de tiempo; proseguiréis esta causa en la forma ordinaria y según estilo del Santo Oficio' (without wasting a minute of time; you shall proceed with this case in the standard form and according to the practice of the Holy Office').

This voice assumes the same role as the voice which emerges at the end of *Quixote* I, viii: that of the 'supernarrator' (as James Parr calls him), who can 'organize and manipulate the discourse of all the subordinate voices',[21] and who makes visible a whole new frame of which the reader had not until that moment been aware. In *Quixote*, of course, this 'supernarrator' does not get the last word – his emergence as an authority is almost immediately undermined by voices from within his own text, to the point where the debates between authorities almost *become* the text, overshadowing the points about which they are arguing.

We do not have any further record of the trial cited above, but something quite similar happens in Bartolomé Sánchez's case. A year after Sánchez's second trial, which had essentially ended with the judges, Riego and Moral, giving up on making heads or tails of Sánchez's culpability and letting him go with a public whipping and the threat that they could reopen the case whenever they deemed it necessary, the prosecutor protested to the *Suprema*. He complained that Sánchez 'siempre ha estado en su juicio . . . y no hay muestras de que lo pasado hubiese sido con enajenación alguna dél sino por maldad' ('has always been in his right mind . . . and there is no evidence that what occurred was with any derangement on his part, but instead [was done] out of evil'). Riego and Moral, presumably hoping to avoid a reprimand like the one delivered above, defended their own actions. In order to strengthen the authority of their narrative, however, they took a 'highly unusual' step:[22] they asked the notary, Juan Ybaneta, who had also served as the notary for Sánchez's first trial, to give a deposition regarding his impressions of the defendant. As in *Don Quixote*, in the battle for authority, the translator became visible, supplying the authority and the text for the author who suddenly found himself without either. Yet from both Ybaneta and the *morisco* translator, what the reader learns is all that he has not learned – all the words and acts that the scribe 'intentionally . . . passes over in silence' (I, ix, 68).

Ybaneta's report reveals both why a scribe's intervention was uncommon and why, in the presence of madness, it would seem so necessary. He reported that in Sánchez's first trial, after he witnessed several *audiencias* in which the wool carder 'entró en la sala . . . como hombre furioso o endemoniado, haciendo muchos personajes de su persona y diciendo y hablando muchos desatinos' ('entered the courtroom . . . like a madman or someone possessed, striking many poses with his person and talking a lot of nonsense'),[23] he went to the Inquisitor and pleaded that, since clearly 'en este reo no se hallaba tan entera capacidad ni el juicio que convenía en tan grave negocio' ('in this defendant there was not to be found enough competence or reason requisite for such a serious affair'), the prosecution be put off until it could be determined 'si éste era endemoniado o había perdido el juicio' ('if he were possessed or had lost his mind').[24] Cortes had answered that 'más adelante se podría proveer en todo' ('later on everything could be decided'), and the trial had continued. A first level of silences is revealed; in the transcript of the first trial, none of this appears. This puts the lie to the idea of a text which can be 'exact, truthful, and absolutely free of passions' and of authors for whom 'neither interest, fear, rancor, nor affection should make them deviate from the path of truth' (I, ix, 68). The scribe's erasure of his own intervention forms the text and shapes its outcome no less than the intervention itself.

This is the very complaint that the second author initially has against Cide Hamete: that, in failing to praise Quixote properly, he has done a disservice to his subject. We might say that Ybaneta's first silence (his silence about his own silencing by Cortes) was 'remedied' by the revelation of such in the second trial, but in the rest of his declaration he reveals a pattern of more systematic and irrecoverable silences. For Cortes, he says, then told him to continue recording the *audiencias* but only 'tomando en ellas de sus palabras lo que más hacía a la materia de sus proposiciones' ('taking down in them those of his words which formed the core of his propositions').[25] This meant leaving out 'muchas cosas de las que decía por ser desatinos e disparates' ('many of the things he said because they were nonsense and more nonsense'). The statements he did write down, Ybaneta continued, 'las fue ordenando sin quitar ni añadir en la sustancia cosa alguna' ('he went along organising them without removing or adding anything in their substance').[26] Even in revealing his editorial intervention, Ybaneta maintains the fiction of transparency, the possibility of reordering thoughts without changing 'anything in their substance', especially when the disorder of those thoughts would have been chief evidence of the insanity of the speaker. The lines between authors, narrators and scribes, between mimesis and diegesis, become tangled, just as they do in *Quixote*. In both, the breakdowns of narrative clarity are tied to madness.

Ybaneta's first intervention, his leap into the narration of the *proceso*, came because he felt compelled to address the Tribunal's failure, as he saw it, to interpret Sánchez's capacity correctly. Cortes had ordered Ybaneta to change the *representation* of the trial, to give up the struggle of representing speech and thought that exceeded reason and instead to record only those parts which were rational, and even then to arrange them coherently. Exploring the limits of language and of human consciousness was not the goal of a legal tribunal charged with keeping all of Cuenca from descent into apostasy. By forcing a confession and repentance, however logically improbable their value, Cortes hoped to skirt the whole madness issue. Yet this madness, having been swept under the rug, proved irrepressible, and the limits of language and consciousness again brought the Tribunal to its knees. Ybaneta's intervention, the moment when he revealed his first intervention and all the other invisible ones along the way, was a direct result of this crisis. This intervention both established his authority and completely stripped him of it. The *Suprema* sided with Riego and Moral, presumably influenced by Ybaneta's testimony. However, after the trial, Ybaneta was fired for overstepping his authority in this and various other trials – for revealing his own *protagonismo* in a genre that insisted on the fiction of his invisibility.

While this was the only trial I saw in which the notary testified, there are multiple examples which feature more subtle scribal interventions: changes in voice, deletions, reorderings, opinions. Often these are unattributed, blended into the narrative as unexpectedly as Cide Hamete's 'I swear as a Catholic Christian' (II, xxvii, 636). The switches in voice are particularly subtle, because of the Inquisitorial practice of recording all testimony in the third person. This shift in voice obviously implies a constant editorial intervention, but through most of the proceedings the scribe gives the impression of direct representation, a mere switch from 'My name is Fulano' to 'He said his name was Fulano.' The record of a session in which various priests attempted to make Juan Egujo affirm more orthodox views begins in this vein, but veers back and forth into an editorial voice which clearly is not Egujo's.

Habiéndole [the Jesuit priests] con razones procurado disuadir, que respondió que había de venir el río en una carroza del cielo diez veces mayor que todo ese cielo, la cual habían de tirar bueyes o animales, y que tendrían mucho refrigerio con el frescor y *otros semejantes disparates que no se pueden reducir a escrito*. Y habiéndole preguntado si los ángeles bajan a la tierra por bastimento para comer, que respondió que no ha dicho que bajan sino que pueden bajar . . . y habiéndole procurado disuadir deste error *respondió, como en lo demás, mil disparates* . . . (italics mine)

[The Jesuit priests] having tried to dissuade him with reasons, he replied that the river was going to come in a carriage from the sky ten times bigger than all this sky, which would be drawn by mules or animals, and that its coolness would offer great refreshment *and other similar nonsense that can't be put down in writing*. And having asked him if angels descend to the earth for provisions to eat, he replied that he hadn't said that they descend but that they can descend . . . and having tried to disabuse him of this error, *he responded, as with the rest, a million bits of nonsense* . . .

Sometimes it seems that Egujo's translator[27] was the editor and the scribe the 'transparent' recorder of this editing ('y dijo a cada cosa el Padre intérprete que no respondía a propósito de lo que le preguntaba y proponía sino que a cada cosa respondía disparates' ['and to everything, the Father interpreting said that he did not respond to the question asked but instead responded with nonsense']), but at other times the translator, although noted as present, is not mentioned ('y preguntado del santo sacramento de la eucaristía y del bautismo y otros misterios, respondió otros semejantes disparates' ['and asked about the holy sacrament of the Eucharist and baptism and other mysteries, he responded with other similar nonsense']).

We see this same tension and blurring of the roles of characters, translators, narrators and authors in *Don Quixote*. Even if we agree with James Parr that much of the conflict between the *morisco* translator, Cide Hamete, the Second Author and the supernarrator is a 'a joke played on unsuspecting readers . . . a transparently parodic literary device',[28] it is still worth taking this joke seriously, as games and jokes are cultural products too. Some of the skirmishes between various levels of narrators may be largely comic or parodic, but the existence and visibility of these tensions is integral to the themes of the work as a whole.

Most critics who have written on the narrative strategies of the *Quixote* note, quite rightly, that the multiple frames and narrators draw attention to the pitfalls and tricks of writing and reading.[29] This, however, is only part of the story; it is quite often specifically in the attempt to represent unreason that these narrators run aground. When the 'sane' characters tell stories, they are generally in command of their narration. Their authority as narrators, and the very possibility of communicating what they seek to convey, is not called into question. Were Cervantes's 'parodic literary device' disconnected from madness, we would expect it to appear throughout these episodes, and yet the only intercalated story in which representation becomes a bigger problem than that which is represented is the account of the mad Cardenio, interrupted by the mad Quixote. It also seems telling that the increasing prominence of the narrative battles parallels the increasing complexity of madness in the work; the first eight chapters are told by a fairly unproblematic omniscient narrator (who, as we have seen, has no problem peeking into Don Quixote's mind and informing the reader precisely which screws have come loose), and Cide Hamete and his translator are far more present in Part II, which, as we have seen, is also when Cervantes increasingly complicates his portrayal of his protagonist's madness.[30]

There are two cases where Cide Hamete's interjection is a direct reaction to Don Quixote's madness: an exclamation of amazement and disbelief that echoes the reactions of so many characters within his narrative. These come precisely at what I have identified as the key transitional points in the portrayals of Sancho and Don Quixote, respectively. Just before the scene in which Sancho recognises his master's madness and takes advantage of it, Cide Hamete announces that he:

> would have preferred to pass over it in silence, fearful it would not be given credence, for the madness of Don Quixote here reached the limits and boundaries of the greatest madnesses that can be imagined, and even passed two crossbow shots beyond them. (II, x, 513)

The inverisimilitude of what he is about to relate causes Cide Hamete to fear that he will lose his credibility as an author, and so he is forced to step outside of his position of invisible, omniscient historian to insist on his veracity. These comments about verisimilitude obviously engage a centuries-old debate about aesthetic representation, and Cervantes' position in this debate has been amply studied.[31] Here Cervantes ties a philosophical or aesthetic discussion to a historical, social one: what must and cannot be represented is the inverisimilar, but, as we have seen, Don Quixote's madness is, in many ways, entirely verisimilar. Cide Hamete's very need to insist that he is telling the truth and nothing but the truth puts the lie to his assertion that 'truth may be stretched thin and does not break' (Ibid.). *Reasonable* truth is strong and will not break. When attempting to represent *unreasonable* truth, however, one must seek new methods of self-authorisation.

This becomes critical again at the crucial turning point in Don Quixote's madness: the descent into the Cave of Montesinos. Once again, the narrator who has frequently boasted of his omniscience is unable to reconcile the improbability of the knight's account of a mad vision with his own previous assertion of Don Quixote's truthfulness. He does not know how to insert his own doubt into the text he is supposed to control, and so he steps outside the text and his omniscience to scribble in the margins:

> I cannot believe, nor can I persuade myself, that everything written in the preceding chapter actually happened in its entirety to the valiant Don Quixote: the reason is that all the adventures up to this point have been possible and plausible, but with regard to this one in the cave I can find no way to consider it true since it goes so far beyond the limits of reason. But it is not possible for me to think that Don Quixote, the truest and most noble knight of his day, would lie . . . if this adventure seems apocryphal, the fault is not mine, and so, without affirming either its falsity or its truth, I write it down. (II, xxiv, 614)

The judgement of verisimilitude and truth depends on 'the limits of reason'; madness upsets the fundamental Aristotelian binary between truth and falsehood because what is truth for the speaker *seems* false, and yet judgement of both the 'objective' truth (did the vision occur?) and the 'subjective' truth (did Quixote really *think* he had that vision?) require access to invisible, interior processes. Cervantes could have endowed Cide Hamete with the power to know the answer to either question, but he chooses instead to revoke his omniscience precisely at this moment in order to emphasise the conundrums that unreason presents for the usual mental processes by which we 'know' and 'judge' others' stories. A frustrated Cide Hamete passes the mantle of authority and omniscience to others, just as the Inquisitors had to call on everyone from soup kitchen servers to cellmates to their own scribes to 'judge it according to your own lights, for I must not and cannot do more' (Ibid.).

The motivation for almost all of the narrative interruptions in the novel is a crisis of coherence and authority. We have seen that these two themes are central to the experience of the *loco* and of those who seek to interact with him or represent his speech and actions. The Inquisition accounts reveal the textual ruptures which occurred when an official who needed to produce an authoritative and coherent text came upon a subject whose experience was defined by incomprehensibility and incoherence. The Inquisitors' job was that of the omniscient narrator *par excellence*: they were to examine the speech, acts and *soul* of the accused, and then pronounce a verdict which told THE story, to be read aloud as the punishment was enacted so that the audience could come to only one conclusion and take only one moral lesson from the scene. Yet we have seen how on both a personal and textual level the madman destabilised this process. Cervantes's text shows the same struggles over the 'proper' way to create a coherent narrative that is made up of incoherent utterances, yet, rather than try to conceal the destabilisation, he foregrounds it.

Thus in Part II, Chapter x – the very same chapter where both Cide Hamete and Sancho reveal their doubts as to Don Quixote's mental state – Cervantes begins to poke holes in the possibility of omniscience in general. From this point on, the narrator will increasingly register indeterminacies, even outside the immediate context of describing Don Quixote's behaviour, and often without explicitly commenting on them, such as when we read that the protagonists 'found a stand of trees or a wood' (II, ix, 512) and in the next chapter, the author, 'continuing his history', refers to Don Quixote's entry into 'a wood, oak grove, or forest near the great Toboso' (II, x, 513). The crisis of narrating madness is the catalyst for a broader destabilisation of narration and narrator.

These lapses in the omniscience of the supposed authority create spaces into which other authorial voices emerge, at the same time competing for and denying the possibility of omniscience and invisibility. Chapter x begins in what we think is the omniscient narrator's voice: 'Coming toward [Sancho] from the direction of Toboso were three peasant girls on three jackasses, or jennies' (II, x, 516); as the sentence continues, however, we find ourselves in narrative no-man's land:

> since the author does not specify which they were, though it is more likely that they were she-donkeys, for they are the ordinary mounts of village girls, but since not much depends on this, there is no reason to spend more time verifying it. (Ibid.)

With that 'since the author does not specify' the reader's sense of who is speaking is suddenly destabilised. And yet this new narrator immediately reveals that his knowledge is as imperfect as that of the previous narrator whom he is criticising, at which point he must hastily invent a pretext to excuse his fault, offering very unconvincingly that the distinction is unimportant. Of course this pretext undermines the necessity of his intervention to begin with, and the net effect is an undermining of both authorial voices. Instead of a greater authority correcting a lesser one, we get two narrators who not only reveal themselves to have incomplete knowledge of their subject but to be untrustworthy in their false profession of completeness. The scene is not about Don Quixote's madness per se, but we recognise the uncertainty and the destabilisation of voices that madness introduces. Cervantes explores these uncertainties in all corners of his text, but they radiate from its centre.

Satire, *Proceso* and the Novel

The fact that the text's formal experimentation grows naturally, almost inevitably, from the madness of its central character and from character-driven narrative is why, despite many formal similarities, it is not, in the end – despite the end – primarily a satire.[32] Not all of the elements of a work as heterogeneous and complex as *Don Quixote* stem from a single idea, but the majority of the parody and polemic in *Quixote* comes from problems suggested by the questions at its core: questions about self-knowledge, ethics and the mind. In satire, the parody and polemic are ends in themselves; if there is any unifying thread, it is generally a desacralising one, aimed at debasing such exalted concepts as knowledge, ethics and mind. Bakhtin writes that the laughter of satire:

> has the remarkable power of making an object come up close, of drawing it into a zone of crude contact where one can finger it familiarly on all sides, turn it upside down, inside out, peer at it from above and below, break open its external shell, look into its center, doubt it, take it apart, dismember it, lay it bare and expose it.[33]

Don Quixote certainly produces laughter, but it is not *this* laughter. The focus on the struggles that a *character* experiences creates a laughter that is mixed with empathy, admiration and self-doubt about the very ethics of laughing. The very diversity of readings of the *Quixote* points to the affiliation with a more ambiguous and indeterminate genre than satire. Satirical laughter depends on an unambiguous identification of the laughable 'object'; the polyphony within the text must be subsumed into a greater structure which allows the reader to laugh confidently at the parodied voices. An all-authoritative narrator must convey to the reader a sense of certainty and superiority that presupposes an ability to peer into, break open and dismember an object. But by the time Don Quixote returns home for the last time, we the readers, like the characters, are unsure of how to categorise Don Quixote: we have ample evidence of his wisdom and his folly, his violence and his suffering, his cruelty and his charity, his self-knowledge and his delusion. That single, omniscient narrator who had once informed us of who Don Quixote was and what to think of him has disappeared some thousand pages ago, replaced by a chorus of narrators and more or less 'false' authors (the Avellaneda text having been worked into the Cervantine to further complicate matters of real and spurious authority) who are hardly more trustworthy than the characters they would describe (and perhaps less so, as the characters themselves have had plenty to say about their own narration). We are in the same position as the Inquisitors or the modern reader of Juan Egujo or Juan Calvo or Gaspar García Tenorio's file: moved, touched, amused, entertained, enlightened and stumped.

Yet there is one huge difference between all of these Inquisition files and the *Quixote*. The lives recounted in these files do not end; the narrative arc of the *proceso* extends only to the end of the trial. The record of Juan Arias's trial shows us the limitations of Inquisitional narrative and the possibilities it opens up for art.[34] Arrested for making heretical statements in public and in a cleric's frock, Arias described his ten-year downward spiral after being, as he himself put it, 'expulso de su religion por incorregible, y por diversas enfermedades que ha tenido de melancolía . . . y por haberse perdido en los sermones' ('expelled from his order as incorrigible, and for various illnesses of melancholy he has had . . . and because he lost himself in the sermons'). For most of the *audiencia*, Arias was able to give at least a semi-coherent representation of episodes in the past. However, after hours of discourse about his life, he said that:

> Había año y medio que estando en Segovia tuvo unas pasiones del alma estando diciendo misa, y con esto empezó un largo discurso de pensamientos que había tenido en que por ser dada la hora y tarde no se prosiguió en la audiencia . . .

> A year and a half ago when he was in Segovia he experienced some passions of the soul while he was saying mass, and with this he began a long speech about the thoughts he had had in which, time being up and it being late, the *audiencia* was not continued.

While speaking rationally of his tendency to 'perderse' ('get lost/lose himself') while giving sermons, Arias 'se perdió' ('got lost').

The reader feels as if a door has slammed in his or her face – the door to Arias's thoughts and feelings. The Tribunal, interested only in making a specific determination on a legal matter, did not find it useful to continue the session or record the discourse. In successive *audiencias*, Arias repeated this movement from reasoned representation of mad experiences to incoherent, mad representation of . . . something we cannot know. Each time, the trigger seems to have been the discussion of his actions during the mass; this is his knight errantry, the black hole into which his reason is drawn and from which it does not emerge. The Inquisitional *genre* was not interested in what happened in this black hole. All that mattered was the determination of unreason itself; they had no interest in the journeys that the mind would make or language would take once it had left the realm of reason. Similarly, they were uninterested in the afterlives of their defendants; the moment a case was suspended or a verdict given, even when that verdict or suspension was forced by a need to move on rather than the resolution of any doubts or the assertion of any truth, the story stopped.

To journey into the unreasonable mind, to take interest in all that went on after the jurist or theologian ceased to be interested, would require a new genre, a genre that made the human mind itself its principal object. Freed from the need to pronounce a definitive verdict of innocence or guilt, this genre could indulge in digression, ambiguity and paradox. Yet Cervantes had learned from his Part I of the dangers of suspending a case, of leaving an ambiguous, open-ended narrative in the public domain. If he was going to kill off his protagonist and declare him off limits to other would-be authors, he would have to reclaim a certain degree of authorial power. To leave Quixote's final moments as indeterminate or ambiguous as his final weeks would be to open the door to uncharitable interpretations and, even worse, sequels. And so Cervantes, having moved steadily away from the black-and-white world of romance and epic madness to the greys of real insanity, decided to reclaim his right as an author to proclaim truth and omniscience.

The Inquisitors also ended their cases with a definitive, omniscient pronouncement regarding the mental state of their 'protagonists'. Yet there are key differences between the Cervantine and the Inquisitorial gesture. The Inquisition files were kept secret precisely so that no one would see the competing narrations, destabilisation of authority and inscribed ambiguity that preceded the definitive sentence. In *Don Quixote*, however, the reader has been privy to a thousand pages of narrative struggle. The final chapter of the book, read in isolation, seems to have the same omniscient narrator as the first chapter. But for the reader who still does not know if the peasant girls came on jennies or she-donkeys and remembers an 'author' who 'does not specify which they were', the narrative certainty of the end rings hollow. It is not so much that we doubt Quixote/Quijano's return to reason – as we have seen, this has been developing for chapters – as we doubt the return to certainty and narrative stability. And indeed Cide Hamete doth seem to protest too much.

Still, the majority of readers have accepted the reality of the re-conversion of Quixote to Quijano (even those who feel it is a betrayal, the *wrong* ending, are implicitly acknowledging that it is *the* ending) and, by extension, the authority of the narrator who tells us this was so. I would argue that Cervantes takes advantage of the power of fiction to leave them this option. On the one hand, he gives them every reason to doubt the final sentence, to accept that madness, and modern literature, may be irremediably ambiguous. On the other hand, for the reader who seeks closure, he also offers a plausible 'happy ending'. And he takes advantage of his power with these readers to define that happy ending on his own terms. He very well could have had Don Quixote die in his delusions or even because of them, flattened to a pulp by a wine press he mistook for a dragon. The choice to reclaim Don Quixote's sanity is an affirmation of Don Quixote's humanity. Cervantes allows his *loco* to escape the ignominious end of the *loco* in Avellaneda – the disappearance into the madhouse – and the ignominious lack of an end of the *locos* before the Inquisition – the disappearance into oblivion the moment the Inquisitors lose interest. Or, at the very least, he allows that escape for those who wish to see it.

Cervantes's end, then, is a windmill-giant, a *baciyelmo*, an *ambigüe-certeza* (an open *and* shut case). This is the power of the novel: not only can it engage the archive in order to then escape it, but it can simultaneously engage *and* escape it.

Notes

1. Manuel de la Puebla summarises the 'many and very serious problems' (117) and various critical responses to this last chapter. He acknowledges the tension between a recognition that Cervantes 'has from chapters far back been preparing this resolution, this return of the protagonist to sanity' (119) and the reader's shock, the sense of 'betrayal' (119) because Cervantes 'had led us to expect another death' (118) .
2. Ortega y Gasset: 303.
3. Grossman has 'causing him to lose his mind'.
4. Felman: 101.
5. Grossman alternately translates 'discreto' as 'wise', 'clever', 'well-reasoned' and 'intelligent', among other things.
6. Juan Antonio Lázaro, AHN, Inq. Lib. 944, fols 261–6.
7. Alonso de Alarcón. AHN Inq. Leg. 11, Exp. 11.
8. In Canto 34 of *Orlando Furioso*, Astolpho rises to the heavens, where the apostle John (*sine qua non* of omniscient, authoritative narrators) puts Orlando's madness into the proper narrative and provides Astolpho with the magical remedy. According to the Prophet, Orlando was 'selected from the crowd / To be defender of his Church's right', but 'such gifts has made Unto his heavenly Lord an ill return . . . Hence God hath made him mad' (34, lxii–lxvii).
9. Durán: 46.
10. Ibid.: 240.
11. Ibid.: 9.
12. They finally decided that Lázaro was insane, and thus voted to suspend the case and have him placed 'en puesto cómodo y conveniente, asi para la aplicación de los remedios' ('in a comfortable and convenient place, for the application of remedies').
13. I have eliminated the references to folio numbers that accompanied each different opinion in the summary.

14. This second author protests the break in the manuscript: '[he] did not want to believe that so curious a history would be subjected to the laws of oblivion, or that the great minds of La Mancha possessed so little interest that they did not have in their archives or writing tables a few pages that dealt with the famous knight' (*Don Quixote* I, viii, 64).
15. Nalle: 4.
16. Ibid.
17. Ibid.: 6.
18. See Chapter 2.
19. Parr, *Touchstone*: 181.
20. The letter follows the summary of the *proceso* of Jacinto Pellicer (Lib. 940, fols 250–4). While Pellicer did claim insanity, the dates of the two cases do not match, and the letter, while exceedingly difficult to read, seems to be referring to a female. For my point, however, it makes little difference whether the letter refers to Pellicer's case or another with similar difficulties.
21. Parr, *Touchstone*: 22.
22. Nalle: 128.
23. Ibid.: 129.
24. Ibid.
25. Ibid.
26. Ibid.
27. Egujo was a native French speaker (although he spoke Spanish fairly well, as we learn by a note following the transcript of an *audiencia* which Egujo himself called, which reads 'no fue necesario intérprete porque se entendía bien lo que responde' ['a translator was unnecessary because his answers were easily understood']), which makes this transcript all the more quixotically polyphonic. In the first *audiencia*, he was not provided with a translator, and answered most questions – even about simple things like his parentage – with 'no lo sabe' ('he does not know'). Once a translator was brought in, he (we suppose – the translations are not recorded) asked him the same questions and reported that 'dice que no lo sabe' ('he says he does not know'). A few *audiencias* later, there is another note asking for someone who 'tenga verdadera inteligencia de la lengua francesa, porque según se ha reconocido deste proceso los que hasta ahora le han tratado, dan a entender que muchas de las palabras que habla este reo no las entienden' ('someone with true knowledge of the French language, because, according to what has been recognised by those who have dealt with him up to now in this trial, it is to be understood that they don't understand the majority of the words this defendant says'), although there has been no record of unintelligible answers (only unorthodox and illogical thoughts) up to then. The interventions of the translator are entirely inconsistent – at times the scribe notes the act of translation, at other times the translator is either not there, is rendered invisible or was speaking on his own (since he was a priest).
28. Parr, *Touchstone*: 34.
29. For example, Forcione, *Cervantes, Aristotle, and the Persiles*.
30. As Howard Mancing notes, Cide Hamete is mentioned 31 times in Part II as opposed to 5 times in Part I (qtd in Parr, *Touchstone*: 35).

31. See Riley and Forcione, *Cervantes, Aristotle, and the Persiles*.
32. Parr and Close, among others, make the argument for reading it as such.
33. Bakhtin, *Dialogic Imagination*: 23.
34. Juan Arias Dávila, AHN Inq. Leg. 213, Exp. 5.

Epilogue (Second Sally)

I have argued that a 'novel' understanding of (or difficulty in understanding) madness in early modern Spain leads to the development of the early modern Spanish novel (or, rather, to the development of a work whose characteristics would come to be associated with the novel). Yet the novel has, as Diana de Armas Wilson notes, 'risen' many times and in many places. It is worth asking, then: what, if any, is the connection between novel and madness is in these other times and places? On the one hand, a quick mental journey through the 'great' Western novels since Cervantes would seem to make an argument for a connection unnecessary: *Moby Dick*, *The Scarlet Letter*, *Jane Eyre*, *Madame Bovary*, *Heart of Darkness*, *The Idiot*, *Mrs Dalloway*, *Ulysses*, *The Sound and the Fury*, *The Bell Jar*, *Catch 22*, to name an arbitrary few. One could, of course, argue that madness is a recurrent theme in many modern literary genres: short stories, theatre, autobiography and, above all, poetry. And there are certainly plenty of novels that do not explicitly engage with madness. So what *can* we say about madness and the novel, or madness in literature?

We could, with Foucault, say that 'madness is contemporary with the work of art, since it inaugurates the time of its truth'.[1] Or with Shoshana Felman that literature is 'the sole channel by which madness has been able throughout history to speak in its own name'.[2] These theorists, however, assume a definition of literature or a definition of madness that is fairly specific to the Modernists and Postmodernists. Modernist authors wrote so explicitly about madness as psychological experience, and Freud and Lacan wrote so explicitly about literature and language, that it becomes difficult to imagine relationships between literature and madness that do not fit their model.[3] Yet the study of the early modern Spanish archives of madness – and their striking difference from the madness of early modern epics, satirical allegories, court and carnival pageants, not to mention eighteenth-century asylum records, Freudian notebooks, Modernist poetry and contemporary neuroscience writing – suggests that madness has *no* set definition and *no* fixed relation to literature.[4] Literature and madness both live in quicksand; precisely when they appear to have settled into recognisable forms (literature *is* the epic or the satire, madness *is* folly or passion) is when we should begin to look for them elsewhere.

Spain in 1605 was *one* of those moments. The new 'place' we had to look was not 'in the archives' or 'in the novel'. Literature *became* 'novel' because it looked outside epic and satire and found a madness in inns, on the road and before the Inquisition that was not epic or satiric. To write of this madness, characterised by ambiguity and a precarious position at the edge of – neither safely incorporated into nor beyond – the social fabric, Cervantes had to develop a new form, one characterised by its ambiguity, its precarious position – neither safely incorporated into nor beyond – traditional strategies of representation. He did not call the result 'a novel';[5] the term, with its current meaning, came later and, in one sense, is entirely arbitrary. Whenever literature and madness meet in new guises and new configurations, new forms will be created, although these may be in poetry, in autobiography, in science writing, in film, in medical treatises or in novels: anywhere we find the written word. What is *not* arbitrary, however, is that, for the last four hundred years, madness and literature, in a process of mutual construction, have never ceased to produce something new, 'novel'.

In the present historical moment, when the quicksand under the mind and the quicksand under literature seem to be shifting with unprecedented speed, it would seem particularly important (and promising) to think about madness*es* – or the things that we have, in past ages, associated with madness: passion; folly; inspiration; social exclusion; a crisis of belief; a crisis of identity; the fragmentation of the self and the world; the unspeakable. And yet criticism continues to be dominated by Modernist paradigms. The frameworks of psychoanalysis or deconstruction are probably the most productive way to read certain texts, just as a framework of the Christian allegory was productive for reading Erasmus. Yet in this study we have seen that allegory was not, in fact, the principal context for 'madness' in *Don Quixote*. To articulate a connection between theme and form, to understand why *Don Quixote* was about a madman and why it was a novel, we had to open our eyes to another madness.

Today, much of what was once described as 'madness' no longer goes by that name. In medicine, psychology/psychiatry, neuroscience and public policy, one does not speak of madness at all, but of anorexia, schizophrenia, bipolar disorder, etc. This does not mean that madness (in the Modernist understanding of the word) does not exist. It does: but only in philosophy, literary criticism and certain works of literature. It will be useful to read *those* works using Lacanian or Foucauldian categories. But since, as we have seen, changes in the idea of reason were fundamental in the creation of a new genre, and it required attention to these new ideas and discourses of reason to recognise this connection, literary critics should, now more than ever, be attentive to the way that unreason is changing, and changing literature.[6]

It is not a question that can be answered from the safety of our libraries, or our preconceptions. Literary scholars may have to recognise that the books and theories we have been working with have either been exhausted or come to an abrupt end. It is certain, however, that if we set forth into the markets of Toledo (the streets, the airwaves, the internet, archives of every sort), we will find new authors and new stories to be told – and questioned – both about the literature of the past (even books like *Don Quixote*, about which one would think there was nothing left to say) and that of the present (and future).

Notes

1. Foucault, *Madness and Civilization*: 288–9.
2. Felman: 15.
3. The subject heading 'psychoanalysis and literature' in the Columbia University online library catalogue has 718 titles. A keyword search of the two words uncovers 1448 hits.
4. The first part of this claim is not far from Foucault's argument that 'madness' does not exist a priori of the discourses that define and organise it. However, Foucault argues that there is a chronology of what 'madness' means: that, in any given period, 'madness' means something particular.
5. Or at least only in the sense of the 'novelas ejemplares' or any of the other short fictions that we would now consider *novellas*.
6. For instance, it has been argued that the genre of the 'Tweet' is born from a culture that experiences psychic instability as Attention Deficit Disorder. 'Made scrambled eggs for dinner' is certainly not literature. But there will be literature that adopts and adapts the rhythms of Tweet, or the experience of constant distraction, and to read it in terms of repressed desire will not be very productive.

Bibliography

Unpublished Sources

ADC = Archivo Diocesano de Cuenca
AGN = Archivo General de la Nación (Mexico)
AHN = Archivo Histórico Nacional (Madrid)
BN = Biblioteca Nacional (Madrid)
BUH = Biblioteca Universitaria de Halle (Germany)
The *Sumario* is a summary of a case, sometimes with considerable detail, but without a transcription of testimony or the proceedings. A *proceso* is the complete case file.

Aguilar, Blas de. AHN Inq. Leg. 31, Exp. 5. 1530.
Alarcón, Alonso de. AHN Inq. Leg. 31, Exp. 11. 1635–6.
Antonia Teresa de San Joseph, Sor. ADC Leg. 547, No. 6880–1 (testimony as part of another *proceso*). 1687.
Arias Dávila, Juan. AHN Inq. Leg. 213, Exp. 5. 1628.
Calvo de Illescas, Juan. AHN Inq. Leg. 103, Exp. 1. 1677–94 (3 *procesos*).
Carballo, Adán. AHN Inq. Leg. 2106, Exp. 39 (*sumario*); AHN Inq. Leg. 200, Exp. 28 (*proceso* up through first votes). 1627–8.
Clariana, Vicente. AHN Inq. Lib. 944, fols 155–60. 1675–8.
Díaz, Fernando. AGN, Inq. vol. 366, Exp. 42, fols 443–55. 1612, 1630 (2 *procesos*).
Dios, Juan de. Testimony from the *proceso* of Francisca de los Apóstoles. AHN Inq. Leg. 113, Exp. 5. 1575–9.
Egujo, Juan. AHN Inq. Leg. 99, Exp. 6. 1647–51.
García, Juan. AHN Inq. Leg. 114, Exp. 7. 1541–2.
García Tenorio, Gaspar. AHN Inq. Leg. 35, Exp. 25. 1650–3.
Hernández Marín, Alonso. AGN Inq. Lib. 285, Exp. 74, fols 305–40. 1609.
Hernández Tejero, Andrés. AHN Inq. Leg. 38, Exp. 6. 1543.
Herreria, Juan de. ADC Leg. 141, No. 1730. 1536.
Íñiguez, Bartolomé. AHN Inq. Leg. 38, Exp. 35. 1562.
Largier, Claudio. BUH fol. 365r. 1608.
Larrea, Juan de la. AHN Inq. Leg. 2106, Exp. 28 (*sumario*); AHN Inq. Leg. 225, Exp. 21 (*proceso*). 1627.

Lázaro, Juan Antonio. AHN Inq. Lib. 944, fol. 261–6. 1688.

Madrigal, Hernando de. ADC Leg. 229, No. 2879. 1563.

Martínez, Andrés. AHN Inq. Leg. 2106, Exp. 5 #1 (*sumario*); AHN Inq. Leg. 40, Exp. 27 (*proceso*). 1605–6.

Mendoza, Alonso de. AHN Inq. Leg. 3713, 8ª pieza; AHN Inq. Leg. 3079, No. 55; AHN Inq. Leg. 3080, Nos 131, 175, 176. 1592–8.

Núñez, Antonia. AHN Inq. Leg. 2106, Exp. 24 #25 (*sumario*); AHN Inq. Leg. 206, Exp. 43 (*proceso*). 1623–4.

Núñez Freitas, Francisco. AHN Inq. Lib. 932, fol. 27r.; AHN Inq. Lib. 931, fol. 380. 1650–67.

Pantalión, Juan Alexandro. AHN Inq. Lib. 939, fol. 140. Date: ? (mid–late seventeenth century).

París, Giraldo. AHN Inq. Leg. 2106, Exp. 3, #49 (*sumario*); AHN Inq. Leg. 100, Exp. 21 (*proceso*). 1603–4.

Pellicer, Jacinto. AHN Inq. Lib. 940, fols 250–4. 1631.

Ramírez del Vado, Francisco. AHN Inq. Leg. 2106, Exp. 3 #1 (*sumario*); AHN Inq. Leg. 101, Exp. 3 (*proceso*). 1601–3.

Rodríguez Herrero, Pedro. AHN Inq. Leg. 101, Exp. 9. 1542–4.

Salinas, Pedro. ADC Leg. 400, No. 5675. 1620.

Sánchez, Bartolomé. ADC Leg. 196, Exp. 2216. 1553–8 (two *procesos*).

Santaren, Juan de. ADC Leg. 708, No. 636. 1582.

Trillo, Juan de. AHN Inq. Leg. 47, Exp. 60. 1567.

Valles, Joseph. AHN Inq. Lib. 944, fol. 266. 1688.

Published Works

Alcalá Galán, Mercedes, *La escritura desatada: poéticas de la representación en Cervantes* (Alcalá de Henares: Centro de Estudios Cervantinos, 2009).

Allen, John Jay, *Don Quixote: Hero or Fool? A Study in Narrative Technique* (Gainesville: University of Florida Press, 1971).

Amaro Sánchez, José, *Los sermones predicables del loco Don Amaro*, ed. Luis Estepa (Madrid: Mayo de Oro, 1987).

Ariosto, Lodovico, *Orlando Furioso*, trans. William Stewart Rose (London: Bohn's Illustrated Library, 1858).

Aristotle, *Nichomachean Ethics*, trans. W. D. Ross <http://classics.mit.edu/Aristotle/nicomachaen.html>.

Atienza, Belén, *El loco en el espejo: locura y melancolía en la España de Lope de Vega* (Amsterdam and New York: Rodopi, 2009).

Auger, Peter, *The Anthem Dictionary of Literary Terms and Theory* (London and New York: Anthem Press, 2010).

Avalle-Arce, Juan Bautista, *Don Quijote como forma de vida* (Madrid: Fundación Juan March, 1976).

Bailón Blancas, José Manuel, *Cervantes y la psiquiatría: la histeria en El Licenciado Vidriera* (Madrid: Necodisne Editorial, 2000).

Bailón Blancas, José Manuel, *Historia clínica del caballero Don Quijote* (Madrid: F. Plaza del Amo, 1993).

Bakhtin, M.M., *The Dialogic Imagination: Four Essays*, trans. Caryl

Emerson and Michael Holquist (Austin: University of Texas Press, [1975] 1981).

Bakhtin, M. M., *Rabelais and His World*, trans. Hélène Iswolsky (Bloomington: Indiana University Press, 1984).

Baquero, Aurelio, *El bosquejo histórico del Hospital Real y General de Nuestra Señora de Gracia de Zaragoza* (Zaragoza: Institución Fernando el Católico, 1952).

Bartra, Roger, *Cultura y melancolía: las enfermedades del alma en la España del Siglo de Oro* (Barcelona: Editorial Anagrama, 2001).

Basile, Bruno, *Poëta melancholicus: tradizione classica e follia nell'ultimo Tasso* (Pisa: Pacini, 1984).

Bataillon, Marcel, *Érasme et l'Espagne: recherches sur l'histoire spirituelle du XVIe siècle* (Paris: E. Droz, 1937).

Bergson, Henri, 'Laughter', in Wylie Sypher (ed.), *Comedy* (Baltimore: Johns Hopkins University Press, [1900] 1980), pp. 61–190.

Beys, Charles de, *L'Hospital des fous* (Paris: 1636).

Blázquez Miguel, Juan, *Sueños y procesos de Lucrecia de León* (Madrid: Tecnos, 1987).

Bouza Álvarez, Fernando Jesús, *Locos, enanos y hombres de placer en la corte de los Austrias: oficio de burlas* (Madrid: Temas de Hoy, 1996).

Brand, C. P., *Torquato Tasso: A Study of the Poet and of His Contribution to English Literature* (Cambridge: Cambridge University Press, 1965).

Bunn, Elaine, 'Fashioning identities in *El Licenciado Vidriera*', in *Cervantes* 24.1 (2004), pp. 119–36.

Caro Baroja, Julio, *El carnaval (análisis histórico-cultural)* (Madrid: Taurus, 1965).

Casalduero, Joaquín, *Sentido y forma de las Novelas ejemplares* (Buenos Aires: Coni, 1943).

Casalduero, Joaquín, *Sentido y forma del Quijote, 1605–1615*, 2 vols (Madrid: Ediciones Ínsula, 1949).

Castilla del Pino, Carlos, *Cordura y locura en Cervantes* (Barcelona: Ediciones Península, 2005).

Castro, Américo, *El pensamiento de Cervantes* (Madrid: Revista de Filología Española, 1925).

Cavillac, Michel, 'Introducción', in Cristóbal Pérez de Herrera, *Amparo de pobres* (Madrid: Espasa-Calpe, 1975), pp. ix–cxciii.

Cervantes Saavedra, Miguel de, *El casamiento engañoso; El coloquio de los perros*, ed. Florencio Sevilla Arroyo and Antonio Rey Hazas (Madrid: Alianza Editorial con la colaboración del Centro de Estudios Cervantinos, 1997).

Cervantes Saavedra, Miguel de, *Don Quijote de la Mancha: edición del Instituto Cervantes, 1605–2005*, ed. Francisco Rico, Joaquín Forradellas and Fernando Lázaro Carreter (Barcelona: Galaxia Gutenberg, 2004).

Cervantes Saavedra, Miguel de, *Don Quixote*, trans. Edith Grossman (New York: Ecco, 2003).

Cervantes Saavedra, Miguel de, *La española inglesa; El licenciado Vidriera; La fuerza de la sangre*, ed. Florencio Sevilla Arroyo and Antonio Rey Hazas (Madrid: Alianza Editorial con la colaboración del Centro de Estudios Cervantinos, 1996).

Cervantes Saavedra, Miguel de, *Exemplary Stories*, trans. Lesley Lipson (Oxford: Oxford University Press, 2008).

Close, Anthony J., 'Algunas reflexiones sobre la sátira en Cervantes', *Nueva revista de filología hispánica* 38 (1990), pp. 492–511.

Close, Anthony J., *The Romantic Approach to Don Quixote: A Critical History of the Romantic Tradition in Quixote Criticism* (Cambridge and New York: Cambridge University Press, 1978).

Cohen, Thomas V., and Elizabeth Storr Cohen, *Words and Deeds in Renaissance Rome: Trials before the Papal Magistrates* (Toronto and Buffalo: University of Toronto Press, 1993).

Cohn, Norman, *The Pursuit of the Millennium: Revolutionary Millenarians and Mystical Anarchists of the Middle Ages*, rev. and expanded edn (Oxford: Oxford University Press, 1970).

Collins, John Joseph, Bernard McGinn and Stephen J. Stein, *The Encyclopedia of Apocalypticism Vol. 2: Apocalypticism in Western History and Culture*, ed. Bernard McGinn (New York: Continuum, 2000).

Covarrubias Orozco, Sebastián de, *Tesoro de la lengua castellana o española*, ed. Ignacio Arellano and Rafael Zafra (Madrid: Iberoamericana Frankfurt: Vervuert, [1611] 2006).

Cruz, Anne J., *Discourses of Poverty: Social Reform and the Picaresque Novel in Early Modern Spain* (Toronto: University of Toronto Press, 1999).

Cruz, Anne J., 'Don Quixote, the Picaresque, and the "Rise of the Modern Novel"', in John P. Gabriele (ed.), *1605–2005: Don Quixote Across the Centuries: Actas del Congreso celebrado en el College of Wooster Ohio, 7 al 9 de abril de 2005* (Madrid: Iberoamericana Frankfurt: Vervuert, 2005).

Cuddon, J. A., and Claire Preston, *The Penguin Dictionary of Literary Terms and Literary Theory*, 4th edn (London: Penguin, 1999).

Cueto Ruiz, Ronald, *Quimeras y sueños* (Valladolid: Universidad, Secretariado de Publicaciones, 1994).

Davis, Natalie Zemon, *Fiction in the Archives: Pardon Tales and Their Tellers in Sixteenth-Century France* (Stanford: Stanford University Press, 1987).

Dedieu, Jean Pierre, 'The archives of the Holy Office of Toledo as a source for historical anthropology', in Gustav Henningsen and John Tedeschi (eds), *The Inquisition in Early Modern Europe: Studies on Sources and Methods* (Dekalb, IL: Northern Illinois University Press, 1986), pp. 158–89.

Derrida, Jacques, *Mal d'archive: une impression freudienne* (Paris: Galilée, 1995).

Deyermond, A. D., *Lazarillo de Tormes: A Critical Guide* (London: Grant and Cutler for Tamesis, 1975).

Durán, Manuel, *La ambigüedad en el Quijote* (Xalapa: Universidad Veracruzana, 1960).

Eco, Umberto, 'The frames of comic "freedom"', in Thomas A. Sebeok (ed.), *Carnivale!* (Berlin: Mouton, 1984), pp. 1–10.

Egido, Aurora, *Cervantes y las puertas del sueño: estudios sobre La Galatea, el Quijote, y el Persiles* (Barcelona: Promociones y Publicaciones Universitarias, 1994).

El Saffar, Ruth S., 'Montesinos' Cave and the *Casamiento engañoso*', *Kentucky Romance Quarterly* 20 (1973), pp. 451–67.

El Saffar, Ruth S., *Novel to Romance: A Study of Cervantes's Novelas ejemplares* (Baltimore: Johns Hopkins University Press, 1974).

El Saffar, Ruth S., and Diana de Armas Wilson, *Quixotic Desire: Psychoanalytic Perspectives on Cervantes* (Ithaca: Cornell University Press, 1993).

Emmerson, Richard Kenneth, and Bernard McGinn, *The Apocalypse in the Middle Ages* (Ithaca, NY: Cornell University Press, 1992).

Erasmus, Desiderius, *Literary and Educational Writings, Vol. 2: De copia/De ratione studii*, Collected Works of Erasmus, ed. Craig R. Thompson, trans. Betty Knott (Toronto: University of Toronto Press, 1978).

Erasmus, Desiderius, *The Praise of Folly*, trans. Leonard Dean (Chicago, IL: Packard, [1511] 1946).

Escandell Bonet, Bartolomé, and Joaquín Pérez Villanueva (eds), *Historia de la Inquisición en España y América*, 3 vols (Madrid: Biblioteca de Autores Cristianos, 1984–2000).

Estepa, Luis, 'Notas introductorias', in José Amaro Sánchez *Sermones predicables del loco Don Amaro*, ed. Luís Estepa (Madrid: Mayo de Oro, 1987), pp. 15–135.

Felman, Shoshana, *Writing and Madness: (Literature/Philosophy/ Psychoanalysis)*, trans. Martha Noel Evans, Shoshana Felman and Brian Massumi (Ithaca, NY: Cornell University Press, 1985).

Fernández de Avellaneda, Alonso, *El ingenioso hidalgo Don Quijote de La Mancha: que contiene su tercera salida y que es la quinta parte de sus aventuras* (Mexico: Editorial Porrúa, [1614] 1986).

Forcione, Alban K., *Cervantes, Aristotle, and the Persiles* (Princeton: Princeton University Press, 1970).

Forcione, Alban K., *Cervantes and the Humanist Vision: A Study of Four Exemplary Novels* (Princeton: Princeton University Press, 1982).

Forster, E. M., *Aspects of the Novel* (New York: Harcourt, Brace & Company, 1927).

Foucault, Michel, *Folie et déraison: histoire de la folie à l'âge classique* (Paris: Union Générale d'Éditions: 1964).

Foucault, Michel, *History of Madness*, ed. Jean Khalfa, trans. Jonathan Murphy (London; New York: Routledge, 2006).

Foucault, Michel, *Madness and Civilization: A History of Insanity in the Age of Reason*, trans. Richard Howard (New York: Vintage Books, 1988).

Friedman, Edward, '"El pobre servicio de mano": Lazarillo de Tormes, Don Quixote, and the design of the novel', in John P. Gabriele (ed.), *1605–2005: Don Quixote Across the Centuries: Actas del Congreso celebrado en El College of Wooster Ohio, 7 al 9 de abril de 2005* (Madrid: Iberoamericana Frankfurt: Vervuert, 2005), pp. 29–50.

Frye, Northrop, 'Anatomy of criticism: Four essays' (1957), in Michael McKeon (ed.), *Theory of the Novel: A Historical Approach* (Baltimore: Johns Hopkins University Press, 2000), pp. 5–13.

Garcés, María Antonia, *Cervantes in Algiers: A Captive's Tale* (Nashville: Vanderbilt University Press, 2002).

García Gilbert, Javier, *Cervantes y la melancolía: ensayos sobre el tono y la actitud cervantinos* (Valencia: Institució Alfons el Magnànim-Generalitat Valenciana, 1997).

Garzoni, Tomaso, *L'ospedale de' pazzi incurabili* (Venice: 1586).

Giles, Mary E., *Women in the Inquisition: Spain and the New World* (Baltimore: Johns Hopkins University Press, 1999).

Gilman, Stephen, *Cervantes y Avellaneda: Estudio de una imitación* (México: Colegio de México, 1951).

González Duro, Enrique, *Historia de la locura en España*, Vol. I (Madrid: Temas de Hoy, 1994).

González Echevarría, Roberto, *Love and the Law in Cervantes* (New Haven, CT: Yale University Press, 2005).

Gorfkle, Laura J., *Discovering the Comic in Don Quixote* (Chapel Hill: University of North Carolina Press, 1993).

Green, Otis H., *Spain and the Western Tradition: The Castilian Mind in Literature from El Cid to Calderón* (Madison, WI: University of Wisconsin Press, 1963).

Guevara, Antonio de, *Menosprecio de corte y alabanza de aldea*, ed. Matías Martínez Burgos (Madrid: Espasa-Calpe, [1539] 1975).

Harmon, William, *A Handbook to Literature*, 10th edn (Upper Saddle River, NJ: Pearson/Prentice Hall, 2006).

Heers, Jacques, *Carnavales y fiestas de locos* (Barcelona: Edicions 62, 1988).

Henningsen, Gustav, and Jaime Contreras, 'Forty-four thousand cases of the Spanish Inquisition: analysis of a historical data bank', in Gustav Henningsen and John Tedeschi (eds), *The Inquisition in Early Modern Europe: Studies on Sources and Methods* (DeKalb, IL: Northern Illinois University Press, 1986), pp. 100–29.

Hershkowitz, Debra, *The Madness of Epic: Reading Insanity from Homer to Statius* (Oxford and New York: Oxford University Press, 1998).

Horozco y Covarrubias, Juan de, *Tratado de la verdadera y falsa prophecía* (Segovia: 1588).

Huarte de San Juan, Juan, *Examen de ingenios para las ciencias*, ed. Guillermo Serés (Madrid: Cátedra, [1575] 1989).

Huerga, Álvaro, *Historia de los alumbrados (1570–1630)*, 5 vols (Madrid: Fundación Universitaria Española, 1978–94).

Iffland, James, *De fiestas y aguafiestas: risa, locura e ideología en Cervantes y Avellaneda* (Pamplona: Universidad de Navarra; Madrid: Iberoamericana; Frankfurt: Vervuert, 1999).

Iriarte, Mauricio de, *El Doctor Huarte de San Juan y su Examen de ingenios: contribución a la historia de la psicología diferencial*, 2nd edn, trans. from German (Madrid: Consejo Superior de Investigaciones Científicas, [1938] 1948).

Jacobellis v. Ohio, 378 US 184 (United States Supreme Court) <http://laws.findlaw.com/us/387/184.html>.

Johnson, Carroll B., *Cervantes and the Material World* (Urbana: University of Illinois Press, 2000).

Johnson, Carroll B., *Madness and Lust: A Psychoanalytical Approach to Don Quixote* (Berkeley: University of California Press, 1983).

Jordán Arroyo, María V., *Soñar la historia: riesgo, creatividad y religión en las profecías de Lucrecia de León* (Madrid: Siglo XXI de España Editores, 2007).

Juliá, Mercedes, 'Prólogo', in Mercedes Juliá (ed.), *Don Quijote y la narrativa posmoderna* (Cádiz: Universidad de Cádiz, 2010), pp. 11–20.

Kagan, Richard L., *Lucrecia's Dreams: Politics and Prophecy in Sixteenth-Century Spain* (Berkeley: University of California Press, 1990).

Kahn, Victoria, and Lorna Hutson (eds), *Rhetoric and Law in Early Modern Europe* (New Haven, CT: Yale University Press, 2001).

Kallendorf, Hilaire, *Conscience on Stage: The Comedia as Casuistry in Early Modern Spain* (Toronto: University of Toronto Press, 2007).

Kamen, Henry, *The Spanish Inquisition: A Historical Revision* (New Haven, CT: Yale University Press, 1999).

Keitt, Andrew W., *Inventing the Sacred: Imposture, Inquisition, and the Boundaries of the Supernatural in Golden Age Spain* (Leiden and Boston: Brill, 2005).

Keitt, Andrew W., 'Religious enthusiasm, the Spanish Inquisition, and the disenchantment of the world', *Journal of the History of Ideas* 65.2 (2004), pp. 231–50.

Klibansky, Raymond, Erwin Panofsky and Fritz Saxl, *Saturn and Melancholy: Studies in the History of Natural Philosophy, Religion, and Art* (London: Nelson, 1964).

Lea, Henry Charles, *A History of the Inquisition of Spain* (New York: The MacMillan Company, 1906).

Longhurst, John Edward, *Luther and the Spanish Inquisition: The Case of Diego de Uceda, 1528–1529* (Albuquerque: University of New Mexico Press, 1953).

López Alonso, Carmen, *Locura y sociedad en Sevilla* (Sevilla: Diputación Provincial, 1988).

López Navia, Santiago, 'Una aproximación funcional al problema de Cide Hamete Berengeli en el texto del Quijote', *Anales Cervantinos* 35–6 (1987–8), pp. 255–67.

Lukács, Georg, *The Theory of the Novel*, trans. Anna Bostock (Cambridge, MA: MIT Press, [1915] 1974).

MacDonald, Michael, *Mystical Bedlam: Madness, Anxiety, and Healing in Seventeenth-Century England* (Cambridge: Cambridge University Press, 1981).

Madariaga, Salvador de, *Guía del lector del 'Quijote': ensayo psicológico sobre el 'Quijote'* (Madrid: Espasa-Calpe, [1926] 1976).

Mancing, Howard, *The Chivalric World of Don Quixote: Style, Structure, and Narrative Technique* (Columbia: University of Missouri Press, 1982).

Maravall, José Antonio, *La literatura picaresca desde la historia social* (Madrid: Taurus, 1986).

Márquez Villanueva, Francisco, 'Erasmo y Cervantes, una vez más', *Cervantes* 4.2 (1984), pp. 123–37.

Márquez Villanueva, Francisco, 'Planteamiento de la literatura del "loco" en España', *Sin Nombre* 10 (1980), pp. 7–25.

Martín, Adrienne Laskier, *Cervantes and the Burlesque Sonnet* (Berkeley: University of California Press, 1991).

Martin Morán, José Manuel, 'La función del narrador múltiple en el Quijote de 1615', *Anales Cervantinos* 30 (1992), pp. 9–65.

Martínez Bonati, Félix, *Don Quixote and the Poetics of the Novel* (Ithaca, NY: Cornell University Press, 1992).

Menéndez Pidal, Ramón, 'Un aspecto en la elaboración del "Quijote"', Discurso leído en la inauguración del curso 1920–1 en el Ateneo de Madrid;

reproduced in Ramón Menéndez Pidal, *De Cervantes y Lope de Vega*, 5th edn (Madrid: Espasa-Calpe, 1958), pp. 9–60.

Merenciano, F. Marco, 'Vida y obra del Padre Jofré, fundador del primer manicomio del mundo', *Archivos Iberoamericanos de Historia de la Medicina* 2 (1950), pp. 305–59.

Midelfort, H. C. Erik, *A History of Madness in Sixteenth-Century Germany* (Stanford: Stanford University Press, 1999).

Molho, Maurice, *Cervantes, raíces folklóricas* (Madrid: Editorial Gredos, 1976).

Monedero, Pilar, 'El ama, la sobrina y Teresa Panza', in Teresa Marín Eced (ed.), *Figuras femeninas en el Quijote* (Cuenca: Ediciones de la Universidad de Castilla-La Mancha, 2007), pp. 60–76.

Moreno Villa, José, *Locos, enanos, negros y niños palaciegos: gente de placer que tuvieron los Austrias* (México: La Casa de España en México, 1939).

Morón Arroyo, Ciriaco, *Nuevas meditaciones del 'Quijote'* (Madrid: Gredos, 1976).

Nalle, Sara Tilghman, *Mad for God: Bartolomé Sánchez, the Secret Messiah of Cardenete* (Charlottesville: University Press of Virginia, 2001).

Ortega y Gasset, José, 'Notes on the novel' ('La deshumanización del arte' 1925; trans. Hélène Weyl 1948), in Michael McKeon (ed.), *Theory of the Novel: A Historical Approach* (Baltimore: Johns Hopkins University Press, 2000), pp. 294–316.

Parr, James A., *Don Quixote: A Touchstone for Literary Criticism* (Kassel: Edition Reichenberger, 2005).

Parr, James A., *Don Quixote: An Anatomy of Subversive Discourse* (Newark, DE: Juan de la Cuesta, 1988).

Pasamonte, Jerónimo de, 'Vida y Trabajos', in José María de Cossía, *Autobiografías de soldados (siglo XVII)*, Biblioteca de Autores Españoles Vol. XC (Madrid: Atlas, 1956), pp. 5–73.

Pavel, Thomas, 'The novel in search of itself: A historical morphology', in Franco Moretti (ed.), *The Novel, Vol. 2: Forms and Themes* (Princeton: Princeton University Press, 2003), pp. 3–31.

Pellicer de Ossau y Tovar, José, *Avisos históricos*, ed. Enrique Tierno Galván (Madrid: Taurus, 1965).

Percas de Ponseti, Helena, 'La Cueva de Montesinos', *Revista hispánica moderna* 24 (1968), pp. 376-99.

Pérez de Herrera, Cristóbal, *Discurso del amparo de los legítimos pobres y reducción de los fingidos: y de la fundación y principio de los Albergues destos Reynos, y amparo de la milicia dellos* (Madrid: 1598).

Pinedo, Luís de, *Libro de chistes* (sel.), in A. Paz y Meliá (ed.), *Sales españolas* (Madrid: [16th c.] 1890), pp. 100–17.

Planes, Jerónimo de, *Tratado del examen de revelaciones* (Valencia: 1634).

Puebla, Manuel de la, 'Las dos puntas del camino: consideraciones sobre el nacimiento y la muerte de Don Quijote', *Revista de estudios hispánicos* 12 (1985), pp. 111–20.

Rabell, Carmen, *Rewriting the Italian Novella in Counter-Reformation Spain* (Woodbridge: Tamesis, 2003).

Redondo, Augustín, *Otra manera de leer el Quijote: historia, tradiciones culturales y literatura* (Madrid: Editorial Castalia, 1997).

Reed, Walter L., *An Exemplary History of the Novel: The Quixotic versus the Picaresque* (Chicago: University of Chicago Press, 1981).

Rey Hazas, Antonio, 'Novelas ejemplares', in A. J. Close (ed.), *Cervantes* (Alcalá de Henares: Centro de Estudios Cervantinos, 1995), pp. 173–210.

Riley, E. C., *Cervantes's Theory of the Novel* (Oxford: Clarendon Press, 1962).

Riquer, Martín de, *Cervantes, Passamonte y Avellaneda* (Barcelona: Sirmio, 1988).

Roncoroni, Luigi, *Genio e pazzia in Torquato Tasso* (Torino: Fratelli Bocca Editori, 1896).

Rosales, Luis, *Cervantes y la libertad* (1985), in Luis Rosales, *Obras completas* Vol. 2 (Madrid: Editorial Trotta, 1996).

Russell Peter E., 'Don Quixote as a Funny Book', *Modern Language Review* 64 (1969), pp. 312–26.

Sacristán, María Cristina, *Locura e Inquisición en Nueva España, 1571–1760* (México: Colegio de Michoacán, 1992).

Salas Barbadillo, Alonso Jerónimo de, *Correccion de vicios* (Madrid: 1615).

Salillas, Rafael, *Un gran inspirador de Cervantes: El Doctor Juan Huarte y su 'Examen de ingenios'* (Madrid: Victoriano Suárez, 1905).

Sampayo Rodríguez, José Ramón, *Rasgos erasmistas de la locura del licenciado Vidriera de Miguel de Cervantes* (Kassel: Reichenberger, 1986).

Sarrión Mora, Adelina, *Beatas y endemoniadas* (Madrid: Alianza Editorial, 2003).

Saunders, Corinne, '"The thoughtful maladies": Madness and vision in medieval writing', in Corinne Saunders and Jane Macnaughton (eds), *Madness and Creativity in Literature and Culture* (New York: Palgrave Macmillan, 2005), pp. 67–87.

Schelling, Friedrich Wilhelm Joseph von, *The Philosophy of Art*, trans. Douglas W. Stott (Minneapolis: University of Minnesota Press, [1802] 1989).

Schindler, Carolina María, and Alfonso Jiménez Martín, 'El licenciado Avellaneda y El licenciado Vidriera', *Hipertexto* 3 (Winter 2006), pp. 81–100.

Schreiber, Flora Rheta, *Sybil* (Washington, DC: Henry Regnery Company, 1973).

Sevilla Arroyo, Florencio, and Antonio Rey Hazas, 'Introducción', in Miguel de Cervantes Saavedra, *La española inglesa*; *El licenciado Vidriera*; *La fuerza de la sangre*, ed. Florencio Sevilla Arroyo and Antonio Rey Hazas (Madrid: Alianza Editorial con la colaboración del Centro de Estudios Cervantinos, 1996), pp. xxxix–lix.

Shuger, Dale, 'Beyond allegory: The meanings of madness in early modern Spain', in Yasmin Haskell (ed.), *Diseases of the Imagination* (Brussels: Brepols, 2011), pp. 181–200.

Sierra, Julio, *Procesos en la Inquisición de Toledo (1575–1610)* (Madrid: Trotta, 2005).

Sluhovsky, Moshe, *Believe Not Every Spirit: Possession, Mysticism, & Discernment in Early Modern Catholicism* (Chicago: University of Chicago Press, 2007).

Soto, Domingo de, and Juan de Robles, *El gran debate sobre los pobres en el siglo XVI, 1545*, ed. and introd. Felix Santolaria Sierra (Barcelona: Ariel, 2003).

Soufas, Teresa Scott, *Melancholy and the Secular Mind in Spanish Golden Age Literature* (Columbia: University of Missouri Press, 1990).

Speak, Gill, 'An odd kind of melancholy: Reflections on the glass delusion in Europe (1440–1680)', *History of Psychology* 1.2 (1990), pp. 191–206.

Spitzer; Leo, 'Perspectivism in Don Quijote', *Linguistics and Literary History: Essays in Stylistics* (Princeton, NJ: Princeton University Press, 1948), pp. 68–73.

Sullivan, Henry W., *Grotesque Purgatory: A Study of Cervantes's Don Quixote, Part II* (University Park: Pennsylvania State University Press, 1996).

Tasso, Torquato, 'Dialogo di Torquato Tasso i del suo Genio Familiare', ed. Giacomo Leopardi *Operette Morali* (Florence: Sansoni Editori, [1578–94] 1969) <http://it.wikisource.org/wiki/Operette_morali/Dialogo_di_Torquato_Tasso_e_del_suo_Genio_familiare>.

Tasso, Torquato, *Le lettere di Torquato Tasso*, 5 vols, ed. Cesare Guasti (Florence: Le Monnier, 1852–5).

Tasso, Torquato (Giovanni Gaetano Bottari and Giovanni Battista Manso), *Opere di Torquato Tasso* (Florence: 1724), Googlebooks.

Thiher, Allen, *Revels in Madness: Insanity in Medicine and Literature* (Ann Arbor: University of Michigan Press, 1999).

Torrente Ballester, Gonzalo, *El Quijote como juego* (Madrid: Guadarrama, 1975).

Tropé, Hélène, *Locura y sociedad en la Valencia de los siglos XV al XVII* (València: Diputació de València, 1994).

Ullersperger, Johann Baptist, *La historia de la psicología y la psiquiatría en España: desde los más remotos tiempos hasta la actualidad* (Madrid: Alhambra, 1954).

Unamuno, Miguel de, *Vida de Don Quijote y Sancho* (Madrid: Cátedra, [1905] 1988).

Urbina, Eduardo, *El sin par Sancho Panza: parodia y creación* (Barcelona: Anthropos, 1991).

Van Deusen, Nancy E., 'Introduction', in Ursula de Jesús, *The Souls of Purgatory: The Spiritual Diary of a Seventeenth-Century Afro-Peruvian Mystic, Ursula de Jesús* (Albuquerque: University of New Mexico Press, 2004), pp. 1–77.

Van Doren, Mark, *Don Quixote's Profession* (New York: Columbia University Press, 1958).

Vega, Lope de, *Los locos de Valencia*, ed. Hélène Tropé (Madrid: Castalia, [1595?] 2003).

Vega, Lope de, *El peregrino en su patria*, ed. Juan Bautista Avalle-Arce (Madrid: Editorial Castalia, [1604] 1973).

Vélez de Guevara, Luis, *El diablo cojuelo* (Madrid: 1641).

Villegas, Alonso de, *Fructus sanctorum, y quinta parte de Flos sanctorum* (Cuenca: 1594).

Vives, Ioannes Ludovicus (Vives, Juan Luís), *De subventione pauperum. Sive de humanis necessitatibus libri II* (Bruges: 1526).

Wasserman, Dale (book), Joe Darion (lyrics), Mitch Leigh (music), *Man of La Mancha* (New York: Random House, 1966).

Williamson, Edwin, *The Half-Way House of Fiction: Don Quixote and*

Arthurian Romance (Oxford: Oxford University Press; New York: Clarendon Press, 1984).

Wilson, Diana de Armas, *Cervantes, the Novel, and the New World* (Oxford: Oxford University Press, 2000).

Zijderveld, Anton, *Reality in a Looking-Glass: Rationality through an Analysis of Traditional Folly* (London: Routledge & Kegan Paul, 1982).

Index